T0268640

ADAM NICOLSON

HOW TO BE

Adam Nicolson is the author of many distinguished books on history, landscape, and great literature. He is the winner of the Somerset Maugham Award, the W. H. Heinemann Award, and the Ondaatje Prize. His books include *Life Between the Tides* and *Why Homer Matters*. He lives on a farm in Sussex, England.

HOW TO BE

LIFE LESSONS FROM
THE EARLY GREEKS

ADAM NICOLSON

PICADOR

FARRAR, STRAUS AND GIROUX

NEW YORK

for Sofka Zinovieff and a lifetime of friendship

Picador
120 Broadway, New York 10271

Printed in the United States of America
Originally published in 2023 by William Collins, Great Britain
Published in the United States in 2023 by Farrar, Straus and Giroux
First paperback edition, 2024

Maps drawn by Martin Brown.

Illustration credits can be found on pages 353–356.

The Library of Congress has cataloged the Farrar, Straus and Giroux
hardcover edition as follows:
Names: Nicolson, Adam, 1987– author.
Title: How to be : life lessons from the early Greeks / Adam Nicolson.
Description: First American edition. | New York : Farrar, Straus and Giroux, 2023. |
    Includes bibliographical references and index.
Identifiers: LCCN 2023014917 | ISBN 9780374610104
Subjects: LCSH: Philosophy, Ancient—Influence. | Existential phenomenology. |
    Conduct of life. | Greece—Intellectual life—To 146 B.C. | Greece—Antiquities.
Classification: LCC B181 .N53 2023 | DDC 180—dc23/eng/20230714
LC record available at https://lccn.loc.gov/2023014917

Paperback ISBN: 978-1-250-33816-7

Our books may be purchased in bulk for promotional, educational,
or business use. Please contact your local bookseller or the Macmillan Corporate
and Premium Sales Department at 1-800-221-7945, extension 5442,
or by email at MacmillanSpecialMarkets@macmillan.com.

Picador® is a U.S. registered trademark and is used by Macmillan Publishing Group, LLC,
under license from Pan Books Limited.

For book club information, please email marketing@picadorusa.com.

picadorusa.com • Follow us on social media at @picador or @picadorusa

1 3 5 7 9 10 8 6 4 2

On the title page: A dynamic sea—the currents of the Mediterranean, as synthesised by
NASA from a combination of satellite and in-ocean data.

Being overly certain, he was relatively sure, was what eventually made one a wacko.

George Saunders, 'The Falls',
New Yorker, 22 January 1996

CONTENTS

HOW TO BE

PHILOSOPHY HAS
A GEOGRAPHY

T his book, which is about the first stirrings of philosophical thinking among the Iron Age Greeks, began a few years ago at sea in the eastern Aegean. My wife Sarah and I were in Samos early one summer and had tied up for the evening at a small quay somewhere on the south coast. Other boats had come in after us, laying their anchors over ours. It happens in busy harbours. And so, first thing in the morning, at first light, with the air as pale as the harbour water, and only the cats awake, I jumped off into its lime-green blue and swam down the 12 feet or so to the sandy sea floor, hand over hand and link by link down the chain, looking for the tangle that needed to be undone.

In one dive after another, I picked up the later anchors, setting them aside. Three dives were enough for ours to lie clear. I was soon back on board, dripping and cold, a towel and then a jersey around me, the engine running quietly under the deck. Whispering to each other so as not to disturb our neighbours, we raised and stowed our anchor and freed the warps from the quay.

With scarcely a wake behind us, we left the harbour, pulled slowly out into the sea south of the island and turned east towards the channel between Samos and the great bulk of Mount Mycale on the Turkish mainland. As the first of the sun touched the tips and vertebrae of mountain and island, we cut the engine, raised the sails, winched them in, felt the hull of the boat starting to lift and surge on its way. We tacked at the far end of Samos, freed the sheets, set the boat on a reach and made for Chios, 50 miles away in the haze. The shadows and ghosts of the blue-grey islands and headlands lay around us all day, as calm as a family of sleeping lions. The Aegean sang and swept beneath us as we took the helm in turn and dozed in turn, heeled over in that wind, driving north and west in the blue and glitter of life.

The whole day felt like a dose of happiness, a moment of suspension, both transient and unexpected, when this earth and this life seemed not only to be wonderful, replete with beauty and grace, but astonishingly, almost overwhelmingly whole, undisturbed by the news-and-noise of daily existence, or any sense of hurry.

I had with me an old and battered copy of a book Sarah's father, who had taught Greek at King's College, Cambridge, had co-authored with his friend Geoffrey Kirk in the 1950s. *The Presocratic Philosophers* by G. S. Kirk and J. E. Raven has been for many generations the guidebook to the beginnings of western thought. Carefully, in both Greek and English, the two friends outlined the first emergence 2,500 years ago of the instinct that understanding was not simply to be learned from priests or elders, or experts, or by imagining a congeries of terrifying metaphysical monsters, but could be gathered by each of us applying the worrying and thinking mind to the conundrums of life. Questions come rippling out of their pages. What is the underlying structure of things? what lasts? what is constant in a world of flux? what is identity? or substance? what is the relationship of thought to world? what is being? what value? what justice? And, in the light of any answers to those questions, how should we be? How should we treat each other?

I never knew John Raven. He died ten years before I met his daughter. But it is one of the miracles of books that through their pages you can start to know a man decades after his death. I could, in a way, hear him and converse with him through his printed words. And as we sailed through the Aegean that day, and as I looked at the chart beside me, I began to ask why this eruption of new thinking had happened in this place and at that time. Almost in view from the cockpit of our small chartered boat was the whole province in which Greek philosophy had begun. Those grey-blue masses of island and mainland hid within them the thinkers' cities. Thirty or forty miles to the south in Miletus was the birthplace of the first theorists of the physical world. Twenty miles to the east in Ephesus was the home of Heraclitus, the first person to consider the interrelatedness of things. Just to the north, in the twin cities of Notion and Colophon, was the country of Xenophanes, the first philosopher of civility. Just over the horizon was Lesbos, the island of Sappho and Alcaeus, the greatest early lyric poets. To the south in Samos, the birthplace of Pythagoras, the man who first imagined an everlasting soul and who when exiled to southern Italy took this intellectual revolution to a new and western Greek world, where it flowered again in surprising and radical forms.

That wonderful day's sailing was the invitation to which this book is an answer. It is an exploration of the sea-and-city world in which, in the western tradition, the great and everlasting questions of existence were first explored. What I have written is grounded in a double belief: first that places give access to minds, however distant and strange, that philosophy has a geography and that to be in the places these thinkers knew, visit their cities, sail their seas and find their landscapes not overwhelmed by the millennia that have passed is to know something about them that cannot be found otherwise; and second that, despite that locatedness, and despite their age, the frame of mind of these first thinkers remains astonishingly and surprisingly illuminating today. Read them and you will find your way of seeing the world refreshed and renewed, as if you had bathed one cool morning in a different sea.

Metaphysical philosophy, that branch of thought which deals with the first principles of things, the nature of being and knowing, is, as Bertrand Russell wrote in an early essay, 'the attempt to conceive the world as a whole'. Philosophy had not begun, he added, as an act of intellectual exclusion but had 'developed, from the first, by the union and conflict of two very different human impulses, the one urging men towards mysticism, the other urging them towards science'. Russell thought that super-rationalists – he named the eighteenth-century Edinburgh philosopher David Hume – may have achieved greatness through science and analysis alone and others such as Hume's younger contemporary William Blake through deep mystic insight.

> But the greatest men who have been philosophers have felt
> the need both of science and of mysticism: the attempt to
> harmonise the two was what made their life, and what always
> must, for all its arduous uncertainty, make philosophy, to
> some minds, a greater thing than either science or religion.

That meeting of impulses is what defines philosophy. Its place is to bridge the transition between the perception of a universal harmony and the daily encounter with the world as it is, in all its difficulty and multiplicity. Both aspects of human experience seem real and yet contradictory. How do they connect? How to reconcile a sense of the whole with the experience of dividedness, the chaos and mutability of things?

These first Greek thinkers, teaching and writing between about 650 and 450 BC, found their life on that boundary. They did not provide a set of rationalist solutions nor of religious doctrines, but again and again explored the borderland between those ways of seeing, holding their position in the shadowy ground between the poetic and the analytic, the physical and metaphysical.

The heart of their approach, in one thinker after another, was not assertion but enquiry, a shuttling between thinking and imagining, and so perhaps should not be called philosophy – the love of wisdom – as if wisdom were a commodity to be taken down off a shelf, but the more troubled and anxious *zetosophy*, the search for wisdom.

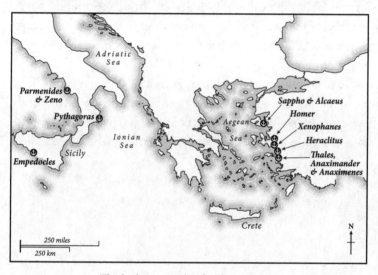

The harbour minds of archaic Greece.

That focus on the uncertain, engaging with the unknown other, was common to every one of these Greek thinkers. This book makes a suggestion: their emphasis on fluidity, on interchange and connectedness, derived from their emergence in the great port cities of the Iron Age Aegean, in the period of Greek history known conventionally by historians as the archaic. They lived in a fluid world and thought with a harbour mind. Their cities' lives were dependent on the sea and on the connections the sea could provide, so that this version of Greece in the centuries between 700 and 500 BC was not land-based. It essentially existed at sea and, where it touched the land, it appeared and manifested itself as the cities from which these philosophers came.

Early philosophy is a harbour phenomenon, a by-product of trading hubs on the margins of Asia, on the islands, and eventually in the rich lands of Sicily and southern Italy. What we think of now as the mainland of Greece, then filled with communities of farmer-warriors, played no part in this. The creators of the philosophical revolution were from the mobile edges, merchants in ideas, people from communities in which exchange was the medium of significance and for whom inherited belief was not enough.

That condition is their lasting value. We may want fixed answers but, along with these great and inspiring early minds, we must know in the end to stay afloat, stay with the questions and entertain doubt as the unlikely bedrock of understanding.

HARBOUR MINDS

THE BEGINNINGS OF PHILOSOPHY
EASTERN MEDITERRANEAN, 1200–650 BC

It is a story of the margins, the product of deep political and cultural changes in the eastern Mediterranean between about 1200 and 800 BC. Nothing about the new way of thinking came from centrality or long-instituted authority; every one of its qualities derived from conditions found on the edges of power, where fusion, manoeuvrability, thievery, deceit, eclecticism and openness were aspects of a vitalized, at times anxious and often predatory life.

To imagine large geopolitical change as human experience is difficult, partly because it occurs on a far from personal scale and over time spans that stretch beyond the individual life. And we cannot think of ourselves as epiphenomena, bubbles on the surface of a much larger stream. But the sources of philosophy were not merely brilliant individuals nor chance happenings. It can be seen in retrospect to have emerged from the intersection of three culture-worlds in the eastern Mediterranean about 3,000 years ago. The meeting of the western limits of Asia, the northern shore of Africa in Egypt and the braided and tasselled fringe of southern Europe gave rise to what we now see as the beginnings of western thought.

The change had been a long time coming. For the centuries after 3000 BC, the great river-based empires of Egypt on the Nile and Mesopotamia in what is now Iraq had been the power centres of the most civilized and enriched region of the world. Vast authoritarian structures, both physical and administrative, had been established by which the dominion of priests and kings ruled for generation after generation. Fat with the nutrients their alluvial valleys could give them, cities, palaces, temples, writing, literature, sculpture, historical records, libraries, accounting systems, mathematics and astronomy had all been developed to serve the purposes of an overwhelming divine and regal authority. All the goods of the world, wines and ivories, spices and scents, fine timbers, precious metals and exquisite goods were drawn in towards them.

Different forms of a palace economy ruled this core of the Bronze Age world. In Anatolia, the Hittite empire played its part as one of these near-eastern power blocs. In Crete, the palace-temples of the Minoans drew on Egyptian and Mesopotamian models, commanding a sea-based empire stretching up into the Aegean and west towards Italy. The warrior-kings at Mycenae in mainland Greece were first the acolytes and then imitators of the Cretans, and after about 1450 BC their conquerors. Where the rest of Europe and most of western Asia remained divided into low-tech, small-scale chiefdoms, these sophisticated literate empires looked as if they could last for eternity.

Almost without exception, this civilization was concentrated in great capital cities, hived around a royal or priestly ideology and arranged in rigid hierarchies. The empires competed with one another, but each was founded on that same centralizing principle. All thought was bound either to the temples or to the great autocratic monarchs. Thinkers were the servants of order; their highly conservative scribal world was singular and fixed for centuries at a time. Precise repetition, not inventiveness, was its virtue. The thousands of texts that survive from them, as the Assyriologist Leo Oppenheim said, are 'stereotyped, self-centered, and repetitious'. No dialogue, no setting out of opposing views and no multilayering of perspectives is ever encountered. This

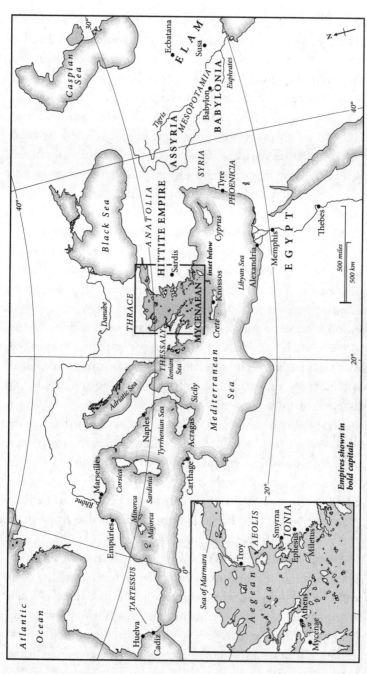

The Mediterranean, a compendium of complementary niches, connected by a sea that extends east and west through similar if ever-varying environments. Any voyage of sufficient length would be sure of a landfall.

was, as Oppenheim wrote, a 'curiously inhibiting and ultimately falsifying [set of] constraints'. Palace and temple ordained a long-lasting imperial reality and the intellectuals were tied to it. The atmosphere was in its way not unlike those of the giant quasi-autocracies of the twentieth century and of China now.

With many vicissitudes, the river empires persisted until about 1300 BC, when for reasons that remain opaque the long-fixed pattern of power started to fray and erode. The authority of the pharaohs began to shrink and Egypt's Mediterranean presence and command faded. Monument-building came to an end. The Mesopotamian cities went into decline. To the north, in Anatolia, the empire of the Hittites collapsed. On the edges of this palace-world, Mycenaean power in Crete, in mainland Greece and on the Aegean shore of what is now western Turkey splintered and crumbled. Settlements returned to poverty and insignificance. Instead of grand bureaucratic dynasties, minor warlords came to control small and parochial territories. The population of the islands in the Aegean and its peripheries fell by three-quarters. Houses became small, poor and simple, filled with basic equipment. The knowledge of writing and metalwork disappeared from the Greek world.

It was the end of the Bronze Age. The causes of this general catastrophe, which unfolded over some 200 years, reaching a nadir in about 1050 BC, are not known. There is no sign of any great climatic change. It may simply have been that the administrative and political systems of the empires had become etiquette-bound, rigidified and overloaded, unable to keep up with the demands and challenges of imperial rule.

The key factor may have been what the Cambridge prehistorian Cyprian Broodbank, borrowing a term from modern economics, has called 'the advantage of backwardness'. When old and deeply established institutions or empires grow to the point where their systems start to inhibit them, and their actions become sclerotic and cumbersome, the advantage moves to the agile and impoverished outsiders who can exploit the opportunities that old and elephantine systems cannot use.

As the authority of the empires began to fall apart, fleets of sailing ships from the north, filled with crews of freebooters, raiders-cum-traders, with Greeks among them and often equipped with a new kind of European slashing sword, began to roam the eastern Mediterranean, terrorizing its inhabitants. In Crete the populations of hundreds of villages deserted their seaside locations and built high, hidden refuges up in the hills. In Egypt, a pharaonic inscription records the bafflement of the authorities when faced with these new and unpredictable enemies:

> The unruly Shardana [their identity has never been established] whom no one had ever known how to fight, came boldly sailing in their warships from the midst of the sea, none being able to withstand them.

These sea raiders were a pan-Mediterranean phenomenon, led by private individuals unencumbered and unburdened by any priority except immediate gain. You could portray them either as pirates or as seaborne entrepreneurs, independent, resourceful and inventive. Unlike the armies of the great river empires, these maritime nomads had no need to attend to centralized control. They could go where they wanted, take what they wanted, sell where they wanted and focus their interest on short-term benefits. They could both service and prey on a world in transition, acting in effect as both symptoms and agents of flux. It is the phenomenon that emerges at the end of empire, whether in post-Roman Europe, the post-Ottoman Balkans or post-Soviet Asia. Overarching control diminishes and everywhere comes a surge of local vitality and demand.

The first beneficiaries of this shift and dispersal of authority were the trading cities on what is now the coast of Israel and Lebanon. Collectively these people were known to the Greeks as the Phoenicians, meaning the 'red ones', perhaps because of the purple-dyed cloth they made and wore. It was a name unknown to themselves, and they were called after the cities from which they came: the men of Tyre, of Sidon, of Byblos. These were the dynamic coastal entrepôts of the years after 1000 BC, providing goods and treasure to the remaining markets to the south and east, intensified by the imperial demands of the newly energized and expansive Assyrian empire, and so developing into multicultural exchange hubs for information, beliefs and goods.

Their reach was long, and by about 900 BC the whole of the Mediterranean was starting to become a single maritime space. Goods travelled its length. A Phoenician hoard deposited then and recently dug out of the river muds at Huelva in the Gulf of Cadiz contained a helmet from Mesopotamia, swords from Ireland and Atlantic France, African ivory and ostrich shell, brooches from the eastern Mediterranean and pottery in patterns that originated in Tyre and Sidon but made of local Spanish clay. The Phoenician merchant oligarchs who had gathered and transported these treasures straddled the entire sea and its connections, founding new towns (for which the Phoenician word was Qārthadāšt, later heard by the Romans as 'Carthage'), and building port installations. In Tyre itself, a city of 20,000 inhabitants in 900 BC, where the water was piped to fountains within its walls, they made a 15-acre harbour basin, protected against all winds and raiders, next to a marketplace and with a channel that led to an inner harbour for extra safety.

The Phoenicians in many ways were the proto-Greeks – rich, adventurous, enterprising, living on the edges of the great Egyptian and Mesopotamian inheritances, aggressive, urban, ruled by nominal doge-like kings but with the real power resting with the merchant oligarchy in city councils. They remain a puzzling phenomenon. They were literate, adopting and developing the alphabet that in the eighth century the Greeks would borrow and adapt from them in their turn, but the Phoenicians left nearly no record of themselves: no poetry, no epic tales, no literature, no history, no drama, no philosophy. The so-called *Annals of Tyre* were kept in that city and much later were sent by Alexander the Great for safekeeping to Tyre's colony of Carthage in north Africa, but the papyri were lost there and next to nothing beyond a few brief Phoenician inscriptions remains. The silence of the Phoenicians is one of the great absences of this story. Did they begin to develop the kind of thought that later emerged and was recorded among the Greeks? Did equivalent conditions in the Phoenician cities not generate an equivalent frame of mind? In several of the early thinkers, there is an explicit Phoenician connection, usually a parent, often a journey. If the texts in which they recorded their thoughts had not disappeared, would this book have been about them? Would the Phoenicians, Semitic and Asian as they were, now be recognized as the progenitors of our world?

From about 900 BC onwards, the Greeks began to insinuate themselves into this Phoenician network, trading to what is now the coast of Syria and to the Italian peninsula (leaving their ceramics as evidence), where the Etruscans were also playing their part in a vortex of change and rivalry. Animated by the ambitions of these seaborne remakers of the world, the Mediterranean was driving itself out of the post-Bronze Age slump. The population of the sea as a whole had reached about 20 million by 800 BC, and was still growing. It was now that the terraces, the identifying mark of Mediterranean ambition and enterprise, were first built on island hillsides. Vines and then cuttings from olive trees were exported from one end of the sea to the other. The house mouse, originally a near-eastern species, gradually spread west and north in the holds and cargoes of the pioneer traders. By about 800 BC, the Mediterranean was in touch with itself, a spinning, fractalizing and hybridizing whirlpool of expanding and interacting cultures in which every voyage could be certain of finding a known destination on a distant shore.

This brief history is the soil in which the seed of early philosophy began to grow: the fraying of ancient, imperial control; the eruption of an unregulated stimulus in the sea-based free-booters; the development by them of trading networks which ran the length of the Mediterranean; and, as a product of those networks, the growth of merchant cities, first among the Phoenicians and then, after about 800 when Phoenician autonomy began to shrink under renewed pressure from the neo-Babylonian empire to the east, the emergence of the Greek cities into their own years of potency.

These are tangled beginnings, more a meshwork than a network, one lattice of interactivity laid over another in a *rösti* of connect-edness, but a pattern can be made out within them: the Greeks would draw on the ancient, inherited learning of Egypt and Mesopotamia; set it in the frame of an adventurous and disruptive approach to life; and then look for a third term, neither wedded to autocratic power nor merely interested in a piratical free-for-all, but seeking what might be called the inventively civic, forms of life and understanding that depended neither on arbitrary authority nor on anarchic violence but were forever in search of the middle ground of social and personal justice, looking for, if perhaps never quite finding, the shared understanding of the three connected realms of soul, city and cosmos that would come to define them.

Absolutely fundamental to it is a sense of justice. For the Greeks, justice was 'the indicated way', the way of things that the arrangement of the universe suggests. If the universe can be seen to have a certain structure, then the self and the city should adopt that structure. The three realms of self, city and cosmos are the points of a triangle within which a coherent understanding can be found.

A microcosm of the interaction between the Greek merchant harbour cities and the world in which they found themselves can be heard in a traditional story told by the second-century AD Greek traveller Pausanias about the harbour city of Erythrae, now on the coast of Turkey, out to the west of Izmir. It was strategically placed to use and benefit from the sea roads that crossed the Aegean and led north towards Thrace and the Black Sea and south towards Egypt and the Levant. As one of the cities that had been founded by the Greeks on the Aegean shores of Ionia in the centuries after 1100 BC it had begun to thrive along with its Greek neighbours on this maritime crossroads.

At some point, at the height of Phoenician success and expansion, before the Greeks had begun their own wide-scale Mediterranean career, perhaps in about 900 BC, a statue of Hercules, whose origins as a demi-god were partly in Greece, partly in the Near East, set out on a wooden raft from the port of Tyre in the land of the Phoenicians. When the raft arrived off the coast of Ionia, it bumped ashore on a headland exactly halfway between the harbour of the Erythraeans and its great rival the Greek island city of Chios.

Hercules floats from the great Phoenician city of Tyre to a point halfway between the young Greek settlements of Chios and Erythrae in Ionia.

The modern frontier between Greece and Turkey now divides these two places – at night you can look out across the channel from Erythrae in Turkey to the lights of Chios on the Greek side, the red pinpoints of its wind turbines on the ridge above them, and the lanterns of the fishing boats catching squid and mullet in the channel between. It is one of the narrow crossings between Asia and the European Union which in the twenty-first century has seen thousands of refugees from Asian wars attempt to find a new life in Europe, and where many have died.

Some 2,900 years ago the two were merely rivals in a contested sea. Citizens from both urgently wanted to bring home the enormous Hercules. For a while neither succeeded, until a fisherman from Erythrae called Phormion, who had lost his sight through disease, had a vision in a dream: the women of Erythrae must cut off their hair and weave a rope with it, and by using it the men of the city would be able to tow Hercules into their harbour.

The women of Erythrae refused to shave their heads for such a crazed scheme from a poor, blind fisherman, but the non-Greek Thracian women in the city – Thrace is roughly equivalent to Bulgaria today – some of whom were slaves and some now freed, offered up their hair. A rope was made and with it the men towed the statue home. Phormion the fisherman recovered his sight and a marvellous temple was erected to enshrine their prize. Hercules became the half-human deity of Erythrae (as of many other places in the Mediterranean), but no women except Thracians were allowed within his sanctuary. Statue and temple were still there more than a thousand years later, in the second century AD, when the image of the god was described as 'absolutely Egyptian' by Pausanias, who was also shown the hair rope, still kept as a holy relic.

The heavy-featured Hercules, fat-lipped, boxer-nosed, brutal-browed, wearing on his head the mane and pelt of the lion he had strangled to death at Nemea in the Peloponnese, came to embody the spirit of this port city, with its acropolis high over the harbour, its cornlands and olive groves stretching into the shallow valleys of the hinterland, and with a scatter of low, sheltering islands across the sea between it and Chios. It is the head that would appear forever stamped on Erythrae's silver coins.

The coins of Erythrae showed on one side Hercules wearing his lion pelt and on the reverse his club, quiver and bow.

What to make of the tale? There seems little doubt that there was a statue of Hercules in Erythrae, one that was not to be recognized as particularly Greek. It had somehow come in from elsewhere, and why not from the city of Tyre in the Levant, where the patron god of the city Melqart was merely Hercules by another name? Hercules was the embodiment of masculine strength, a tough, god-defying, god-becoming man, who had adventured down to Hades to wound the king of the underworld and returned unharmed, who was an ex-slave himself but with club and bow had dominated creation. All animals shrank before him; mice on the Black Sea coast would refuse to eat the grapes from a vine that grew around his statue, or even to be on the same island when it fruited, for fear of his vengeance.

A gigantic stone head from Old Smyrna, perhaps the kind of statue
Pausanias saw in Erythrae and described as 'absolutely Egyptian'.

An undatable statue excavated from Old Smyrna, quite
un-Greek, and of which only the giant head now survives in
the museum in Izmir, may well have something of the raft-borne
Hercules about it: huge, semi-abstract, battered, irreducibly
masculine. This Hercules represented dominance and would
surely protect any person or place that gave tribute to him. Any
small harbour city would want him to hand. Perhaps to those
first Greeks in Erythrae he embodied the success and reach of
the Phoenicians who had already made their way to the far end
of the world. Here was a god who could bring good fortune.

There is something more: the weak and disenfranchised had
brought Hercules to Erythrae. In the face of opposition from the
rich women, the blind fisherman and the Thracian slaves and
ex-slaves had come together to welcome the Phoenician/Herculean
power to Erythrae. That combination makes this an epitome of
these sea-edge stories: significance dragged in from elsewhere;
potency found afloat on the sea; foreignness welcomed in *by*
foreigners; a sea fisherman given, even in his blindness, a vision

of the future; and the slave or ex-slave class contributing to that acquisition of potency. The underlying significance of this counter-intuitive alliance of shorn-headed slave women and the most dominating of Mediterranean male figures is that the wellbeing of a city was dependent on such an alliance. Strength was to be derived from drawing in the strange; more often than not, the understanding of the poor, the blind and the enslaved was central to that success. A city would thrive only by accommodating all that it was offered and by defeating its rivals in doing so.

This world built on exchange, connection and openness to the foreign has left one supremely articulate trace: the coins, like Erythrae's, that these cities made and used. The Greeks, as great borrowers and transformers, had initially taken the idea of coinage from the metal-rich Lydian empire just to the east of the Aegean, whose king Croesus would acquire a proverbially moneyed status he has yet to lose, but it was the Greeks who were the first to use coins as travelling emblems of the cities from which they came.

For centuries the power of silver money irrupting into their world retained a kind of mythic presence for the Greeks. It was said (admittedly by a late source) that the first of the Phoenicians who perhaps in about 800 BC sailed to Tartessus, the ore-rich country of south-west Spain,

took on board so much silver that, when they had loaded up the olive oil and other merchandise of lesser value, they had no more room to take on the silver, so before their departure they had no choice but make the silver into the objects that they used, including all of their anchors.

The Greeks soon followed. Herodotus thought the people from Phocaea in Ionia were the first to get there, welcomed by the tyrant of Tartessus, Arganthonios, whose name means something like 'Silver King' and who urged them to stay. They would not, but with the rich pickings from their voyage they fortified their city with a long and expensive wall. Soon after the Phocaeans, by about 640 BC, a merchant explorer from Samos called Colaeus also found his way to Tartessus, claiming to have been blown there by a storm, returning from his secret destination with a vastly rich cargo of silver with which he beautified the great sanctuary of Hera on his island.

Silver enabled the making of sea connections, the establishment of cities and the adornment of temples. This sounds mythic, but it was not. The scale of the works at Rio Tinto in south-west Spain is some indicator of how vast the silver business was. Between the ninth and sixth centuries BC, something approaching 3 million tons of waste rock was dug from and deposited outside the silver mines.

One set of extraordinary archives preserves a record of this foundational metallic moment. Like most of the silver in antiquity, the Spanish ores were mixed with lead. They could be roasted and smelted in wood-fired clay furnaces, from which, when the fires reached 1200°C, the two metals could be run off and separated, but the furnace smoke always contained traces of metal. Tiny fragments of lead were carried away on the prevailing winds, blown north on the eastern edge of Atlantic lows, gradually falling out over Europe and the north Atlantic. Most of that Tartessian dust has been eroded or dispersed but a few grains have been miraculously preserved and encased as distinct layers under the falling snow that became the Greenland ice sheet and in peat bogs in various places on the continent.

In the layers of ice and peat the silver boom of the Iron Age Mediterranean left its mark. Cores taken down to the bedrock from the ice sheet in the centre of Greenland, some 300 miles from each coast, or through the floor of the bogs, can be read year by year. These physical calendars show that where lead pollution had dropped to almost nothing after the collapse of

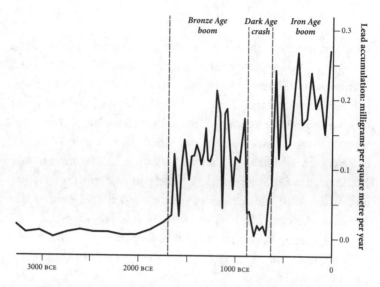

Bronze Age
boom

Dark Age
crash

Iron Age
boom

The specks of lead found in the peat of a Serbian bog chart the vicissitudes of Mediterranean civilization: a Bronze Age boom, a post–Bronze Age slump, followed by the sharp rise of smelting in the early Iron Age as the Phoenicians and Greeks returned to work.

the Bronze Age civilizations in about 1100 BC and remained low for centuries thereafter, from about 800 BC onwards, as the fires in southern Spain were lit to satisfy the appetites of the Phoenicians and then the Greeks and to feed the growing metal-hunger of the Mediterranean, the lead content of the winds began a rise that marks the emergence of what we call civilization. The later stories of silver riches were not wrong. The pollution created in its smelting was the sign of a world getting back to business.

Thousands of coins have survived. For a few tens of pounds or dollars you can buy one today that was made on the shores of this sea 2,500 years ago. To hold one of them in your hand is a reorientating experience. We easily assume that the materials of the past were large and monumental, that the miniature or the delicate would not have entered such ancient lives. But look at a silver obol on the tip of your finger, made in Ephesus in about 550 BC and weighing about two-hundredths of an ounce, and you start to feel in touch with this Greek Iron Age. It is a coin, but hardly in the sense we would recognize; no more than a fragment or suggestion of metal, but stamped with the bee that is one of the emblems of Ephesus because Artemis Ephesia, the presiding goddess of the city, was queen of the bees. She was not the Artemis known throughout classical Greece, the hunter sister of Apollo, but an older, more earthy deity of Anatolia, in all likelihood a transmutation of the ancient east Mediterranean mother goddess Kybele, for whom the bee was an emblem and whose priestesses were known in Greek as the Melissas, the bee girls. And so at the heart of this most famous of Greek Ionian cities was a deity and her cult that could scarcely be less Greek and which derived their potency from those deep and borrowed roots.

The coin with its bee emblem, now sitting balanced on my fingertip, is proof that the Ephesians saw value and fertility in the gatherings of a hive. And what was a hive but a bee city running with liquid riches? The coin is a nugget of value almost exactly the size of a single cell in a honeycomb. It is wealth both concentrated and portable and it connects with an earlier object, from the Bronze Age and now in the museum in Chania in Crete, of a boat, about 9 inches long and made in about 1400 BC, with honeycomb cells in its deck designed to be filled with honey for the voyage to eternity.

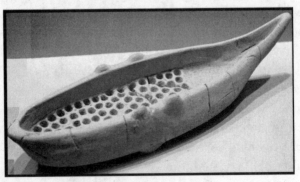

A Minoan honey boat for the afterlife, its deck
peppered with honeycomb cells.

Bees, honey, money, trade goods and voyaging were not aspects of business marginal to the central concerns of life but a set of mind-shaping elements and connections by which this thought-world was made. Plato famously compared the Greeks to ants or frogs sitting expectantly and warily around the edges of a pond. But just as vivid a picture is provided by these bee analogies: every city a hive, every ship running with liquid gold, every mind busy for gain.

Emblems stamped into the silver, or electrum, a silver–gold alloy, were chosen to demonstrate the governing realities of different cities. The Ionian harbour city of Phocaea, among the most enterprising of all these Greek adventurers, the founder of Marseille, marked its money with the figure of a harbour seal, sometimes with an octopus clamped between its teeth, as *phoka* is the Greek for seal and the city was named after a small island at the entrance to the harbour that looks, if you are willing to believe it, seal-like in profile, perhaps even with the tentacles of an octopus spilling from its jaws.

Athens had her owl, the grey-eyed bird of wisdom, sometimes with an olive sprig beside her; the holy island of Delos had Apollo's lyre; Larissa in Thessaly, with a grand reputation for breeding horses, a high-stepping stallion; and Metapontum in the great cornlands of southern Italy an ear of barley on whose bristles a grasshopper perches, ready to spring.

Many of these micro images also embraced the sea connections that made the coins both possible and necessary. Sicilian Acragas had a crab, the island city of Aegina a sea-swimming turtle and the Black Sea port of Apollonia an anchor with crayfish near by. The island of Thasos in the northern Aegean off the coast of Thrace has the most disturbing image of all: a naked satyr, a bearded, bug-eyed and bulbous-nosed wildman, with a huge and engorged penis, carrying off a girl, conventionally called 'a nymph' – but the Greek word *nymphē* can be applied to a young woman of marriageable age as much as to a semi-divine

Coins from Larissa, Delos and Metapontum.

daughter of Zeus – who with open-handed shock is protesting at the horror of her rape.

The Thasos coin is a warning that this beginning of our civilization is not to be sentimentalized. The island, which had hugely valuable seams of silver and gold, was one of the great consumers of slaves captured in Thrace to the north, and conducted a business exporting them to cities further south. Brutal dominance and subjection of the weak played central roles in its gathering of riches.

Coins from Aegina, Apollonia and Thasos.

The facts of slavery recur throughout the story. The philosophers consistently interact with them, and for slavery to have been significant in the ancient world there must have been a slave trade. That is what the coin of Thasos means: the woman is in the act of being enslaved. Enslavement is rape. One of the structural myths of Greek culture, the Rape of Europa, describes the stealing of a Phoenician princess by Zeus the king of the gods disguised as a bull and her rapid transport to Crete; there she gave birth to Minos, who became king of Crete. It may be disturbing to our sensibilities that this early Greek world of achievement, ambition and beauty was not only dependent on slavery, and not ashamed of the presence of slavery, but sexually excited and stimulated by the act of enslavement. To be engorged and erect as a slaver/rapist was a badge of pride for the Greeks of Thasos, and by implication of the world they served. To be a slaver was to be potent, to replay Zeus' foundational act.

It may be – and this is one of the themes this book will explore – that the increased presence of slaves in these cities is central not only to their growing commercial heft but to the changing ways in which the citizen-merchant-oligarch-philosophers of archaic Greece thought of the world: full of distinctions made between the valued and the valueless, the high-minded and the domestic-ordinary, the noble and the degraded. In the words of Walter Benjamin, the twentieth-century cultural critic:

> Without exception cultural treasures have an origin which cannot be contemplated without horror. They owe their existence not only to the efforts of the great minds and talents who have created them, but also to the anonymous toil of their contemporaries. There is no document of civilization which is not at the same time a document of barbarism.

Benjamin's famous words represent a sobering truth underlying every one of these chapters. A world full of pleasure in the sunlight of one of the most beautiful places on earth sat alongside a form of human exploitation that was fundamental to its existence.

It was assumed that every citizen had a slave or two. At the peak of production, in the silver mines at Laurion in Attica,

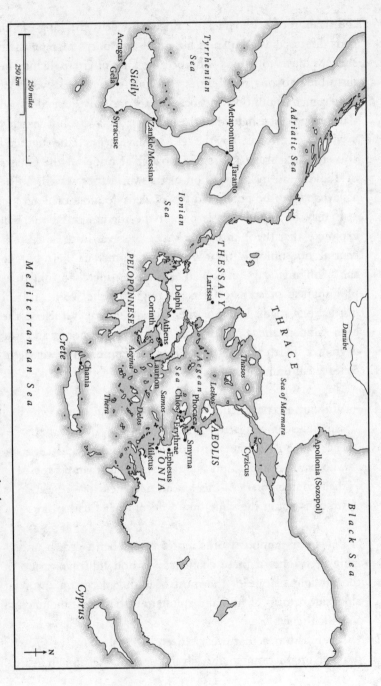

Archaic Greece, a culture with its life as much at sea as on land.

on which the economy of Athens relied, perhaps as many as 20,000 slaves at any one time worked to extract the ores. The number of Athenian slaves was perhaps 80,000 to 100,000 in all, or roughly 30 per cent of the population. Other ancient estimates are much higher. Mnason, a trader from Phocaea, the seal city north of Smyrna, had more than a thousand slaves himself.

It was a giant enterprise. Slaves were set to work in households – one Greek family of eight members was known to have had five domestic slaves to run their lives. They were bought to provide the workforce in the fields, in pottery, sculpture and metal factories, and for onward sale to the Near East. Prices were generalized: one adult slave was worth about half a ton of wheat. An educated slave was worth a good horse. You could buy six or seven children for the price of a man who might be able to manage a household. One merchant from Chios, called Panionius, specialized in boys, castrating them and selling them in Anatolian slave markets from where they would be transshipped to customers deep in the Persian empire. A skilled craftsman would have to devote nine years' earnings to buying a high-class Athenian courtesan of the kind aristocrats owned.

Slaves came from the northern shores of the Black Sea, from many parts of Anatolia and from further afield in Syria and even Ethiopia, people whose black skins meant they commanded exceptional prices. Inland tribes would funnel captives – or the children of the poor – towards the Greek entrepôts on the coast. Many of these slave origins are known because the Greeks, like the English later, would rename their slaves: many were given Greek names but others were called simply 'the Phrygian', 'the Scythian' or 'the Thracian', part of the dehumanizing process on which slavery depends. The name 'Thratta', meaning female Thracian, was a straightforward synonym for slave in Greece. Without doubt, many of them were sex slaves. A fragment

A fifth-century BC plate, made in Attica and found in
Taranto in southern Italy, portraying an African boy, labelling
him *kalos kalos*, meaning 'beautiful beautiful'.

survives from the archaic and notoriously unbuttoned poet
Archilochus in which he says a woman 'was sucking like a
Thracian or a Phrygian sucking beer through a tube, and she
was bent over working hard', which the modern editor footnotes:
'The fragment almost certainly describes a woman engaged in
fellatio.' A small fifth-century plate discovered in the Greek city
of Taranto in southern Italy carries the image of a young African
boy standing beside a water basin, with the words KALOS KALOS
written on the surface of the plate around him. The words mean
'beautiful, beautiful', the usual attribute a Greek man would
give to his younger boyfriend or 'beloved'. Perhaps his given

slave name was Kalos and that was the joke: here for your delectation is a picture of beautiful Beautiful.

The nameless names of slaves confirm a conceptual prejudice. As the archaeologist Timothy Taylor has said, the institution of slavery is founded on 'the absence of a universalizing category of "human being"'. These people were not seen entirely as people. They were chattels, depersonalized and commodified. One term used by the Greeks to describe a human slave, typically of captives taken in war, was a 'man-footed animal', *andrapodon*, equivalent to the *tetrapodon*, the 'four-footed beast'. According to Aristotle, friendship with a slave was as impossible as it would have been with a horse or an ox.

Greece was not alone in this: between a quarter and third of the population of Babylonia under the Persian empire may have been enslaved, but the point needs to be made that the civilization of archaic Greece saw the co-emergence of a slave society and an unprecedented flowering of thought. It seems as if the more advanced the Greek city state, the more likely it was to have large numbers of slaves. The cities in which Greek civilization flourished most fully were those in which slavery played the biggest part. Where freedom of speech, thought and action was most cherished, slavery was always to be found. Philosophy and autocracy may have been incompatible; philosophy and a slave-based society certainly were not.

There is one further witness to the presence of slaves in this world: the relative emptiness of the ancient shipwrecks found on the floor of the Mediterranean. Many of them appear to be half empty and quarter laden because the slaves that represented a good proportion of their cargo would have swum or been washed away as the vessel went down, leaving no trace for the archaeologists to find.

It is impossible in the early twenty-first century not to associate these grim and terrifying journeys with those of the poor and afflicted who have drowned here over the last decade. Every headland and bay is a reminder. These seas alongside the philosophers' cities have been filled with the terror and sorrow of a modern exodus, whether in the channels between Turkey and the near Greek islands, or at the Mediterranean's own narrows, its wasp-waist between Libya, Sicily and southern Italy. The UN High Commission for Refugees reckons that, between 2014 and the middle of 2022, about 2,300,000 people made these desperate crossings by sea, all in search of asylum, however defined. Of those, more than 26,000 drowned or are now missing, about a fifth of them children. The philosophical ideas may have persisted over the millennia; so has the chasm between the potent and the powerless.

Any evidence of the scale of the slave business is patchy and often late, paradoxically, as Timothy Taylor has written, 'because the phenomenon was so widespread and highly organized – just as one might vainly scour newspaper after newspaper today, searching for figures relating to total national electricity or water consumption'. Slavery was not the focus of what these cities thought about themselves, and so the figure that appears on more silver coins from more cities in this newly metalled, connected and enabled world was not the slave on which the enterprise depended but an emblem of the network itself: the dolphin. It appears everywhere: as dolphin-shaped money from the Greek city of Olbia on the Black Sea coast of what is now Ukraine; from Thera in the Cyclades, where the dolphins swim in opposite directions, dramatizing precisely the coming and going and interchange of the voyages themselves; on the coins of Syracuse in Sicily where in issue after issue four dolphins circled the head of Arethusa, the nymph who, wanting to escape the attentions of Alpheius the Peloponnesian river god, became a river herself and flowed under the sea from the Peloponnese to the island of Ortygia where she founded the city.

Dolphin coins from Thera and Syracuse.

In Dankle or Zankle (now Messina) at the north-eastern tip of Sicily, founded by Greek colonists in the eighth century BC, the coins showed on one side a dolphin leaping within the near-enclosing walls of its perfect harbour and on the other a sea shell, perhaps a cockle, within a geometric matrix.

Dolphin coins from Dankle, Taranto and Cyzicus.

At Taranto in southern Italy, founded from Sparta, Taras, son of Poseidon, rides a dolphin on his voyage across the Ionian Sea, his left arm outstretched, as if pointing the way to a new world on the back of an animal that embodies the sea route that took him there.

Dolphins proliferate from sea city to sea city: alongside wolves, lions and eagles, or as magical transporters of lost mariners, as emblems of dominance and potency at sea. A wonderful silver-and-gold coin from Cyzicus on the Sea of Marmara shows two powerful dolphins trapping and enclosing a tuna, for whose fishery Cyzicus was famous.

The sixth-century dolphin discus from Gela, Sicily,
about a foot in diameter, weighing 9 lbs.

Even those cities that made another animal prominent on
their coinage often included a small accompanying dolphin or
two, subscript or superscript, as if to suggest that the voyage
was the element in which all the city's riches swam.

That emblem of the dolphin as the voyage in animal form
is also what lies behind the consistently repeated imagery in
the stories of encounters with dolphins that spread across the
Greek sea world: the great singer Arion was rescued by one;
in a Homeric hymn, Dionysus was captured by Etruscan
pirates who eventually flung themselves into the sea where
they were turned by the god into dolphins; the sea nymphs,
the Nereids, rode dolphins; Eros, the god of longing, rode them;
in the Greek port city of Gela in southern Sicily a sixth-century
bronze discus, now in Vienna, was unearthed in the nineteenth
century, deeply etched with the form of a dolphin so that it
would fly as far and fast as the sea mammal whose image
it bore.

The *Homeric Hymn to Apollo* cannot be dated but may be
just earlier than the first philosophers in the mid-seventh century
BC, perhaps contemporary with the *Odyssey* and sharing much
of its language. The hymn is a vision of the Greek world,
surveying seas, headlands, islands and cities as if from thousands
of feet above them, and describing how Apollo himself, wanting
to find people who could be the priests and guardians for his
newly acquired oracle at Delphi, became aware of 'a swift ship

on the wine-like sea filled with many handsome men, Cretans from Knossos, the city of Minos'.

In the open sea Apollo leapt on to their swift ship, like a dolphin in shape, and lay there, a great and awesome monster. None of the crew could understand but they tried to throw the dolphin overboard. But the god kept shaking the black ship every way and making the timbers quiver. So they sat silent in their craft for fear, and did not loosen the sheets throughout the black, hollow ship, nor lowered the sail of their dark-prowed vessel, but as they had set it first of all with oxhide ropes, so they kept sailing on; for a rushing south wind hurried on the swift ship from behind.

The dolphin god was in command, the ship would not obey the helm, and he led it to the sands at Crisa on the Gulf of Corinth below Delphi and grounded it there at the head of the harbour, when 'like a star at noonday, the lord, far-working Apollo, leapt from the ship: flashes of fire flew from him thick and their brightness reached to heaven'.

This spark-haloed, dark-bodied, forge-like sea-mammal god was Apollo Delphinios, Dolphin Apollo, equipped with both lyre and bow, vast-bodied in the mind of any crew who encountered him. He became the presiding deity at the great harbour city of Miletus in Ionia and of its many colonies to the north, including Olbia on the Black Sea where the dolphin currency was made. The central sanctuary in the marketplace of Miletus, from which the annual processions set out along the sacred road to the oracle at Didyma, was the Delphinion, a holy site in which the god of understanding, beauty and brilliance was fused with the sea creature that was most inti-mate with human voyaging. This meeting of city and voyage, of culture and nature, the spirit of the dolphin voyage, stood at the foundation of the city itself.

The foundation of the altar of Apollo Delphinios in Miletus,
the holiest place in the greatest port city of the archaic
Greek world, caked in silt from spring floods.

There is one other illuminating presence in this archaic Greek consciousness. On the marble base of his giant gold and ivory statue of Zeus in Olympia, Phidias, the prince of fifth-century sculptors, carved all the great gods of Greece and arranged them in pairs: the Sun with his sister Moon; Apollo with his sister the huntress Artemis; Aphrodite, the goddess of love, with her son Eros; Zeus with his Queen Hera; Poseidon with his sea queen Amphitrite; the smith god Hephaestus with his wife, the grace Charis; and Athena with her foster son Hercules. No gathering of the divine could be more glorious than these. Among them, given equal status, was another pair, not brother and sister, nor guardian and ward, nor husband and wife, but bound to each other as deeply as any two gods in Greek mythology. They are not one of the beauty couples of the Greek pantheon but they are the presiding spirits of the harbour city: Hermes and Hestia.

They belong together because they don't belong together. Hermes is the god of movement and change, of unreliability, of the imminent presence of the foreign. Hestia is the goddess of the hearth, the central, the immovable, the safe and the domestic. She is habitat, he is journey. She is navel, he is gesture. She is centred, he disperses. They represent those two irreconcilables: the urge to settle and the urge to explore. In a house, she is at the hearth, he on the threshold, as on the borders of a city, where he can protect it from thieves because he is the king of thieves himself.

He brings luck and can slip sidewise through the keyhole of a door, 'like the autumn breeze, even as mist', as a Homeric hymn says. He treads softly and makes no noise: 'As a sudden thought spikes into a man's heart as his cares crowd about him, or as an eye flashes across a room from one to another, so glorious Hermes planned both thought and deed at once.' He made for himself wickerwork shoes 'by the sand of the sea, wonderful things, unthought of, unimagined; for he mixed together tamarisk and myrtle-twigs, fastening together an armful of their fresh, young wood, and tied them, leaves and all, securely under his feet as light sandals'.

Hermes is the spirit of transaction, 'a bringer of dreams, a night-watcher, gate-lurker'. He carries in front of him his vastly erect phallus and is the god of lucky finds. He recognizes no locks and no enclosures. For him, everything is available for exchange. He can live on crossroads or tombs, the gateways to other worlds, but also in the marketplace and the stadium where outcomes are in contention, and certainty to be had only through struggle or contest. He attends as a witness to agreements and truces, to oaths sworn between contending parties. He can act as herald, messenger and ambassador. He lives at the boundaries of sleep and death. Of all the gods, he was thought to be the most friendly to men. It was Hermes who conveyed souls to Hades.

If Hermes is the dolphin-like spirit of movement, Hestia is the fixed place, the shelter within which safety is to be found and goods stored. Whatever is to be negotiated finds its conclusion in her. Her name is nothing but the Greek word for hearth. Each house had a *hestia* and each city a communal *hestia* in temple, shrine or council chamber. Even in the temple of Apollo Delphinios in Miletus, there was a perpetual hearth from which all those Milesians setting out to found a colony in the northern Aegean or Black Sea would take a flame to make a new hearth in the new country. The ever-burning hearth in the temple of Apollo at Delphi was sometimes seen as the communal hearth for the whole of Greece. Offerings were made to her at the beginning of meals or public events, the small sacrifice on the fire of home. For Socrates, there was a connection between Hestia and *essia* or *estia*, meaning 'reality'. Hestia, the hearth and home, the fire that did not go out, the certain middle, was the essence of things. The Russian-American philosopher Patricia J. Thompson has called her 'the divinity of dailiness'. Hermes was the god of 'what might be', Hestia of 'what is'.

Both were gods that were here with us, dwelling in this world, called the *epichthonioi* in Greek, the *on-earths,* present in all that we do, in all of our goings and stayings, not in some distant and inaccessible Olympus but everywhere here and now. They could both be found, Patricia Thompson wrote, 'where people make fire, trace limits, build walls and a roof over their heads. Together, they are the gods of orientation.' Hestia settles; Hermes opens. He barters, buys and sells; she gives and keeps. She is the goddess of granaries, whose value lies in the storing of what is good; he of the deal, of which the virtues are in the quick and responsive. She must be wise; he must be clever. She knows; he plots and hopes.

And so together they define the harbour city, both open to the world and fiercely distinct within it. Ancient Keos (now called Kea), one small island in the Cyclades, 12 miles long by 6 wide, but with good harbours for anyone making the cross-Aegean voyage, was home to four independent archaic city states. Each was based on its harbour and each dependent on exchange and on the fruits of exchange, interlocking safety with adventure, knowledge and ignorance, stability and mobility, the security of attachment and the possibilities inherent in the exploration of the strange.

All this is the seedbed of the philosophical moment some 2,600 years ago. But the harbour mind is not something confined to this one instant. It is an attitude to the world that is dependent on a particular amalgam of fixity and liquidity, the threats, rivalry and violence with which any melting pot is infused. In the modern world and above all with containerization, as Jan Morris said of Trieste, 'the jumble of port life, its stinks, noises and clashing colours, has been removed from city centres, and so from public consciousness', so that 'the agents, the financiers, the warehouse companies, the valuers, the ship repairers, the chandlers' have all gone, to be replaced on the one hand by the closed efficiency of the container port and in old harbour cities themselves by the neatened orderliness of the restaurants and museums of a tourist economy.

The fusion of nationalities and businesses that defined a harbour city, the way a Triestino could rail at his enemies with the anglo-loan insult *sonababic* (to be pronounced with an Italian accent and a soft c), the 'multi-ethnic, multi-lingual, multi-faith' conglomerations and 'the longshore thieves' hanging out between 'the crates of lemons and sacks of coffee beans' – all have now largely gone from the modern world. But not long since. The port–city amalgam was still there in the twentieth century. 'Here everything ostensibly permanent is broken up,' Joseph Roth, the great Austrian novelist-journalist, wrote of Marseille in the 1930s.

Here, it is re-assembled again. Here, there is continual rebuilding and demolition. No time, no power, no faith, no understanding for ever here. What is foreign? The foreign is at hand. What is at hand? The next wave will wash it away. What is now? It's already over. What is dead? It comes bobbing up again.

The harbour city melts all definitions and that Hermes-like fluidity of exchange finds its mate in the Hestia-like love and nostalgia felt by its émigré sons in other lands, dreaming of their harbour home as if it were an earthly paradise. 'I recommend that the sensitive traveler, if he goes to Algiers,' Albert Camus wrote of his beloved port city before the Second World War,

> drink *anisette* under the archways around the harbour, go to La Pêcherie in the morning and eat freshly caught fish grilled on charcoal stoves; listen to Arab music in a little café on the rue de la Lyre whose name I've forgotten; sit on the ground, at six in the evening, at the foot of the statue of the duc d'Orléans, in Government Square (not for the sake of the duke, but because there are people walking by, and it's pleasant there); have lunch at Padovani's, which is a kind of dance hall on stilts along the seashore, where the life is always easy; visit the Arab cemeteries, first to find calm and beauty there, then to appreciate at their true value the ignoble cities where we stack our dead; go and smoke a cigarette in the Casbah on the rue de Bouchers, in the midst of spleens, livers, lungs, and intestines that drip blood on everything (the cigarette is necessary, these medieval practices have a strong smell).

This is not the mode in which archaic Greece spoke of itself. But there can be little doubt that the anxious excitement of a Roth or the fond, half-disenchanted attachment of a Camus would have found its echoes in the harbour cities of the first philosophers.

No one has given more persuasive voice to this port–city alloy, with all its sense of flux and indeterminacy, loss and presence, than Constantine Cavafy, born in Alexandria in 1863, from a Greek family on his mother's side that had been prominent in Constantinople since the eighteenth century. The family had long experience in the offices of Greek commercial houses in London, Manchester and Liverpool, and all the trade routes between them. Cavafy himself never lived in Greece, 'the tight-lipped little kingdom' he despised, but remained in the far more dynamic and ever-mobile Greek world of his polyglot cosmopolitan port city.

With his own fusion of the erotic and the lonely, Cavafy advised us, his readers, that we should not hurry to our destinations but hope that the voyage we take should be a long one, 'full of summer mornings' when:

> with what pleasure, what joy,
> you enter harbours you're seeing for the first time;
> may you stop at Phoenician trading stations
> to buy fine things,
> mother of pearl and coral, amber and ebony,
> sensual perfume of every kind –
> as many sensual perfumes as you can;
> and may you visit many Egyptian cities
> to learn and go on learning from their scholars.

We are not to forget that an Ithaca – or a Tartessus or a Smyrna – is our destination.

> But don't hurry the journey at all.
> Better if it lasts for years,
> so you're old by the time you reach the island,
> wealthy with all you've gained on the way,
> not expecting Ithaca to make you rich.

And if you find her poor, Ithaca won't have fooled you.
Wise as you will have become, so full of experience,
   you'll have understood by then what these Ithacas mean.

The Ithacas we must look for are not in that final harbour
but out on the sea roads, in the bright wakes that cross and
recross the Mediterranean, the dolphin paths which are the
ligatures of that sea. Cavafy's famous poem, full of a calm and
unlikely optimism, echoing the world of Odysseus, written in
early twentieth-century Alexandria, describes a harbour mind
in which destinations matter only as much as the journeys they
generate. This is the Hermes–Hestia world, a dolphin-coinage
and dolphin-god world, one that is ready for – in fact pregnant
with – the philosophy that began to emerge in Ionia in the
seventh century BC.

2

MUST I THINK MY OWN WAY THROUGH THE WORLD?

ODYSSEUS
SMYRNA, AEOLIS/IONIA, 650–600 BC

The *Odyssey* stands at the threshold of this philosophical moment. It is the first work of our literature in which thinking plays the part of the hero – and Odysseus' first adjective, in line 1, is the definition of a multiple, agile, ever-thinking mind. He is *polytropos*, many-wayed, meaning not only that he travels to many places, but that the ways in which he travels are many, that he is many. He is protean, slipperily capable of many ways of being. He is many because the world he meets is many. Only by being many can a man survive in a many-wayed world. Many were the men he met, the poet says, many the cities he saw and – this the culminating term – many the minds he learned. The Greek word for mind, *noös*, is etymologically close to the word for ship, *naös*. Odysseus is essentially the navigator of mind and world. Navigation is what defines his vitality in a universe formed by its multiplicity. Many-ness requires a hand on the helm. To exist in a world of unexpectedness is to steer. Fully to live is to be Odyssean. To live is to think. Nothing could be further from the old imperial forms of thought in which to live was either to rule or to obey.

Only a few minutes into the telling of this story, even before the story itself has begun, with the troubled atmosphere merely conveyed, it is clear that Odysseus is away from Ithaca. The island is dominated by his absence when a stranger arrives at the door of the palace, like the herald of a new world. Odysseus' son, Telemachus, approaches him.

Who are you? where are you from? your city? your parents? what sort of vessel brought you? Why did the sailors land you in Ithaca? Who did they say they were? I hardly think you came this way on foot. Is this your first time here? Are you a friend of my father's?

There is some subtle characterization here: these are indeed the questions the moment generates. In a world of such mobility, it is difficult to know who is who. Everyone is a stranger and doubt over identity must colour the first steps in any encounter. But this cataract of questions is too much – a rush, a half-awkward joke about coming to an island on foot, from a young and anxious man, over-aware of the 'polished spear-rack' at the side of the hall where his father's weapons stand upright but unused, waiting for his return.

The stranger is calm and exudes *savoir faire*. He is Mentes – a name which is the Indo-European root of the word for 'thought' or 'mind' – and he arrives as a representative of this new world, a declaration at the beginning of the poem that it belongs in the now of about 650 BC. This Mind-man is an operator, quite explicitly not from the Iliadic past – he had not been to Troy – although an old friend of Odysseus. He is one of the Taphians, a people from the mainland opposite Ithaca, with a reputation known to every member of this audience as pirates, but now on a trading voyage to the west, to Temesē, a city in the south of the Italian peninsula, with a cargo of iron, already smelted and gleaming, looking to exchange it for copper in Italy.

The pirate captain seems to know a lot. He has heard that Odysseus is alive and well, somewhere on the broad sea, but he is no soothsayer or reader of the signs that some divine in birds. He is Mentes, a man of the Mind, and it is his thinking, information-processing self that has come to this conclusion.

In the sophisticated way of commerce, and not unlike Odysseus' own habit with strangers, he begins to flatter and charm. How handsome Telemachus is, his head, his eyes. Surely he is the son of Odysseus? But uncertainty rules this world. Who knows? Telemachus says to this impressive stranger. They say I am his son. My mother says so. But who of us can say where we are from? Are we not *thrown* into this world?

The smooth-talking pirate-trader-captain continues full of advice. Telemachus must begin to decide. He must take control, think how to be, how to remove the men from his mother's halls who are intent on marrying her and taking the kingdom. What Mentes recommends is hard. Think how to do this, he says confidingly, 'down in your heart and down in your spirit' – *kata phrena kai kata thumon*. To think is a matter not of surfaces but of depth and interiority. To think for Mentes is to make a distinction between outer appearance and inner truth; it is to enter the core of one's own person, to be concealed in oneself. Thinking is not social but the opposite of sociability, the denial of accepted wisdom. In some ways to think is to deceive.

Mentes recommends what a thinking trader-captain will always recommend: Telemachus must consider how to kill his enemies, either openly or with a trick. The word he uses, *dolō*, is the word Homer uses to describe the Trojan Horse, Odysseus' own great trick by which Troy was finally defeated. And the reason Telemachus must learn to lie and deceive? Because he is no longer a child and there is no dignity in childishness when one is a man. To be a man is to think about things, to devise tricks, to lie to one's enemies and to kill them.

This new world is a stirring sea. Motive in it is neither noble nor dignified. Those with any wisdom are prepared to behave in the ways that formal morality cannot condone. A pirate-captain-king is the source of this understanding. And he knows something about Odysseus – or says he does – not mentioned elsewhere in Homer: before Odysseus went to Troy he travelled up into the mainland of Greece to find poison for his arrows. His favoured way of killing was not the old heroic method of courageous face-to-face encounter but covert like this, killing as a trick. A glancing scratch from his arrows would poison an enemy. Mentes knows that Odysseus was refused the poison by people who thought the gods would not have approved. He acquired it anyway. And so even here in his absence, the first we have heard of him in this poem, Odysseus belongs to the world of hidden powers, a user of subtlety and secrecy, of dealing and dishonesty, of holding in his quiver the weaponry of deceit. The whole scene sets one's expectations on edge. Must I lie? Must I distrust the inherited ways of doing things? Must I somehow think my own way through the world?

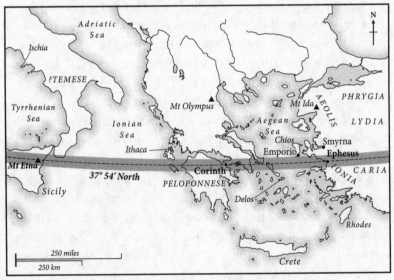

The Homeric sea-world, in which an understanding of the night sky allowed navigators to follow lines of latitude across open seas.
(See pages 68–71)

The argument over exactly where and when the *Odyssey* was made has come clear only in the last few years. Its roots are multicultural and ancient, with undoubted elements going far back into the Bronze Age and even before, but the *Odyssey* in the form we have it certainly came from somewhere on the coast of what is now Aegean Turkey. Homer knew the mountains and geography, winds and currents of the eastern Aegean, all of which he describes and refers to far more accurately than those he portrays on the distant west coast of Greece. Odysseus' fictional homeland, the island of Ithaca in the Ionian Sea between Greece and Italy, was clearly almost unknown to him. Nowhere does he describe it correctly. Nor on Ithaca, despite careful searching, has anyone found anything resembling Odysseus' palace. As much for Homer as for Cavafy, that island stands for a remote and longed-for place, out on the north-western edge of the known. The coast of Ionia was Homer's country.

The second hint as to Homer's origins is the language in which the epics are written. Apart from the forms inherited from the Mycenaean Bronze Age, Homer's poems fuse two kinds of Greek: the usual Ionic dialect – where *pente* means 'five' and *einai* 'to be' – which has been transmitted to modern Greek and was spoken both in Attica and in the southern end of the eastern Aegean; and another branch, the Aeolic, which developed in northern Greece and in the northern half of the eastern Aegean, in which 'five' is *pempe* and 'to be' *emmenai*. Wherever Homer sang was at the meeting of those language worlds.

Third, there is the geographical tradition. The written Homer, as the culmination of a centuries-long, anonymous, oral, bardic tradition, is claimed by many islands and cities but nowhere is mentioned more consistently as his birthplace than the ancient city of Smyrna, now called Izmir, at the head of its long gulf that dives deep into the west coast of Turkey. One ancient source after another says this is where Homer was born. And his name was not originally Homer, which is probably more of a title, meaning 'a singer at competitive gatherings', but Melesigenes, meaning 'born by the River Meles', which is the name of the river that runs down to the sea at Smyrna.

Finally, and critically, there is the question of Homer's date. In the past, the emphasis, perhaps because of the glamour of antiquity, pushed him as far back in time as possible, originally into the Bronze Age. Until recently the consensus hovered around 750 BC, just at the moment alphabetic writing was starting to appear in the Greek world.

A silver-gilt bowl of a kind made by the Phoenicians that was circulating in the seventh-century Mediterranean. This one was found in the Etruscan city of Caere north-west of Rome. Its concentric panels show an armed procession and a lion hunt, and may be the model for Homer's description of the many scenes of peace and war on the shield of Achilles.

That date now looks possible for the *Iliad* but too early for the *Odyssey*. It seems likely that there were two Homers, each a monumental composer of a great epic, separated by a generation or so, and that the *Odyssey* Homer is the later. Already in the *Iliad* there are references to the wealth of the Egyptian city of Thebes (which only grew to world standing in the early seventh century); allusions to certain kinds of Assyrian siege tactics; and the long description of the scenes and cities on the Shield of Achilles, which reads like a transcription of one of the great Phoenician bronze and silver dishes that were made and exported west and north into the Mediterranean only in the seventh century. Everything in the *Odyssey* is clearly aware of everything that was said in the *Iliad*. It is framed as a sequel and so all this suggests, as the great Oxford scholar and polymath Martin West wrote, that 'the *Odyssey* can't be earlier than the second half of the seventh century'.

If those assumptions are true and those conditions met, the poet of the *Odyssey* sang the epic and had it transcribed in about 650 BC, in the eastern Aegean, where the tradition remembered him singing beside the River Meles, in a sea-connected place that had absorbed the miracles of Phoenician craftsmanship, that knew of events and fortunes in the great river civilizations of the Near East, and where different forms of Greek were meeting and fusing. Seventh-century Smyrna, the point at which Ionic and Aeolic Greek intersected, and which fulfilled all those conditions, looks almost certainly like Homer's city.

Miraculously preserved and meticulously excavated in the mid-twentieth century by a series of joint Anglo-Turkish expeditions, the archaic Greek settlement of 'Old Smyrna' is hardly visited now. The earlier datings of Homer did not allow this place to be identified with his city, but if the *Odyssey* is as late as the mid-seventh century, these excavated streets feel revelatory, a sudden access to the place in which the *Odyssey* was made.

You will find it just to the north of modern Izmir, in the conservative and rather poor suburb of Bayrakli – few cars, women in the street wearing the niqab, an air of marginality, tiny vegetable plots caught between the houses, with the blue and silver sheeny towers of the business district standing to the south high above row on row of bland mid-century apartment blocks. Across the bay, beyond the gantries of the container port and the flyovers and interchanges of the modern highways, is 'New Smyrna' – new in the fourth century BC when it was refounded. The River Meles is here, but its waters, held between concrete banks, are black and polluted. Methane bubbles pop to the surface like a slow-glooping stew and one or two cormorants stare disconsolately into its poisoned depths. Bulk carriers lie out at anchor in Izmir Roads while small, double-ended tortoise-backed ferries crawl across the bay, connecting suburb to suburb. In the distance, the modern city hums with its business.

Old Smyrna occupies a low hill – it is the *tell* or occupation mound of a much older Bronze Age settlement – with some dusty black-grape vines in one corner and a few creaking olive trees growing in the volcanic soil. Nobody is there and you can walk all morning alone in the company of Homer and his poem. The ancient site is now boxed in by modern highways and is set some way back from the sea, but in the seventh century this low hill formed a peninsula surrounded on three sides by the waters of the gulf so that vessels could be drawn up on the beaches of the twin harbours on both sides – one open to the Gulf of Smyrna, the other a more protected haven, accessible by a narrow entrance beside the high city walls.

Old Smyrna does not cover a large area – about 15 acres – but it is clear enough from the orderly remains left open by the excavators that this was more than a village or the mere clustering of houses around the presence of a great man or war leader. This was a civic place, well organized and carefully sited to make the most of its sea connection.

Earlier guesses, placing Homer deep into the eighth century BC, had imagined him in small, fortified enclosures, not unlike the hill forts and brochs of the Iron Age in northern Europe. One such place is Emborio in southern Chios, a settlement on a high and austere ridge above the deep scoop of a bay, but it is a village not a town, pre-urban, with no more than fifty houses on the lanes leading up to its little acropolis. It is a hard climb to the top and there is nothing city-like here, but a rough,

Emborio on Chios, its defended early Iron Age settlement
high on the ridge above the harbour beach.

militaristic structure, almost like an encampment, small, well
defended, away from the threat of pirates, with a tiny, chapel-
like temple to Athena. In a hall house or *megaron,* perhaps forty
or fifty people could gather around their lord and master to
hear the heroic songs. The high point, with that hall house and
temple, is surrounded by a wall but the houses of the village
are left outside it. One could perhaps imagine the war poem
of the *Iliad* sung in a place like this, not unlike an Anglo-Saxon
mead hall and its associated village, but it is not somewhere
that could have given rise to the *Odyssey.*

Before about 700, Old Smyrna may have had something of
Emborio's quality: not set on a steep rocky hillside but clearly
non-urban, with rudimentary, curved huts crammed in higgledy-
piggledy, each with a grain store and a threshing yard, with
pigsties and cattle sheds. The inhabitants had a few imported
odds and ends, wine from the famous vineyards of Chios and
Lesbos, good olive oil in full-bodied amphorae from Athens,
but the essence of their lives was agricultural.

In 700 a disaster, probably an earthquake, struck Smyrna and
the shock gave the Smyrneans the chance to make a change.

After it, the houses were rebuilt as elegant, rectangular structures with many rooms and some with two storeys. The number of houses was reduced. A sudden planned spaciousness filled the city, organized carefully on an orthogonal plan with a north–south axis. A new sanctuary to Athena was built at the north-west corner, above the inner harbour, and a wide straight street led from one of the outer harbour gates towards it.

Old Smyrna and a model of its streets.

If the Homer of the *Odyssey* is to be dated around 650, this was his city. It is incontrovertibly urban. Something like 2,000 people would have been able to live here in comfort. The low rubbly walls of volcanic rock that survive today are only the footings and plinths for house walls that were made of large smooth clay bricks, the clay mixed with sand and straw, coated over with a pale clay plaster so that the city would have been fundamentally white, inside and out, probably painted and coloured in places, with stone paving in the streets. The continuous façades by which house was joined to house would have given little away. It was a pale and sophisticated city, washed and brushed, a place of distinction and order.

Internally, the flat roofs of the better houses were supported by rich and carefully shaped timber ceilings. Where the houses before the earthquake usually had only one room, these new houses were often centred on a little courtyard with a clear division between service rooms at the back and more refined apartments nearer the street. Stone kerbs outlined the central hearths for the fires that enshrined Hestia. It may be that these divisions reflect the arrival of domestic slaves in households, so that a social and psychological distinction was drawn between the spaces and lives of the slaves and those who owned them.

Old Smyrna.

Walking the streets today in the autumn sunshine, with starlings chattering in the palm trees, and the archaeologists clearing the grey, sandy soil from the large *megaron* somewhere near the central crossing of the city, it is not difficult to sense the urbanity here. It is a place given form by abstraction and civility, all of it probably dependent on the free time made available by slave labour.

Distinctions are drawn between public and private space, with narrow doorways giving on to the internal shelter of the house away from the street. Communal life would have focused on the harbours, the temple precincts and perhaps on an agora on the narrow neck of the isthmus connecting the city to the mainland. Even now, in its state of ruination, one can feel the meeting of Hestia and Hermes in these spaces. However small it is, Old Smyrna is undeniably a city, organized for trade and mutual support. This is not the clustering of a war band around a leader but a community, a society, what the Greeks called a *polis*.

Signs were everywhere that the large houses were the dwellings of the merchant oligarchs. Polished metal bowls from Cyprus, blue-green faience vases from the Phoenician cities, glossy dark drinking vessels from trading ports on the coast of Etruscan Italy, pieces of jewellery and little metal figurines from Egypt and Mesopotamia: all were found in the inner layers of the houses. Alongside them were the bronze clasps of tight-fitting women's belts from Phrygia, the Anatolian state inland of Smyrna, beside gold and ivory plaques that would have been sewn on to dresses. Both sexes wore heavy silver finger- and earrings, some perhaps from Italy. Amber beads, which must have come from the Baltic, perhaps via Etruria, were a lovely dusky red, glowing deep crimson when held up to the light. In the kitchens were iron spits and knives, the spaces lit by clay lamps that burned olive oil. Most houses had in store the fishing nets and lines of which only the lead net weights and single-barbed fish hooks survive.

These were the possessions and arrangements and life materials of the audience for the *Odyssey*: a cosmopolitan, active and dynamic set of traders in an ambitious coastal city, enclosed by its strong stone and earth-brick wall, for whom the Mediterranean was not the realm of mysterious monsters but a network of allies, rivals, markets and opportunities, a sea of the deal. The stories Homer told them were set in the sea they knew but were not the life of that sea as they knew it. The *Odyssey* was a romance for the trading oligarchs of Smyrna, populating their world with the figures of myth, dream and nightmare.

John Cook, the Director of the British School at Athens who conducted the excavations here in the late 1940s, recognized that the *Odyssey* contains a description of a city strikingly like the one in which it was being sung and heard.

Odysseus has been out in the wilds for years. He has been trapped like a wasp in the delicious honeypot of Calypso's island. At last he has escaped and sailed away from her, nearly drowning in a storm raised by Poseidon, the sea god who loathes him, and finally with the help of Athena and a white-ankled goddess Leucothea finds himself cast up stark naked, starving, hungry and full of lust, on a beach where a river comes down to the sea next to a city.

A sketch of Old Smyrna as imagined by the
Cambridge scholar Richard Nicholls.

This was the island of Scheria, a half-real wonder-world full of golden palaces and self-sailing ships but also a peninsula city by the sea, surrounded by a high wall, with twin harbours on either side and a place of assembly next to the ships. Like Smyrna's, the entrance to Scheria's harbour was narrow (and so safe from swell) and a roadway ran to the city along the neck of the peninsula.

The curved ships are drawn up along the road, for they all have stations for their ships, each man one for himself. There, too, is their place of assembly around the fair temple, fitted with huge stones set deep in the earth. Here the men are busy with the tackle of their black ships, with cables and sails, and here they shape the thin oar-blades.

And Odysseus marvelled at the harbours and the stately ships, at the meeting-places where the heroes themselves gathered, and the walls, long and high and crowned with palisades, a wonder to behold.

There are poetic fusions at work here. The Phaeacians who live in Scheria are the audience for most of Odysseus' tales. They hear from him the stories of the Cyclops and of his visits to Hades, Circe and Calypso. They are identical to the audience Homer has himself in the Smyrna *megaron*. As Homer tells the tale of Odysseus telling the tale of his adventures to the Phaeacians, he is telling the tales to the Smyrneans. There must have been nods of recognition among his audience in his describing Scheria as if it were the very city from which they all came. But his Scheria is also a glamorous near-eastern port city, drenched in riches, far more potent than anything in Ionia. The young men of Scheria are arrogantly pleased with themselves, patronizing Odysseus as a provincial and mercantile nobody, not likely to be good at the sort of athletics in which heroes excel. They tell him he seems to be 'a man unused to manly sports, more like the captain of a merchant crew, trading to and fro in your well-benched ship, careful about the cargo, keeping a greedy eye on freight and profit'.

These descriptions surely raised a rueful smile in the Smyrna audience. Without the depth of culture enjoyed and luxuriated in by the grandees of Scheria, they may have been filled with unease at the vulgarity of their new mercantilism. Or more likely they would answer as Odysseus answers, riled by the condescending tone of his hosts:

The gods seldom grace men equally with their gifts, of mind, form or speech. One man is inferior in his looks, but the gods set a crown of beauty on his words, and men look on him with delight, and he speaks quite fluently, with sweet modesty, and is conspicuous among the people gathered around him, and as he goes through the city men gaze upon him as upon a god.

Scheria might believe in aristocratic excellence but Smyrna loves the power of the word. The lack of vanity marks out the man of the city. Besides, Smyrna *was* good at sports. A Smyrnean called Onomastus was the first man to win a boxing contest in Olympia in 688 BC. Nevertheless, the ambivalence remains: the mercantile reality of their modern lives as traders-cum-pirates, dealmakers and experts in trickery and deceit has summoned the reproach of a far more established world. The Smyrneans are living in a threshold condition, hovering between heroic and post-heroic.

A gold necklace from Rhodes, almost exactly contemporary with the poet of the *Odyssey*, 150 miles to the north, now in the British Museum. A fringe of golden pomegranates hangs beneath the golden plaques each bearing the image of a winged angel or goddess whose origins are in Assyria or Persia.

Imagine this in the pale polished spaces and cypress-roofed apartments of seventh-century Smyrna, the ships drawn up outside, the room full of men who have sailed the Mediterranean, who have brought back the goods and begun to acquire the

Part of a silver banqueting service, including a Greek-style wine jug, a two-handled cup, a hemispherical cup and fluted bowls all typical of the Near East. These objects, contemporary with the *Odyssey*, were found in an Etruscan grave north of Rome – the owner's name was chiselled into the silver – and would have represented a vision of ultimate luxury for Homer's audience.

riches for which they have longed. They have made their way, made the bargains and engaged with the compromises that mean there are luxuries here now.

When Homer describes the great *megaron* in Scheria, it is clearly fantastical, with acres of gold and silver, huge numbers of slave girls, but in other ways it is conspicuously like the *megaron* – or *andron*, the room of the men – to be found in many Smyrna houses of the seventh century: benches for guests along the walls; a central hearth, whose stone kerb is ashy; columns within the hall (usually in Smyrna of timber with stone bases, in Scheria of bronze). All you need add are those soft and transient things Homer describes: for the benches cushions and 'rugs of soft fabric, cunningly woven, the handiwork of women'; torchères for banqueters at night; a good supply of chairs for distinguished guests to sit up off the floor; handmaids bringing water and towels with which to wash and dry one's hands; heralds mixing wine in silver bowls; a polished table, on which a basket full of bread and 'a cup of thirst-quenching wine' can be set; a bed made for the stranger's night in the portico. Beautiful silver banqueting services have been found in Etruscan graves of exactly this date. Homer's story imagines something that is a wonderful example of everything his audience knows, not a sci-fi world entirely alien to them.

Friezes of wild goats graze around the belly of a bowl made in Rhodes in about 650 BC, found in a house in Old Smyrna.

The reception rooms of the houses in Smyrna contained sets of dice and seven-stringed lyres, vases and plates from Rhodes and Corinth, decorated with wild goats, grazing around the belly of the bowls, miniature Phoenician nudes of men and women carved in ivory, beaded dresses in an Egyptian style, with the beads sewn on to the fabric in polychromatic flowers, hawk figurines derived from the Egyptian god Horus. All of these can be seen now in the Izmir museums. Many of the houses had deep terracotta baths, with the rim high at the head-end where the water was likely to splash off the bather's shoulders and lower towards the foot, making it easier for the old to step in and out. The baths had rounded floors, sinking lower at the foot-end of the bath to make a shallow circular basin for the bather's feet. In most of the baths, the edges of these basins were polished by the constant rubbing of the bathers' heels.

Above: A bath from Old Smyrna with a lowered end to make it easier
for the old and infirm to get in.
Below: Capitals from the archaic temple in Old Smyrna, now in
the Izmir History and Art Museum.

In about 630, a new temple of Athena was built next to the
city walls, exactly 100 feet long, first with huge mushroom
capitals to its columns, soon replaced with the rough ram's horn
form known as the Aeolic capital. The temple, in various succes-
sive forms, was drawing on the imagery that Ionian Greeks,
either as mercenary soldiers or as traders in the Nile delta, would
have seen and been amazed by in Egypt, Canaan and the
Phoenician cities, where many contemporary shrines were decorated with capitals of the same pattern. It has a claim to be the
first Greek temple ever to be surrounded by a colonnade and
the first to be built entirely of stone. Somewhere in its precincts
stood huge, loll-tongued lions and the statue of an enormous
man, reminiscent of the Hercules who on his Phoenician raft
drifted into Erythrae at the far end of the gulf (see p. 15).

Capitals from seventh-century Canaanite shrines now in the Israel Museum, Jerusalem, explicitly the models for the capitals on the first stone temple in Old Smyrna.

The Near East was arriving here in Smyrna. These are the physical raw materials of the revolution this book describes: the infusion into a previously small and marginal Greek world of the power, the scale and some of the riches of the aeons-old culture of the Nile and the Levant.

One of the loll-tongued lions from Old Smyrna.

Among the imports was the easily used and easily adapted alphabet, coming from the Phoenician cities, arriving in the Greek lands in about 800 BC and, by the time of the composition of the *Odyssey*, widespread in Greek cities from Italy to the Black Sea. Seventh-century Smyrna was a pervasively literate society. The dust of its remains is full of fragments scratched, written on and graffitied over by the people of the city. Some are no more than an owner's mark – a trident, a simple branchlike gesture, a five-pointed star, a couple of letters or even initials – with which an amphora from Chios or a wine jug was labelled. These signs spread across the language communities gathered in and moving through the city, so that Lydians, Phrygians and Carians all wrote a word or two or parts of their names on cups and bowls. A Phrygian called Hyagnis was here, and a man called Gorgos who may or may not have been a Greek. Three fragments have been found in which the writer was practising the letters of the Greek alphabet in order – alpha, beta, gamma – and nothing more. A piece of a bronze greave or shin guard was found scratched on either side of its central rib with what

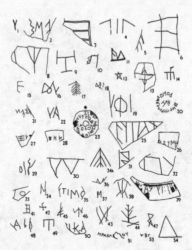

The ownership marks, logos and graffiti found on
various pieces of pottery in Homer's Smyrna.

might be part of the word *aristeia*, meaning that moment of glory in which a warrior wades with undeniable force down a road paved with his enemies; or more likely *aristeion*, a prize awarded in a contest between citizens.

Left: The graffitied shin guard or greave, with the word on the lower level spelling out *aristei-* (to be read from right to left), meaning 'prize' or 'moment of triumph'.
Right: Part of a rim of a bowl saying (from left to right) *Istrokles me.*

One rim of a big wine-mixing bowl, a *dinos*, was painted by its maker with his own name and the beginnings of a phrase most of which has not survived: 'Istrokles [made] me' or perhaps 'drew me'. Istros was the name both of the colony of Miletus at the mouth of the Danube and of the river itself where it entered the Black Sea; it is likely that Istrokles came from there. One large vessel was marked in a spiral of letters on the foot: 'I am the drinking cup of Dolion', but 'Dolion' is not merely a person's name.

A spiral graffito proclaiming Dolion as the owner of this cup.

It means the 'crafty one', the 'trickster'; has the hint of a joke about it; is a word that hovers constantly in the air around Odysseus; and might be taken as the signature of this first moment when the canny man, the man who can make the subtle decisions, who can weigh the evidence and take the risk, who is not entirely straight with those around him, begins to make his presence felt in the world.

Old Smyrna is the world out of which Odysseus grew: literate, adventurous, hungry, urban, careful, witty, sly, on the edge of things, demanding and complex. It was a society more about cleverness than about heroism and dominance. The steps of that seventh-century temple of Athena in Old Smyrna, with the repro-duction Aeolic capitals set on their remade columns, surrounded by the olive trees that remain in the old town and with the towers and cranes of Izmir's new business district to the south, is the place, if you have read the *Odyssey* once, to read it again and find in it not the miraculously strange but the entrancingly familiar. It is the first poem to describe the world we know.

The reconstructed temple of Athena in Old Smyrna.

Odysseus' qualities as a trickster and tale-teller are not his alone but are infused in the world of which he is a part. To be overt in it is to risk victimhood; naivety is impotence and clarity vulnerable. Besides, the conveyor of this gospel of deceit is himself a deceiver. Mentes is not real. The smooth-talking pirate-trader-captain, the man of Mind, is nothing of the sort. He is the goddess Athena in disguise, the radiant transgender goddess of brilliance, the advocate of cleverness, pretending to be what she is not, telling a naive young man that he must become a pirate-captain-trader too, that he must learn to cheat because the only adulthood which will succeed in the new world is one that is not true.

Even that formulation is too definitive. Athena is here only because she is profoundly loyal to Odysseus and his family. She has come to earth to save them from their enemies, and so her lies and her advocacy of lying are in service of a truth and a commitment to the good and great. Her form of deception is itself subject to shifts and changes. The liar following in the path of Athena-Mentes, the Goddess-Mind, will learn how to shift himself between true and untrue, blurring those boundaries, acting now the trader, now the pirate, now the teller of tales, now the liver of them, now loyal, now disloyal, now subtle, now bruisingly and blindingly obvious. Essentially, Mentes is teaching Telemachus how to deal.

There is a moral change in the gods here too. Part of the earlier generation was Poseidon, one of the great, blocky divinities, capable of vast and lumpen violence, coarse-grained and essentially unthinking in every large and destructive gesture he makes. One of his sons is the one-eyed, clump-minded Cyclops Polyphemus. They are the enemies of Odysseus and the two of them stand on the other bank of the great divide that separates the past from the future: Poseidon and the Cyclops for large brutishness and being no other than what they are; Athena and Odysseus for nimble light-footedness, the spirit of the thinking mind, able to appear in the world unrecognized but imparting a kind of glow to it, a dawn presence.

Homer's psychology is subtle and careful. His characters are rarely sure that a god is there with them. Something is usually sensed but it has no name. These arrivals of godliness are not *epiphanies*, actual appearances of gods on the surface of the earth, but something broader and less defined, a feeling of emergence, a haze of power or wellbeing. Homer, and so his audience, always knows that it is a god and which god it is, but people in the poem rarely do. They think merely that some extraordinary weather or sunlight or sudden inexplicable bright-ness has arrived without being able to put a name to it, a signifying of a presence more than the everyday.

There is something transitional in this, an elision between a sense of divine power and a sense of human capacity. The boundary blurs between the two. Even now, Telemachus only half-guesses that Athena has been with him as Mentes, or that the feeling of new purpose and clarity in his mind was put there by her. As she leaves him, he finds his spirit (or his heart – the Greek words are themselves transitional) filled with strength and courage. In his mind, he suddenly sees her for a god and is filled with wonder at this visitation, but then the categories shift and, as Telemachus goes to confront the suitors who are battening on his mother, Homer sees the young man in a different light: as *isotheos phōs*, a man equal to a god, a man like a god himself.

It is one of the scenes that makes the *Odyssey* feel as if it is on the verge of a new form of understanding. The meeting of Telemachus and Mentes is either an aspect of deep inheritance, the visit by a god to a favoured son on earth; or uses that ancient rhetoric to express something else: the realization of a capacity in a man then growing into adulthood, learning that brightness is a close cousin to resolve, and having come to that recognition stands back in delighted wonder at the change that has overcome him, the sense of potential growing in him, the opening of a more capable future. Although much in the *Odyssey* was borrowed from the great near-eastern epics, and from the

Greeks' own past, nothing like this had appeared before. It marks the beginning of the autonomous self.

That is one of the clear differences between the two epics. In the *Iliad*, at moments of crisis, it is more often than not a god that decides. When for example, in the opening scene, Agamemnon insults Achilles and threatens to take the slave girl Briseis from him, Achilles, who loves her, is grief-stricken. He thinks of murdering the king with his sword.

> While he pondered this in mind and heart, and was drawing
> from its sheath his great sword, Athena came from heaven.
> She stood behind him, and seized him by his fair hair. None
> of the others saw her. Achilles was gripped with wonder, and
> turned around, and immediately recognized Pallas Athena.
> Terribly her eyes shone.

Why had she come? Was it to punish Agamemnon? Not at all: 'I have come from heaven to stay your anger, if you will obey. Do not grasp the sword with your hand. With words you can taunt him, telling him how it shall be . . . But refrain from hurting him, and obey.' The goddess is unanswerable authority; she makes Achilles' mind up for him.

In the *Odyssey*, decisions are not made like that. Odysseus, Penelope and the others often 'ponder', 'consider' and 'think about' things. They turn things over in their minds, tossing to and fro at night. Odysseus thinks of himself as a sausage on a griddle, turned one way and then the other. He beats his own chest to calm his troubled heart. Penelope's heart is just as anxious, flitting from branch to branch like a nightingale singing in a thicket. And more often than not – the line between the two epics is not quite sharply drawn – the decisions they make are theirs alone, as autonomous people. Pondering scenes in the *Iliad* are resolved by divine intervention in over 70 per cent of cases; in the *Odyssey*, the people themselves decide quite unaided in over 90 per cent of cases. Athena may often be alongside them as they do so, for the simple reason that she is the goddess of the mind, but it is unthinkable that she might grab Odysseus or anyone else by the hair.

Athena became central to the life of the harbour cities. In one after another the temple of Athena occupies the summit of the acropolis, presiding over the harbour far below. She can be seen from a ship far out at sea and is the goddess of the high points of the city, as if the city formed the skirts around her presence. The temples of Athena were usually the site of enormously rich dedications by grateful citizens, becoming the treasuries of the societies over which she reigned.

That Athena-crown is an important part of the psychogeography of the harbour cities. In one after another, the pattern is repeated: walk up from the beach and quays of the harbour itself to the ship sheds and warehouses, on into the commercial quarters, to the marketplace, the agora which was the meeting place of the citizens, with the council chamber, the *bouleuterion*, beside them. Above them the theatre and then on the very heights of the city, the temple of Athena itself.

This repeated geometry is a movement from the sea to the gilded and enshrined space of the deity who embodies the powers of the mind. To walk through these ruined streets, to climb from harbour to heights, is to experience a model of social existence that might also stand for a model of a balanced mind.

Athena appears as the great ally of the men she loves. She helps them at every turn, full of transformations, ready to steer those she loves and protects into the paths of autonomy, encouraging them to decide for themselves what is right; not relying on inheriting from others the moral or political structures of their lives, but thinking, wrestling with their consciences, not victims of fate but the navigators of an existence in which hazard will always be the price of vitality and autonomy.

We may assume the naturalness of thinking for ourselves, but there is nothing natural about it – nor anything more natural than obeying the powers that be, thinking as we are told to think. To think for oneself is a cultural choice, and often a difficult one. Society has all the instruments to prevent you: ridicule, contempt, exclusion, punishment. And it may not always be the right path. Odysseus himself fails as king, trader and sea captain, largely because he fails to fulfil any responsibilities that extend beyond his own life. He returns from Troy poor and filthy, with no treasure to show for his twenty years' adventuring, his men dead or lost, his ships sunk, the kingdom he has abandoned on the verge of collapse, his queen on the brink of dishonour and saved only by her own courage, wiles and virtue. The *Odyssey*'s exploration of thinking for yourself is no adulation of it but the dramatization of the tragedy and marvellousness of a man out alone on the seas of life. In the way of the tradition of philosophy to which the *Odyssey* opened the door, Homer animates the questions of existence. He provides no answer to them.

The need to navigate the seas was no metaphor. Clearly, even now, it is possible to sail across the Aegean without losing sight of land, but the connections of the harbour cities went further and longer than those island-hopping routes. The sailors of the Greek Iron Age did not cling to coasts, nor only sail on the brightest and clearest of summer days. Homer's world is full of hints and suggestions that highly evolved mental maps played their part. In a famous moment from the *Iliad*, the goddess Hera travels with divine swiftness across the Aegean from Mount Ida near Troy to the heights of Olympus on the Greek mainland where the other gods are gathered. The geography, as usual in Homer, is tangible and specific, but it is Homer's comparison of her speed that throws a sharp light on the mental structures of the world in the seventh century BC:

Just as the mind of a man who has sailed to many lands starts to race when, in the wisdom of his heart, he thinks 'I wish I were here! I wish I were there!' – that's how fast the regal Hera flew in her eagerness.

The distant places are intimately known; they are to be dreamed of and longed for. The sea and the lands beyond it are, in 650 BC, zones not of terror but of desire and nostalgia. Homer's audience would have nodded at that comparison, at their adventures when young, the lastingness of the connectivities in their minds. The sea and its distant shores were not places of disturbing otherness, but a territory – in fact a 'maritory', an area of sea as known and held as a territory on land – to be imagined and reimagined, in storm and calm, terror and triumph.

Sailing was, apart from anything else, a mental exercise. Homer's description of Odysseus' navigation away from Calypso's island in the *Odyssey*, driven by his tearful longing for home and wife, is the *locus classicus* of those intellectual qualities.

And he sat and guided his raft skilfully with the steering oar, nor did sleep fall on his eyelids, as he watched the Pleiades, and Boötes, the Herdsman, slow to set, and the Bear, which men also call the Wagon, which ever circles where it is and watches Orion, and alone has no part in the baths of Ocean.

These were the most familiar of constellations, named like this in the Bronze Age by the Assyrians and Babylonians, described with the same words in the *Iliad* when the smith god Hephaestus drew them into the grand cosmic patterns he made on the shield of Achilles.

These phrases are no landlubber's romantic glance at the stars but an essentially dynamic picture of the movement of those

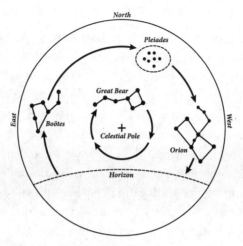

The simplified heavens of Odysseus' voyage: constellations turn through the night around the fixed point of the celestial pole. One after another, Orion, the Pleiades and Boötes, the Herdsman, rise in the east and eventually sink into the sea to the west. The Great Bear, near the celestial pole, circles around it and is never lost from sight.

constellations in the northern sky at night. Each is prominent, rising in the east and circling around the north pole to set eventually in the west. As Homer describes them for Odysseus, they come in two pairs, of which one is early, one late. The Pleiades, which is a star cluster in Taurus, is among the first to rise and first to set; the Herdsman or Boötes, the oxman, among the latest, appearing on a summer night quite quickly, his body laid out almost horizontally at the north-eastern horizon, and as the spinning of the earth turns him around the north pole, it brings him vertical, so that after a long journey lasting most of the night his body slowly sinks in the north-western sky, legs, trunk and head disappearing in turn until the first hint of dawn appears. Slow to set.

The other two constellations also look at each other across the pole: like the Pleiades, the huge and heroic figure of Orion, armed with sword and bow, rises early and so is also early to drop into the western sea; the Great Bear, or the Plough or Wagon, begins the night to the east of the pole but circles close to it and unlike the others never drops into the baths of Ocean, merely fading with the rising of the sun.

The configuration of the night sky today is not quite as it was 2,600 years ago, as the axis of the earth has shifted, but these four constellations still now in the dark of an Aegean night behave as Odysseus knew them. It is ancient knowledge, inherited from far beyond the Greek world, and in a way it is a perception that has philosophical implications. To know the stars is to recognize realities that go beyond the daily flux of things. A kind of eternity is evident in the sky every night. Watch these constellations, understand their relationship and you will grasp something of the everlasting nature of the universe. It is one of the paths towards the metaphysical.

Understanding this pattern is also the means of holding a course at sea at night. If the unsleeping man at the helm watches these constellations revolving above him, he will find, unmarked by anything but relatively faint stars (Polaris today, Kochab in Ursa Minor in the Iron Age), the point around which the heavens turn, known as the celestial pole. If he can hold that night pole at the same place in the rigging of his ship, measuring it against the yard of the mainsail or the main stay that comes down from the mast to the stern, he will be able to keep to a steady latitude. If he loses concentration and diverges from his path northwards, that point in the night sky will seem to rise against his mark; if he drops south, it will sink.

A system of navigation that understood that the altitude of the celestial pole was a way of measuring the latitude of the viewer was a central part of the Mediterranean sailing enterprise. It may be that one of the reasons the eastern sailors reached the Mediterranean west so early is that the alignment of that sea itself is along the lines of latitude. It meant that anyone in Ephesus (latitude 37° 54′N) would be seeing that celestial pole at virtually the same angle as someone in Delos (37° 24′N), in

Corinth (37° 54'N) or on the slopes of Mount Etna in Sicily (37° 45'N). A natural ligature ran between them.

It was the heavens that connected these places. A voyage between them traced a celestial path and the sailor who looked to the stars was not only equipped for trade and adventure; he was aware, at some level, of the nature of the cosmos. Many years later, Plato would point out that it was one of the qualities of the enlightened man to shift his perspective from things on earth. In the *Republic*, whoever is released from his chains in the cave of the ordinary world, and allowed to look beyond it towards the light of an eternal truth, will at first be successful only 'in distinguishing shadows; then he will discern the reflections of men and other things in water; and afterwards the realities; and after this he will raise his eyes to encounter the light of the moon and stars'.

And so when Odysseus sails the path that Calypso has set him he is not only running down a line of latitude that would have been deeply familiar to Homer's audience but engaging in a form of practical astronomy that lay at the foundations of the sailing and adventuring city from which those listeners came. The connection between heaven and earth is a silver thread in the story of this intellectual revolution. In one sense, the fundamental question concerns that connection: what is it that unifies the change and trouble of this world with the stillness and permanence of the world above? The harbour mind is also a mind that seeks to navigate by the stars.

The small volcanic island of Ischia looks across the Bay of Naples to the pudding basin of Vesuvius 25 miles away. A milky haze rests all morning over the almost motionless sea at the foot of the volcano. On Ischia, the woods spread up on to the pleated skirts of Mount Epomeo. Giant magnolias surround the villas, bougainvillea and mounds of ipomoea tumble down towards the beaches. An incomparable spaghetti allo scoglio is to be had in the Ristorante Delfino by the sandy beach in Lacco Ameno.

There is more here than the view or the endless saltwater aqua-detox spas. In the 1950s, a German archaeologist, Georg Buchner, discovered the earliest Greek colony in the west, contemporary with the emergent cities in Greek Ionia. At the same time, the much loved parish priest of Lacco Ameno in Ischia, Don Pietro Monti, decided to start digging in the crypt under his own church. A rivalry, perhaps a kind of enmity, developed between the two of them, as Buchner began to discover the graveyard of the eighth-century colony, full of tantalizing objects: pots made by Greeks from Euboea, graffiti by Phoenicians from Tyre, Sidon, Byblos and Carthage, bronze figures made by peoples from the Italian peninsula, precious stones carved by Aramaeans from what is now northern Syria. Suddenly alive in front of Buchner was the world of Odysseus, a slippery, connected, adventurous universe, exploring the limits of the known.

While Buchner dug into the graves, Don Pietro down the road was digging into the working quarters of the colony beneath his church, where the Iron Age potters made the ceramics that were exported to the Italian mainland. The archaeologist begged the priest to stop, as he knew nothing and was destroying any evidence of what had happened there. The priest continued to dig away, claiming that the ancient layers were confused anyway, looking for prizes, discovering kilns and buildings from the potters' quarter.

Don Pietro died in 2008, aged ninety-three. His underground workings and archives are now closed, as they are thought to be dangerous. There is, of course, no money to make repairs. After a few visits to local luminaries I managed to get access to them. I was accompanied by Immaculata Castagna, a parishioner of Don Pietro, who seemed as much in love with him as when he was alive.

Immaculata, in her golden-buttoned peach linen suit, as perfect as her name, showed me his many finds, still housed in the gloomy dusty dark under the church. A cavern full of ancient streets and crumbled buildings, the burned red marks of hearths and kilns. Shattered pots in hidden backrooms. And there, among the endless remains, one unforgettable marvel. Immaculata brought it out from its tissue-paper wraps: a fragment, a green-glazed sherd from a large late eighth-century or early seventh-century wine-mixing vase, a *krater*, probably made in Ischia but modelled on pots made in the Aegean 900 miles away to the east. Scratched into its glaze, accompanied by the letter B, is a depiction of the constellation Boötes, the Herdsman described by Homer, as he guided Odysseus sailing away from Calypso's island, with its brilliant central gathering of stars accompanied by outliers which are held to represent the Herdsman's arms.

Immaculata showed me, holding it above her, how the sherd came from the rim of a bowl whose inside had been decorated with all the constellations, so that when held upside down it would represent the heavens by which the sailors could plot their course. Imagine the base of the *krater* as the celestial pole: the constellations could be turned around it as they would be in the night sky, slowly revolving, slow to set. She gave me the sherd to hold and for an unforgotten moment I had Odysseus' stars in my hand.

3

WHAT IS EXISTENCE
MADE OF?

THALES, ANAXIMANDER, ANAXIMENES
MILETUS, IONIA, 600–575 BC

The first story about a Greek philosopher is a tiny parable of the relationship between what lasts and what changes. Is it better to think of eternity? Or the here and now? The cosmic realities or the everyday facts? Should we look at the stars or do the laundry?

It is set in Miletus, the great Greek commercial port city 100 miles south of Smyrna, tucked into its own deep gulf driving miles back into the body of what is now Aegean Turkey. The story, first told by Socrates, reported by Plato, describes an encounter between Thales, the archetypal first thinker, and a young female slave. It is, in its way, a story about philosophy itself, what it's good for, what it isn't and how those categories meet.

The scene is somewhere in the depths of the booming sixth-century trading city. Walking now through the wonderful, dusty ruins, out beyond the pomegranate-juice café housed in a Turkish caravanserai, below the huge Roman theatre and past the modern museum into the fields and olive groves worked by the farmers from the Turkish village of Balat, I found something that might have been this ur-place: a stone wellhead over the mouth of a cistern, with a rough marble basin beside it, the stone split and rope-worn from centuries of work hauling water from its depths.

74

The sort of well-head in Miletus into which
Thales, the first philosopher, stumbled.

The philosopher is out strolling at night in the streets and
open spaces of his city. He is a distinguished man, with many
cosmopolitan connections. His father had been a Carian, the
people who lived here before the Greeks arrived (they were allies
of the Trojans in the *Iliad*) and who were still part of everyday
life in Miletus. His mother was Greek but from a Phoenician
family. Thales had been to Egypt and learned from the Egyptians
how to use the shadow of a building to measure its height. He
was an astronomer and had written a book on navigational
techniques, advising the Greeks against using the Plough as the
fixed point of the night sky, as it was too far from the celestial
pole, and instead urging them to pay attention to the fainter
constellation of Ursa Minor, as the Phoenicians did. It was
nearer the hub of the night and any course that kept it constant
in the rigging would be truer. He was, in other words, the agent
and conveyor of near-eastern wisdom.

He knew, probably from Babylonia, almost certainly through
the Phoenicians, when the movements of sun and moon could
allow him to predict an eclipse of the sun – at least roughly.
He understood, perhaps also from Mesopotamia, the manip-
ulation of water and could advise on the diverting of rivers
into alternative channels when needed. He was an astute
businessman, one year making a corner in olive presses when
no one else had predicted a heavy harvest, and renting them

out for the highest possible price when the demand was greatest; and he was politically distinguished, having suggested that
the cities of Ionia should sink their chronic rivalry in a unifying
league, with its centre in the city of Teos (near the geographical middle of Ionia), and he had written a constitution for the
league.

A great and polymathic figure, an inheritor of eastern learning
and no fool but an embodiment of all that was best in the
multiplicity and ingenuity of his harbour world.

> What is difficult? he was asked.
>   To know oneself.
> What is easy?
>   To give advice to someone else.
> What is pleasant?
>   To be a success.
> What is the most unheard of thing?
>   An aged tyrant.

He is out tonight looking at the heavens, as one does, occasionally taking a step backwards to get a better look.

While he was studying the stars and looking upwards, he fell
into a well, and it is said that a beautiful and witty Thracian
slave girl laughed at him because he was so keen to know
the things in the sky that he could not see what was there
behind him, right at his feet.

Philosophers, Socrates says ruefully, will always be

a laughing-stock not only to Thracian girls but to everyone
in general, because they are always falling into wells and all
kinds of trouble – through sheer unworldliness. They're
chronically gauche. Philosophers always look like idiots.

Thales has his bottom stuck in the wellhead, and the laughter of the wonderful Thracian is ringing around him in the starry night. It is a scene to pause over. He is 'the ornament of Miletus' (the city would later build a shrine to his memory) and she is a slave. He is the heir to all the wisdom of the known world; she is a victim of trafficking. He is in touch with the eternal verities; she knows only the reality of her life and the absurdity of philosophers.

This story has been told and retold over the centuries as an endorsement of the virtues of thinking, its magnificent indifference to the ordinary aspects of the world, to the shopping and the washing up, admirable because disconnected from the everyday. That disconnection has always looked like the essence of philosophical virtue. Plato describes in the *Symposium* how when Socrates was walking to a drinking party, he would wander off to a stranger's porch to enjoy a period of silent contemplation, not even considering he might be late or where he should go next. And how in the middle of a military campaign, as the other soldiers tried to get some anxious sleep before battle, he stood up all night 'inspecting' a philosophical problem.

These were the first absent-minded intellectuals, contemplative thinkers lost to the world as they laboured in thought. They never knew where they were, had no idea of the layout of a city, where the marketplace or law courts were, nor what went on in those places, let alone in nightclubs or at outrageous dinner parties. 'It never occurs to them even in their dreams to indulge in such things,' Socrates says. People's ancestry or breeding were 'matters to which they pay no more attention than to the number of pints in the sea'.

The philosopher does not even know that he does not know these things. He does not keep aloof from them for the sake of looking good. Really, it is only his body that is at home in the city; his mind, considering all these things unimportant and trivial, looks down on them and is off away in all sorts of directions . . . investigating the universal nature of everything, each in its eternal aspect, never lowering itself to anything actually close to hand.

This high-minded distractedness may be part of the DNA of philosophy, but does it now hold much attraction for us? Is unworldliness still a virtue? Isn't it in some ways reprehensible? Besides, there is another way of hearing this story. The enslaved woman, dragged from her homeland north of the Aegean, in a scene not unlike the terrifying depiction of rape on the coins from Thasos, has been brought to a city where she has no liberty and no rights, is thought of as a piece of property, where anything she owns technically belongs to her master, where she can be forced to have sex at the will of her owner with no recourse to the law, can be sold on by that owner to other owners who will have the same rights over her, and must attend in the meantime to the tasks on which the workings of the city rely – the drawing of water, the washing of houses and their inhabitants, the provision of her labour. The testimony of a Greek slave means nothing at law (unless given under torture). Slave girls can habitually be bought by citizen-madams to be housed in brothels and raised as prostitutes. Cruelty is implicit in her condition; slaves are whipped, fettered, tattooed and otherwise violated at will.

A question raises its head: is the birth of philosophy, with its clear distinction between the things that mattered to it and the things that mattered to everyone else, a function of this increasingly polarized world, between those who were enslaved and attended to the actual, and those who owned slaves who could attend to the high-minded? Whose side are we on? The thinker staring at the stars? Or the beautiful girl laughing at his ridiculousness? Would Thales have been able to look at the stars had the Thracian girl not been there to carry his water

WHAT IS EXISTENCE MADE OF?

from the well in which he stumbled? Whose work was it that wore the grooves in the marble wellhead?

The story may be a fable of the conflict in all of us between thought and common sense, the imaginative and the practical, but it also has a social and political dimension. Socrates thought Thales' absent-mindedness 'the price of entry for philosophy', but the Italian philosopher Adriana Cavarero sees this story, at the very start of western philosophy, as an origin myth of the wrongness of philosophy itself, the diminished value it puts on the real (and often female) world and its privileging of the theoretical (usually male). The laughter of the Thracian slave, she says, 'recalls us all to the actual phenomena of worldly experience', and the reality of their value. It is a reproach at the root of our civilization because, ever since, western philosophy has failed to love that girl and admired only the heaven-orientated speculations of the philosopher.

Cavarero asks the awkward question: who is philosophy good for? Does the very idea of philosophy – that thinking can give access to a kind of structural understanding of existence that stands above and is in some way better than everyday experience – actually create and reinforce a set of social and conceptual wrongs?

And so the story is more than a joke at the expense of a professor. It addresses the foundations of every philosophical question: what is the important reality – the shape of the cosmos or the tangible facts of life on earth? And what is the relationship between them? In a world that is full both of stars and of unsuspected pitfalls, which is the reality to which we should attend? What is it to understand Being? To think only of the wellhead and the daily commonplaces performed there might be a form of blindness, or at least indifference to important aspects of life. But so is wandering about at night gazing upwards at the changeless universe. Neither is good enough. But how to connect them?

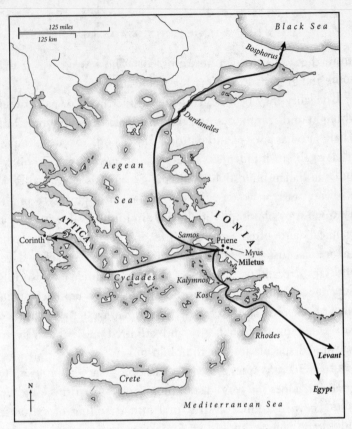

Miletus at the maritime crossroads of sea lanes.

It might be no coincidence that these first questions about the nature of reality were raised in a port city where shiftingness and exchange were its lifeblood. The country around it was not the source of Miletus' prosperity. Its life systems were out to the west, beyond Samos, in the sea lanes on which it relied, the sailing routes that threaded through the Cyclades to Attica, 200 miles away, and from there on to Corinth; or running south under the north wind, past Cape Poseideion and on towards Rhodes and Cyprus, Phoenicia and Egypt. Northwards lay the rich pickings of Thrace and the lands bordering the Black Sea.

No description survives of Miletus at this moment of its first glory when it was, as Herodotus called it, 'the ornament of Ionia'. But there is a contemporary and parallel account of another eastern Mediterranean city which in rich detail paints something of what must have been the life here.

Ezekiel, one of the great Hebrew prophets, who lived in the years around 600 BC, a contemporary or near contemporary of Thales, made a long proclamation against the Phoenician city of Tyre. That city, the prophet thought, was both despicable and enviable for the wonder of its riches and its glamorous trading connections across the Mediterranean. As an island city, Tyre commanded 'the entrance of the sea, merchant of the peoples on many coastlands'.

Ezekiel portrayed Tyre as a place whose 'borders are in the midst of the seas', defined not by its limits but by its connections. He sang of it as a ship: her planks were of pine from what is now southern Turkey, her mast a cedar of Lebanon, her oars of oak from the woods above the sea of Galilee. Her bulwarks were inlaid with ivory carved in Cyprus, her sail and pennants of Egyptian linen.

The crew of the ship were as cosmopolitan, many of the sailors and merchants from the Phoenician trading cities of Sidon and Byblos, the armed mercenaries from more martial centres further afield:

> Those from Persia, Lydia, and Libya
> Were in your army as men of war;
> They hung shield and helmet in you;
> They gave splendour to you.

Homer's descriptions of the Phoenicians are jealous and mean-minded, as if they were little but sea criminals, hawking jewellery from port to port, parasites who lied and stole from the Greeks. Ezekiel's vision of the sea network over which Tyre presided saw it as entirely materialistic, godless and worthy of destruction by a jealous Jahweh, but nevertheless a place of scale and quasi-imperial dignity.

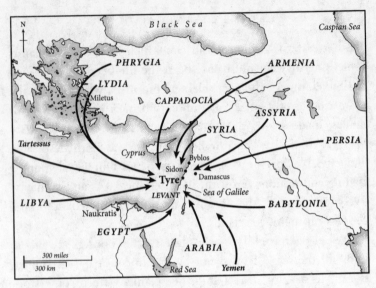

Tyre's commercial connections as described by Ezekiel.

The list of Phoenician commercial partners is dazzling: Tartessus, the kingdom in southern Spain, exchanged silver, iron, tin and lead for the luxuries Tyre could provide. Horses and mules came down from Armenia. Arabian cities brought elephant ivory tusks and ebony, saddlecloths, lambs and goats. Syria could sell them emeralds, purple embroidery, fine linen, corals and rubies. From Judah and the land of Israel came wheat, millet, honey, oil and balm. Damascus sold them white wool. From the Red Sea and Yemen the best spices, all kinds of precious stones, and gold. From Assyria purple cloths, embroidered clothes, chests of multicoloured coats bound with 'sturdy woven cords'.

All came and went on the Tyrian quays. In the absence of any equivalent description of Miletus, Ezekiel's Tyre must stand for the unprecedented multifariousness of this harbour city's life. Its bloodstream was difference, its metabolism exchange, its purpose riches. And what of the Greeks, referred to in Hebrew as *Javan*, the Ionians? Ezekiel's knowledge of what they could provide is starkly expressed. They, along with others called Tubal and Meshech, perhaps people from Cappadocia and Phrygia, were the slave traders.

The Tyrians sold them wrought iron, cane (perhaps for furniture or internal walling) and cassia, a medicinal spice. 'Javan paid for your wares, traversing back and forth. They bartered human lives and vessels of bronze for your merchandise.' This city was a slave port. The Greeks carried the human goods in their own hulls. The great majority of Miletus' forty-five colonies, connected by the dolphin routes across the Aegean and Black Sea, were not to the west but out to the north, to the borders of Thrace and the Scythian territories of what is now Ukraine and southern Russia. The implication of that geography is that the Milesians were not in search of luxuries. Wheat could come from Egypt and soon southern Italy, oil from Attica, wine from Chios, Samos and the Levant, fine things from elsewhere in the Near East. The single most valuable commodity to be sourced from the northern wild lands was people.

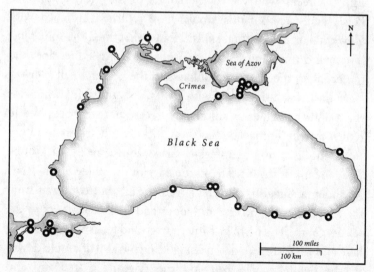

Slave ports: colonies established by archaic Miletus, including the colonies later established by those colonies, on the shores of the Sea of Marmara and the Black Sea.

Miletus had a designated slave quay, on the eastern side of the city, where the waters of its gulf came into a shallow beach. It is a field planted with sunflowers now, beyond the ruins of the Hellenistic market, a row of multicoloured beehives set out beside it, with dunnocks dancing between the flower heads and picking at the seeds. Tall willows catch the sunlight. Now and then a grey heron pulls up and away and clumsies out across the valley. All you can think of in this silent and alluring place is the history of grief it represents. And the absurdity of imagining that a phenomenon such as archaic Miletus could have come at no price. The gathering of riches is also the imposition of pain.

Rivers of influence were flowing the other way in return for this human traffic. The idea of making a map of the world found its way here from Babylon. Knowledge of the stars and methods of measuring the sky were coming from Babylon and Assyria. Understanding of building in stone and sculpture came from Egypt. Greeks who visited the courts of the great empires in Persia and Mesopotamia would have returned enriched with quiverfuls of polycultural skills. Homer described the four most in-demand travelling specialists of the ancient Mediterranean as the prophet, the poet, the builder and the healer. In all four the Near East was burgeoning with riches. It is possible to imagine them and their skills as among the goods that were acquired in return for the human bodies the Greeks could sell them.

Miletus is a forgotten-feeling place now, a reedy backwater. The remains of the city are on the edge of the valley of the River Meander, a sluggish, dirt-grey-green stream that comes in from the mountains to the east and loops and wriggles its way to the sea. Its course lives up to its name, curved and recurved, wandering here and there, repeatedly meeting its own bed half a mile downstream before finally reaching the Aegean in a soggy and sludge-thick delta. On the islands at the edge of the sea, flamingos prod into the mud, pin-legged beauties nose-down for prey. The shallows between them look like the aftermath of a wedding, a carpet of confetti in pink and white drifting feathers.

Curlews cry from the headlands. Herons stand to attention at their hidden stances. A buzzard slides across them. A cotton crop fills the whole valley from one side to another for 20 miles inland. In this theatre of ever-shifting identities, find the rough track up to the hill called Zeytintepe, just to the west of the ancient city. From its heights, it takes little imagination to see that the whole valley is only an arm of the sea now thickened with the silts brought down by the river. The hills look like the islands they once were, the promontories like headlands in a sea of mud. Small mounds out in the plain are off-lying skerries buried in silt. Two thousand six hundred years ago this was the site of the greatest port city of the Greek-speaking world. The mouth of the river was 25 miles further inland and seagoing ships could sail up under the foot of this hill to the harbours just beyond it.

The hill is one of the keys to understanding the mentality of Miletus. Its chalky, limestone soil is covered nowadays with olives that in autumn bear a few dusty black-blue fruits. Little else is visible on the surface beyond the dry grasses, the limy rubble of the trackways and a few fragments of an Ionic temple, but in 600 BC this was the setting in which the people of Miletus celebrated the goddess at the heart of their lives. It was the one place dedicated to Aphrodite, the queen of love and desire.

For a returning ship, the way into Miletus and home was marked by a series of sacred sites: on the tip of Cape Poseideion to the south an altar to the god of storms burned continuously as a signal to mariners. Just north of it, at the beach of Panormos, near the great oracle of Apollo at Didyma, the harbour entrance held a shrine to Hermes, the god of arrivals and departures. Further north still, and turning into the gulf of Miletus itself, past a monument to the founder of the city on a small isolated sea rock called Asteria, the adventurers would find the hill of Zeytintepe above them, before reducing sail and coasting into the main harbour of the city, where the shrine of Apollo Delphinios was there to welcome them. Above him, on the acropolis, was the temple of Athena Polias, the goddess who presided over the spirit of urbanity. From there, the returning crews, perhaps with their families and friends, or their lovers, could make their way up to the shrine of Aphrodite on Zeytintepe itself.

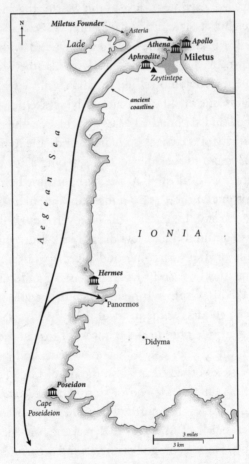

A ship returning to Miletus from Egypt or the Phoenician ports moved through and into a sacralized world.

In this way, sailors coming home would find themselves gradually enfolded in the embrace of their city world, moving in turn from Poseidon the god of wildness to Hermes the god of transitions, tying up at the city quay beside Apollo the god of culture, passing by the Acropolis with its temple to Athena the goddess of city life, before coming finally to Aphrodite presiding over the hill of love.

Souvenirs brought back from Egypt to Miletus by returning Greeks: a bronze head of the falcon-god Horus and a stary-eyed Egyptian.

A simple temple building stood on its summit, its ridge tiles decorated with partridges, as Aphrodite was also the goddess of birds. All over the hill, not in any organized way but deposited in pits and natural hollows, almost like the leavings of picnics, archaeologists have found thousands of votive offerings, in little clusters, no part of a municipal or state religion, but a set of private gestures, left there by a ship's crew or a small party of those who had risked their lives in a venture at sea or by reunited lovers. In many of them, the excavators found the remains of what the people ate as they made their offerings to the love goddess: more often than not a simple lamb stew.

Many of the objects buried here came from where the sailors had been, from the cities of the Phoenicians on the coast of Lebanon and many more from Egypt, where with other Greeks, on the orders of the pharaoh, the Milesians had set up a trading post and town at Naukratis – the name means 'Ship Power' –

on one of the branches of the Nile: hieroglyphic scarab seals, surprised, open-eyed terracotta heads and heavy bronze hawks brought back from the centre of world civilization.

Partridges stalk along a ridge tile from the temple on Zeytintepe dedicated to Aphrodite, the goddess of love and birds.

Just as much as the worldly luxuries discovered in the houses of Old Smyrna, the trinkets in Zeytintepe represent something of the matrix from which archaic Greece emerged. There were miniature animals, including scent bottles in the form of a dove and another as a panther. These are souvenirs of foreignness, signs of having been away. They are not necessarily merchants' goods. The Greeks were often working as mercenaries in Egypt. Some served the warrior-king Nebuchadnezzar II, who reigned in Babylonia from 605 until 562. Others fought for the kings of Judea. The martial spirit was alive in them. A full-sized bronze battle shield was found buried here, still with its wooden backing attached, ready for war.

Oil jars from Zeytintepe in the form of a dove and a panther.

Above all, though, this was a place for love. A group of later marble plaques were carefully placed underground, each inscribed with a simple statement: the name of a woman – Artemisia, Antiochis, Apollonia, Atalantē and Aischra, the last meaning the disfigured or dishonoured one – above her appeal to the goddess, ΑΦΡΟΔΙΤΗ ΕΥΧΗΝ, 'Aphrodite hear my prayer', and, carved into the marble, a listening ear. Nothing more need be said. Hear me. Bring me to the man or woman who is not here. Listen. Bring me love.

The listening stones: Aischra, the dishonoured one,
Atalantē and Antiochis pray to the goddess of love.

The pits and hollows held hundreds of figures of the goddess herself, most of them in terracotta, some in marble, originally painted in the brightest of colours. This was a hill for love and perhaps for sex, but in her journeys across the Mediterranean and arriving among the Greeks, Aphrodite had acquired a kind of reticence. In the Near East, where she was known as Astarte in Tyre and Ishtar in Mesopotamia, her images are almost always naked, holding their life-giving breasts aloft. Only rarely on Zeytintepe has a naked image of the goddess been found, less fertility goddess than nubile girl, her hips just turned in what looks like the movement of a dance. Most of the images here are clothed in the long, tightly waisted and belted chiton of the Ionians, often with a veil, the cloth folded over the curves of

Canaanite figurines of the ancestor of Aphrodite, the love
goddess known in the Near East as Astarte or Ishtar.

the body. Some hold a hand to their breasts, recalling their
near-eastern ancestry, others have their hands folded in their
laps, or held firmly to each side in the Egyptian way. Some are
crowned and some have long braided hair, both fashions drawing
on Egyptian or Assyrian models.

Figurines found at Miletus that represent Aphrodite
wearing the tight-waisted chiton of Ionian fashion.

For the Greeks she was Aphrodite Pandemos, the deity of pandemic love, the love goddess of all the people. She was the goddess of *mixis*, of sexual 'mingling', of longing and yearning, and her constant companion was Peitho, the nymph of persuasion. She could mend and cure separation and distance. In that way, she was the goddess of homecoming.

In that Greek transmutation, as she was brought here by sailors from the Near East, she also became a sea goddess. The Greeks guessed that her name (in fact of near-eastern, probably Semitic origin) was derived from *aphros*, meaning 'sea spume'. But as a sea goddess she did not lose the heavenly associations she had in Mesopotamia, and so as Aphrodite *Ourania*, she was the linkage between sea and heaven for a navigating world. For the navigators themselves she was Aphrodite *Euploia*, favouring sailors with a good voyage, Aphrodite *Pontikē*, goddess of the sea itself, and Aphrodite *Limenia*, of the harbour. Her image has been found in the Mediterranean on over a thousand lead anchor stocks – the horizontal arms at the head of an anchor – as the deity who could bless and guarantee that the anchor would hold in a world riven with storms. And so she formed a pair with Poseidon, as the goddess of the good and friendly sea set against his cruelty.

Already here, expressed in the terms not of philosophy but of cult, is a sense of balance. A cult of love had come to be central to the life of this city, a valuing of stability and calm rather than struggle and heroism. In that way it might be said that Aphrodite herself was the midwife for a new frame of mind in which an Aphrodite-like mingling occurred of a near-eastern divine potency, with a sea culture, a longing for and celebration of homeliness, for the life of the city.

Up here in her sanctuary on a gleaming morning with the sea to the west, and the ruins of Miletus spread out over hundreds of acres on the far side of the hill, you have to imagine what time has not preserved: the scarves and dresses, the flowers, the fruits, the songs. Small hints come from another great sanctuary, dedicated to Hera, across the water on the shores of Samos. The soils are damp there and have preserved soft things which have gone from Zeytintepe but were surely once here too: small wooden statues of the goddess, fragments of wooden chests and bowls.

Alongside that, the fruits and flowers used in the sanctuary for garlands and wreaths. The remains are what you might expect from an Aegean picnic: bunches of grapes both wild and cultivated, the pips of pomegranates and figs, a rare peach (originally from China) and both watermelons and honey-sweet melons. Unknown here were any northern fruits: no apples, pears, plums or berries (except one or two wild blackberries and black mulberries), but the parties giving thanks to the goddess were fond of almonds. Their shells were everywhere. The summer salads were made of lettuce, capers, celery and amaranth, with okra and purslane, sea beet and wild sea radish picked from the shore.

The stony rubbish of Miletus, shoved aside to make room for the plough.

For flowers, they had the pink, sweet-scented buds from myrrh bushes, and the smoky-seductive scent of cinnamon, as well as hollyhocks and the open, airy gold-green umbrellas of dill. This is the scene in the sanctuary here, shaded by the blossom of myrrh bushes in spring, with frankincense smoking in the sunlight on the altar, garlands in the hair of the girls, 'the whole place shadowed with roses', where the adorants of Aphrodite came to worship and, having worshipped, slept.

The gentleness and civility of this love-worshipping cult are often forgotten parts of the culture from which the first thinkers came. It might be easy to imagine the seventh-century Aegean as a rough-edged world of rivalrous cities, hard-dealers and brutal pleasures, but Zeytintepe revises that and is a reminder that delicacy and longing were part of this mental landscape; that the borrowings from the Levant and Egypt had been subtly adapted to Greek purposes; and that we cannot patronize these people. There was nothing 'early' or primitive about them.

Walk down from Zeytintepe towards the old centre of Miletus. The whole ruined city now feels bombed. Parts of the grid of the rectangular street system can still be made out but all is quiet. There is scarcely a person to be seen. Puppies lie asleep in the shade of small field sheds. Black hens pick through the dust beside the farmhouses. The silty fields that fill the harbours are ploughed and sown and everywhere the stones of the ancient city are simply pushed aside, like the rubbish of an attic that might perhaps be looked at one day. Objects that would be valued and curated elsewhere are here treated as no more than the sort of stony annoyance that could damage a plough or a harrow.

Nowhere is more marvellous than the mouth of the great central harbour. Skylarks sing above the late Greek and Roman theatre on the acropolis and brown, orange-tailed lizards skitter across its seats. Down below them, on the silty seabed of what was once the harbour, tamarisk bushes have been ravaged by goats. And there, surrounded by a slick of mud in which sheep and goat hooves have sunk, is the great symbol of Miletus, a huge old marble lion abandoned by time.

It once stood at the entrance to the harbour and has a twin on the far side that has been reburied in the mud to preserve it, both of them a few centuries later than the first thinkers but redolent of the spirit of the city. The lion was the beast of

Archaic lions of Miletus, still in the city (left)
and now in the Louvre (right).

Miletus and appeared on its coins. Everywhere you looked in the sixth-century city you would have met its marble brothers. One, now in the museum here, had a hole drilled straight through it so that it could be used as a mooring stone, but this one, with the empty cartridge-case of a wildfowler's twelve-bore in the mud beside it, presides over the silt city, more beautiful for being settled into his damp bed, with his muzzle blunted, his eye sockets scarcely distinct from a mound of leonine hair, crystalline mica chips glittering in the surface of stone that is visibly spalling and exfoliating. Flooded each spring, tide marks step up his body and on to his face, as willow warblers sing in the bushes around him.

In his tolerant and time-worn nobility, the harbour lion is the chance for Thales, the first of the Milesian philosophers, to have his say. His great question was simple enough: what is the world made of? And his answer, at least initially, was odd. Everything comes from water, and in that way everything is water. Egyptian mythology had long thought that water underlay the world and Homer that the world was surrounded by the great river of Okeanos from which all earthly water came. But Thales stepped beyond that simple mythological and speculative description to an explanation. Change in the world is undeniable. It is what happens. Time itself is the process of change and yet beyond that changefulness is a kind of constancy, a lastingness. The lion is bruised and his stone spalling. Every year he becomes less distinct but he is still here. And the idea of him, once known, will last whether the physical fact of his body survives or not. The lion is both lasting and not lasting and so is emblematic of existence itself. Thales' explanation of these contradictory qualities was that the world seems to fuse change and changelessness because it is fundamentally liquid. Water is the ever-changing changeless thing and so, he suggested, if you reduced everything to its essence, you would be left with nothing but water.

The idea can seem incontrovertible here: water is the fundamental reality of Miletus, a city dependent on the sea for its commercial and cultural life; in a valley where waterborne silt transforms the landscape, turning liquid into solid, or at least half-solid; where change and changefulness are all-apparent. The city of Priēnē, across the gulf, became so clogged with silt that its citizens abandoned it and moved to a new site high on the hillside above the gulf. The old Priēnē was lost and has never since been found. Just to the east, Miletus' tiny neighbour city of Myus, the smallest in the Ionian league, also gave up the struggle; its citizens abandoned its increasingly useless harbour and moved their buildings and statues stone by stone to Miletus itself. Even now one can find at the end of a long dusty track the vast masonry of its city wall and harbour works embedded in the remote cotton fields in which it drowned.

If you can accept that all is water, you can begin to think beyond the ordinariness of things. The world may look reliably solid but, if only you could see it, you would understand that we are afloat in existence and the process by which this floating world goes on through time is like the life of a living thing. Every living thing begins and continues in water and wetness – a corpse desiccates on death and without liquid neither the

The harbour works and city wall of Myus, one of the twelve cities of the Ionian league, abandoned to malaria and the silt brought down by the Meander. The citizens left for Miletus with their statues and most of their buildings.

egg of an animal nor the seed of a plant would become what they were intended to be – and so water is life. But the language Thales used to express this idea was transitional. All things, he said, are full of gods, even objects such as a dead stone that is moved by a magnet. The world as a whole is animate, as if it were a living thing, going through its cycles of life and death, as we must ourselves in the passage from birth to grave. The wet, the living and the divine are in Thales' view one and the same.

What remains of his thought is a set of alluring, half-connected, poetic conceptions, scarcely a logical system. Nevertheless, a switch has been thrown: no Olympian gods are in play. Thales describes a worldly world, one that is addressed on its own terms. The silt is clogging the harbours inland. The slaves are coming down from the north. Trinkets and ancient mysteries are arriving from Egypt and the east. Aphrodite restores returning sailors to happiness and Apollo is a dolphin in the sea roads that run through the islands out to the west. We are alive because, like water, we are full of change and the change-fulness in us is the spark of divinity.

His ideas are, however obliquely, a kind of invitation to mental freedom. He was surrounded by men and women who dared to set out for distant parts of the world which could offer rewards that staying with the familiar could not have matched. If you can decide to cast off, set your own course, act for yourself in a life where there is none to oversee or judge you, a kind of divinity has a chance of shaping your life. The beauty of liquidity and fluency as qualities central to a healthy life and mind is Thales' great gift to us.

Walk on to the head of the Lion Harbour and you will find a large complex of buildings of many ages, most of them adapted and enlarged at times well beyond the early philosophers, but in one ruin here there is a memory of the life of a harbour city. It must have come from the very last moment before the mud enclosed and killed the sea connection of Miletus. The Turkish baths are probably late medieval or early sixteenth century, millennia later than the time of this book, but their walls are covered in something that dives straight into an earlier atmosphere: ship graffiti scratched into the plaster of the rooms. They are the marks made by men who have just come in from the sea and are now here talking in the grey, steamy toplight of the hammam.

The drawings concentrate on the rigging. The hulls, the fixed part of the ship, are no more than sketched in, but everything that is mobile in a ship, the lines aloft, the braces, sheets and halyards, the shrouds and stays, all are carefully and quickly drawn by people who knew them and knew their audience would know them. Sailors are meeting. What kind of vessel have you been in? Was it good to work? How was it in a gale? Could it point up into the wind? Did it rest easy at anchor? How do you tack a lateen sail? Should the bowsprit be braced into a downward curve? These are ships as the men encountered and worked them, the central instruments of their mobile, ingenious, inventive and adventurous world, as much to be discussed in AD 1550 as 2,000 years before.

Late medieval or sixteenth-century ship graffiti scratched
into the walls of the Turkish baths in Miletus.

Here at last, and paradoxically out of synch, you can feel
yourself in the presence of the archaic city. It is a complex
world. A trading city, a place that needed the sea. Rough edges
everywhere in contact with the polished and perfumed. A
hybrid exoticism flourishing on the quays. The stony, dry
country inland not fertile. Any fertility to be found here now
is in the modern silt brought down by the river. Nor had it
ever been a land-based settlement. There had been a small
colony here a thousand years earlier in the Bronze Age, when
Cretans and then Mycenaean Greeks had lived and traded from
this harbour. As much as for Homer's Phaeacians, the sea
connection had always been part of Milesian identity. Next to
nothing would be here without the sea. There was some relationship with the Lydians inland – the Milesians shared a
standard of weights and coinage with them (it derived in the

end from Babylonia) – but overland trade to the east was made difficult by the boggy and shifting terrain of the Meander valley. And the city's immediate lacks were multiple: papyrus, linen for cloths and sails, hemp for ropes and rigging, valuable metals, salt, textiles, dyes, even the mussels and fish whose shells and bones have been found throughout the ruins – all needed to come by water.

In the light of that, should one be surprised that Thales thought liquidity the underlying fact of the world?

Thales had opened a door and others in Miletus began to walk through it. Anaximander was his friend, the first of his followers and a man engaged with the realities of life. He probably led a party of Milesians to found the colony of Apollonia on the Bulgarian coast of the Black Sea. He was almost certainly a writer. Later Greeks quote directly from his works and his supply of papyrus from the Milesian colony at Naucratis on the Nile would have been constant. There is no doubt that he had connections with the Near East and Egypt. He was said later to have invented the *gnomon*, the stick by whose shadow one can tell the time on a sundial, and to have made the first map of the world. These stories were only Greek provincialism: the *gnomon* had been in use for millennia in Egypt and a Babylonian map of the world, showing an encircling sea and a highly mythologized geography of the Near East, stretching across Mesopotamia from the Mediterranean to the Persian Gulf, had existed for many centuries. Besides, graphic depictions of the heavens as a sphere above us had been known to the Greeks and to many cultures in the Near East since at least the eighth century. It would not have been that large a step to have applied that spatial imagination to a depiction of the earth.

Nevertheless, Anaximander was a man of genius. He imagined much of the way we still look at the world. Having listened to Thales' idea that all of existence was, in essence, water, he found it wanting. If all was water, how could fire exist? Water was the extinguisher of fire and yet fire is a radiant presence in the world. It is inconceivable that fire comes from water. And so, taking on Thales' understanding that change is implicit in being, and that what we perceive must come from some other substance, Anaximander named that ur-substance, the stuff from which everything comes, the *apeiron*. The word means the 'without-limit' and it is what exists before anything that we know and perceive in the world comes into being. Homer had called the sea *pontos apeiresios*, the boundless or immense or uncountable or unfenced sea, a word that itself comes from *a-*, meaning 'without', and *peirar*, meaning the 'end' or 'verdict' or 'final decision'. *Peirata* were the very tail ends of the ropes with which the sailors tied Odysseus to his mast so securely that he could not succumb to the hymns the Sirens sang.

Anaximander's *apeiron* is in that sense the endless, the undefined. It is not clear whether he meant the infinite – a substance that went on for ever – or the indefinite – something that could never be precisely identified or subdivided. But that distinction does not finally matter: the *apeiron* is eternal and exists before and outside everything in the world. It is the limitless and everlasting reservoir of being, the imagined state of calm, from which everything that is, the liquid, the solid and the airy, all emerge and to which all eventually return.

This mystic vision of the still world of eternity is not disconnected from our lives. It is the substrate on which our lives are built because out of the *apeiron* comes the actual, in a constant process of coming-to-be, matched only by the equally constant process of ceasing-to-be. The two are balanced with each other: as something comes into being, something else sinks back into the *apeiron*.

And here Anaximander took his idea a step further: the *apeiron* is not only the pre-existing substance; it is the *archē*, the origin, rule or frame of all being. But how, one might ask, can the indefinable be the frame of anything? Surely its very indefinability excludes the possibility of exerting a power or sovereignty over the world as we know it?

Anaximander's response to that doubt is that the paired process of coming-to-be and ceasing-to-be, which is the great function of the *apeiron*, is the source of a kind of justice in the world. There is no wastage. The world cycles and recycles in an ever-shifting but essentially closed loop, one that is overseen by the *apeiron* as the eternal and unageing element that surrounds the world.

> The source of coming-to-be is that into which destruction also descends, according to their obligation, for they pay penalty and retribution to each other for their injustice according to the assessment of Time.

The passage of time means that everything returns to its source in the indefinite. It is time, Anaximander says, which 'steers' this process. He uses the maritime word *kubernaō* – the piloting of the helmsman, the verb at the root of our word 'govern' – to describe the actions of time in the service of a balanced justice, giving out and taking in the different and opposed elements that make their claim on the *apeiron* as aspects of this differentiated world.

It is an intense interlocking of cosmological, psychological, social and political ideas: final justice resides only in the balance of the *apeiron*. The world we know makes unbalanced and selfish demands on the *apeiron* which only time can restore to justice by reabsorbing those transient elements back into the undefined.

One might be sceptical that this can mean anything to us now, with our highly evolved understanding of the physical universe, but it contains a valuable truth, which has within it the first hints of an ecological vision. The universe is a closed and limited system. All actions have consequences and nothing can be done without implication. Every action makes a claim

on existence and in doing so exacts a price. Every benefit in
one part is a loss in another. We live in a profoundly interactive
universe and not to be conscious of the price imposed by individual demand is to ignore the reality of those consequences.
By implication the picture of the world undergoing an endless
recycling through the *apeiron*, a recycling which is Anaximander's
definition of justice, means that if you want to live a just life,
to live in a just city, you have to understand the nature of the
world and respond to its demands. You cannot know how to
be if you don't know how the world works. Or, to put it another
way, lives can be good only if they fit with the infinitely
connected nature of the world as it is. Nothing exists singularly.
Every life generates a death and every death a life.

The politics of Miletus throws some light on the context in
which Anaximander came to this understanding. The city experienced endlessly shifting enmities and friendships. It had been or
would be in alliance with and then at war with the city of Erythrae;
and at war with and then in alliance with Chios; the same oscil-
lation with the Lydian empire to the east; often in conflict with
Samos, then allied with Samos against the city of Priēnē across
the gulf, before once again taking up arms against Samos.

Life here was defined by the alternation of peace and struggle,
friendship and enmity, the very structure of coming-to-be and
ceasing-to-be that Anaximander imagined for the universe as a
whole.

Within the city, political life was permanently on the churn.
Dates are uncertain, but during this period an ancient aristoc-
racy had given way to a tyranny, then to a double tyranny,
followed by a period of civil war in which the great struggle
had been between the city's merchants and the populace.

For all the worship of Aphrodite, Miletus was no pool of
calm. The city found itself caught between two *hetaireiai* –
factions, brotherhoods or alliances – one of which, in a naked
description of political realities, was called 'The Rich', the other

'Those who worked with their hands', perhaps the Artisans, perhaps simply Labour.

The Rich came out on top in the power struggle. Plutarch calls them 'the strong ones', using an adjective that can be applied just as well in describing a ship fit for sea, and then mentions a practice that seems to lie at the very centre of the harbour-city phenomenon:

> When the men of influence, the Rich, gained the upper hand and brought matters into the control of their party, they used to consult on questions of the greatest importance by embarking on their ships and putting out a long way from the land. Only when they had come to a final decision did they sail back; and because of this they acquired the name of 'Always Sailors'.

In a vindication of Thales' watery vision, the city council of Miletus found its home and frame at sea. Understanding was liquid. The ships became Miletus' council chamber, even its agora, a place for the meeting of minds and exchange of views. Water was the frame of wisdom. It may have been that water was the nearest thing to the *apeiron* that could be found on earth.

It is not unlikely that Thales and Anaximander, with their learning, connections and sophistication, were members of the 'Always Sailors'. Both of them embraced uncertainty and promoted the idea that only by recognizing the liquid and formless nature of fundamental reality could you understand the structure of the world. If the world was afloat, or within the frame of the boundless, political wisdom could also come from being out on the water.

Should the city fail to embrace the floating world, brutal catastrophe followed.

> At first the Populace got the better, and drove out the Rich, and, collecting the children of those who fled into some

threshing-floors, herded in a lot of oxen, and so trampled the children to death, destroying them in a wicked and godless way. Therefore, when in their turn the Rich got the upper hand, they took many of the Populace prisoner and smeared them with pitch, and so burnt them alive.

This story of mutual injustice is precisely what Anaximander's vision addresses. Whatever makes a claim on dominance is inherently unjust. Only with the actions of time on the sublunary world will justice be restored. Justice lives in the process by which things change. And so change itself is justice.

The city and the cosmos share the same prescription. Beyond the daily wrangle of life is Anaximander's intuitive grasp of the earth's position in space. Thales had thought that the earth floated in space like a ship on the sea or a log in water. Not for Anaximander. His vision saw it resting calmly and eternally in the very centre of space, supported by nothing, at a distance equal from all margins of the universe, a balanced cylinder 'like the drum of a column', still and perfect, witnessing the struggles and see-saw lives of the creatures on its surface.

One last aspect of this great man's imaginative reach: he was the first person to consider that human existence itself might have its own evolutionary history, a gradual becoming. As his master Thales had taught him, life certainly began in the wet.

The first living creatures were born in moisture, enclosed in thorny barks; and as their age increased, they came up on to the drier part and, when the bark had broken off, they lived a different kind of life for a short time.

It was as if he saw early life as a set of sea urchins, from which later life would emerge into the air as soft-bodied creatures. But the softness and vulnerability of human beings called for a further explanation:

In the beginning man was born from creatures of a different kind; because other creatures can soon manage themselves [the word he uses, *nemesthai*, is the one used to describe a helmsman managing the tiller of a boat at sea, or a shepherd his flock] but only people need to be nursed for a long time. That is why man would not have survived long if this had been his original form.

The actions of the world, its habit of nurturing things that come-to-be, produced a new kind of life:

There arose from heated water and earth either fish or creatures very like fish; in these man grew, in the form of embryos retained within until puberty; then at last the fishlike creatures burst out and men and women who were already able to feed themselves stepped forth.

We are not fixed. No god has ordained our nature. We, like all phenomena of life and world, are emergent. The workings of this life can explain us and we come and go with them. We are as fluid as the world that made us but there is no tragedy in that understanding of our transience. Transience and being are inseparable. The grand Homeric vision had been the grief of existence, the tragedy of necessity in which our lives are caught. But these philosophers went beyond that in recognizing and accommodating – it is tempting to say 'philosophically' – the fact that we are unlasting. Everything I love will die. Only the *apeiron*, the ungraspable eternal, persists beyond the rolling injustice of this world. Our only calm is in recognizing that eternity.

Anaximander had speculated on the nature of the skies. Those heavenly bodies we can see circling above us were only that part of an eternal fire that blazed inside giant unseen rings.

Each ring, he imagined, was like a hollow cartwheel, in which a mouth or pipe, like the nozzle of a bellows, revealed the fire to us below. The rhythmic opening and closing of breathing holes through which the light came down to earth, like the lid of an eye, could account for the waxing and waning of the moon. An occasional blockage could explain the eclipse of moon or sun.

We can know such explanations to be wrong, but it can at least be said that they are steps on the path to explanation itself. Homer had seen the sky merely as a great bronze hemisphere, like the Odyssean wine-mixing bowl, on which the stars were inscribed. Anaximander, like all the thinkers from Miletus, substituted for that fixity a vision of an essentially mobile universe. He knew everything to be on the move. Nothing beyond the *apeiron* could be still. The entire universe was both coming to be and passing away. There were many more worlds than the one we know, a multiverse of which one cosmos succeeded another, just as the phenomena of this world were an endless sequence of changing scenes. Or perhaps – the fragments are not clear – those endless worlds coexist unseen in the unknowable flux of space and time.

It is difficult to guess how these almost-Yeatsian, near-shamanic visions would have been received by the ships' captains sitting in the quayside tavernas in archaic Miletus. But that unfamiliarity is the point. The harbour city would have assembled hard-bitten traders, slave girls, philosophers, the followers of Aphrodite and the many strangers from elsewhere in a melting pot of identities, without singularity or resolution. That is the pool of framelessness from which this new world emerged.

Anaximenes, the third great figure of these Milesian thinkers, of whom next to nothing is known, played his variation on the themes the other philosophers had introduced. His first and ultimate material was neither Thales' water, nor Anaximander's *apeiron* but the air itself, which through variations in its density gave rise to all other materials. If finer, air became fire. If thickened it became wind, then cloud, then water, then earth, then stone. A variation in density generated a variation in material. There was no atomic or molecular theory to this but the perception was essentially right: differing dispositions of the same ingredients of matter generate different kinds of substance. In some ways we still live in the self-cycling and recycling world Anaximenes imagined.

Better than that, he was the first to turn to the human and psychological dimensions of this vision of universal change. Some phrases of his were preserved by Aëtius, an early Christian bishop of Antioch:

> Anaximenes of Miletus declared the air to be the principle and frame of all that is. For all things come-to-be from it and into it they are again dissolved. Just as our soul, he says, being air, holds us and controls us, so does *pneuma* [either 'wind' or 'breath'] and air enclose the whole world.

We are as the world is. We live in an envelope of breath. The air enters us as we are born and leaves us as we die, dissolving back into the constituents of which we were first made. Only for a time does the cosmic breath-soul distinguish us from our surroundings. It is as if the universe infuses us for that moment, inhabited by a world spirit that both pre-exists us and lasts long after us. It is Anaximenes' great recognition that we are no more than an emanation of the cosmos. The lightest of substances inspires us for a few years, and for that time we are as present and as transient as a cloud or a breath of wind.

This conception may not have been original to him. Contemporary with him, perhaps a little earlier, Iranian thinkers were imagining that the wind god Vayu, the vital breath of the world, was identical with the vital breath in a human body. Cosmos and person were one. At the same time in northern

India, it was maintained in the earliest Upanishads that Brahman, the changeless life-soul of the world, was identical with Atman the individual self. Across the eastern Mediterranean, and far off into Asia and India, the same one idea was coming to seem like a description of how we are. Our personal awareness of being is only a local and imperfect observation of a universal reality. Traffic was already rolling on the Silk Roads.

4

HOW TO BE ME

SAPPHO, ARCHILOCHUS, ALCAEUS
LESBOS, AEGEAN, 625–560 BC

How much do I matter? How much does my view of the world put a claim on it? How far can I pursue my own ends? And how much must I listen to the needs of others? How much am I something apart from the life that surrounds me?

The archaic world of floating, negotiable identities in these trading cities generated a double phenomenon: the emergence of the idea of the self, and the recognition that the self must be integrated with the workings of the city. The essence of a person is profoundly part of a city but it is also something set apart from the city, a soul that in the words of the anthropologist and Greek scholar Jean-Pierre Vernant 'is a power that lives at the very heart of the living [person]'.

These two forms of human identity lived in vital tension with each other. The poems and songs that came out of this moment have that double impulse at their heart: a selfhood that can be playful, strident or anxious, both competitive and vulnerable, wanting to command but haunted by loss or the prospect of loss. And alongside that, a sense of companionship, of an essential togetherness in a drinking party, or a wedding, a ship's crew, or a political party set against tyranny. This is quite unlike the god-, king- and hero-dominated world of Homer, where in Vernant's phrase a soul is nothing but an 'insubstantial wisp of smoke', and it is in the lyrics of Sappho, the great sixth-century poet from Lesbos, 10 miles off the coast of Asia Minor in the northern Aegean, that the new voice flowers.

She is sitting somewhere, perhaps in a room, perhaps on a shoreside terrace in the harbour at Mytilene, and looks across to a person she suddenly longs for. There is a man there, handsome, happy and strong, 'equal to the gods', but Sappho says nothing much of him. He is indeterminate, semi-significant, 'whoever he is'. It is the woman beside him who draws her gaze.

The woman is speaking and the man edges close to her and listens to her 'entrancing voice', a phrase in which *adu,* the word Sappho uses to describe her speaking, means 'pleasing', 'pleasurable', hovering on the edges of the seductive.

This is not a Homeric scene. The sensibility has moved on from Homer's public, declarative and essentially external depiction of people. Something more intensely inward is happening. The man and the lovely woman are not seen from the outside, nor from any clearly objective point of view. We see them as Sappho sees them. They are not unreal; they are undoubtedly there, but what matters is not their presence. The governing fact in the room is the longing in the poet for a person beyond reach. It is a description – astonishingly brief: we are less than twenty words in – by which the poet's private sensibility, her most unspoken thoughts, spring up in her heart and balloon out into the room in front of her, shaping and colouring every aspect of the world she perceives. There is nothing more important here than her own self. She looks across at them and the air is filled with the erosive risk and undeniability of desire.

The woman is speaking and as she speaks she laughs in a way that is *imeroen,* lovely, delicious, sexy. It is the word Homer used of the goddess Hera, in the most erotic passage of the *Iliad,* as she prepared herself in her chambers to seduce her husband Zeus.

She entered, and closed the gleaming doors. First with ambrosia she washed every last mark from her desirable flesh, *chroòs imeroentos*, rubbed herself richly with oil, ambrosial, soft, and of rich fragrance . . . She spread that oil over her beautiful body, and she combed her hair, and with her hands plaited the bright fair locks that streamed from her immortal head. Only then did she dress herself in the ambrosial robe Athena had made and embroidered for her with all the skill a goddess can command.

Homer allows us to see Hera naked in the privacy of her innermost room but we are not there with her. We look up at her almost as if she were on stage. She is, after all, divine. But Sappho is clearly present with this desirable, longing-arousing girl. Elsewhere, she says that the nightingale is the *ēros angelos imerophōnos*, the desire-voiced herald of spring, and this girl's liquid laughter, like the run and break of the nightingale's music, reaches across the room to entangle the poet.

As it does, Sappho falls. In the great translation by Anne Carson, the Canadian poet-scholar, Sappho feels how the laughter suddenly:

> puts the heart in my chest on wings
> for when I look at you, even a moment, no speaking
> is left in me.

Sappho sang these poems with a lyre – they are the first lyrics – and you must imagine her singing this, perhaps among a group of her own friends, perhaps with wine, perhaps in the sort of spring-lit apple orchard that appears in her poems, perhaps in a ceremony celebrating beauty in the great shared cult centre at Messon in the centre of Lesbos. In elegant Greek phrases, she sings of her silence when struck with love. This singing-about-not-singing toys with the convention of the publicly enunciated song. In Homer, whoever sang in the *megaron* of heroes and voyages was always perfectly and almost miraculously gifted in the powers of speech and language. They were the grounds on which Odysseus congratulated himself for his standing in the world. But Sappho, famous among Greeks for the effortless grace of her music, becomes so much herself in this moment of revelation that all she can sing, all she can be, is her silence.

'Tongue breaks,' she says, briefly, even curtly – Sappho's word means to 'splinter' or 'shiver', or to disintegrate uncontrollably in the way a wild boar hurtles and smashes through the branches of a thicket, or even as a description of the way the reverberations of music can ricochet and ripple around and across a room. The scale is suddenly both intimate and huge, as if a battle were being fought not on the plain outside Troy but here in this room where a girl is laughing with some unknown man for whom one does not care. It is a moment of self-dissolution in which no distinction lasts between the vast and the intimate. Wordsworth in *The Prelude* wrote of 'a grandeur in the beatings of the heart', and that scale-reshaping thought is here in Lesbos at the very foundations of lyric poetry.

Sappho plunges inwards, revealing a self that exists beyond social expectations. The man disappears – he is not mentioned again – and the atmosphere becomes free-floating. Even the girl vanishes. The geography of life is shaped by Sappho's own longing. There is a madness to the poet as she moves inside her own self:

> tongue breaks and thin
> fire is racing under skin
> and in eyes no sight and drumming
>   fills ears

Thin fire – a disconcerting panic, hot but lean, not in her gut or heart but invisible to an outsider, hidden and overwhelming, a hair's breadth below the surface, underrunning face and arms. She sweats and shakes. Her skin turns as green, she says, as grass. She addresses us her listeners. 'I am dead – or almost, I seem to me.'

This revolutionary poem uses all the vocabulary by which Homer's warriors shook and sweated and died, but turns the words towards a moment of unaccommodated sexuality and to an intensity of private anguish no previous literature had expressed. Public utterance slips under the skin of private reality; it is as if the individual human voice has been invented.

Those who read or heard Sappho's poems in antiquity (she disappeared from view after the sixth or seventh century AD) on the whole loved and preserved those elements that showed a world that was sunlit, fresh, full of the beauty of newness, a dawn in which the women and girls by whom she was surrounded all glowed. Her companions were the 'honey-voiced', 'pink-armed', 'lovely-footed' girls, the ones with the 'beautiful face', 'the gleaming hair' and 'gentle eyes'. Those girls as brides wore dresses the colour of violets. Hands gestured in the dance and meadows came into flower. Dawn wore golden sandals in which the gold was more golden than gold. The best apple reddened and ripened on a high branch, not because the pickers had forgotten it; like so much that was to be longed for, it was too high to reach. Her 'earth is embroidered with its many garlands'. In the mountains the shepherds sometimes trod without care on the blue-purple flowers of the grape hyacinths, but friends and companions could gather and wear them entwined around their necks and garlanding their hair. The qualities of this poetry – poignant, evanescent – are enhanced for us by its preservation in fragments. Much of it has been found on torn and broken Egyptian papyri, in which the lacunae, when printed, are conventionally shown by half-brackets.

I want
To remind you
                    ]and beautiful times we had.

For many crowns of violets
And roses
                    ]you put on beside me

And many woven garlands
    Made of flowers
Around your soft throat

And with sweet oil
    Costly
You anointed yourself.

One girl Sappho asks to:

    bind your hair with crowns
Weaving stems of dill with your soft hands
As the blessed Graces love to look on one who wears
    their flowers
And turn away from those who are not crowned.

The scenes in which these poems or songs were spoken, sung or performed remain entirely uncertain. Was it at a public festival? Or at parties, gatherings of men or of women or girls? Or at weddings? Sappho seems to be both the speaker of an individual self and the celebrant of an ecstatic jointness in the pleasures and beauties of her companions. She lives on the boundary of self and city, often celebrating the bridegroom, sometimes as 'a slender sapling', sometimes as a man 'as strong and large as the god of war', the individual human being seen either as a vulnerable young plant or in the grandeur of his public and martial role.

In the great lines where she melts and shivers in her longing for the girl across the room, her confession of that love-death is not quite the end of the poem, nor of the fragment that was preserved, almost by chance, in a first-century AD treatise *On the Sublime*. One further line was quoted by the author to continue Sappho's thought:

But all is to be dared, because even a poor man . . .

That is all there is but a guess has been made at the final line:

May grow rich and a rich man find his heart expanding.

The word translated here as 'to be dared' is *tolmaton*, usually understood to mean doing something that takes courage, to face down a risk and endure the pains it imposes, and to do it with grace and patience, to be dignified in the face of a task undergone. It is a verb that belongs not to any kind of private sexual encounter but to the world at large. All can be lost, but daring is the price of survival. Sappho's language in this moment of passionate, private selfhood has absorbed the adventuring and entrepreneurial spirit of the seventh-century Aegean world of which she is a part. To act on private desire is of a piece with the risk-taking exploits that had become central to Greek experience and it may be that the daring she considers here – even as *tolmaton* carries echoes of a voyage in search of markets and riches – is in the singing of this very lyric, in saying this like this, when this is not what might have been said before. A life of adventure involves a self as much as a world.

She was a poet of many voices, an aristocrat, part of a family that was engaged with the furious and violent political struggles of sixth-century Mytilene and with trade abroad. Like her male contemporaries, navigating the seas between Lesbos and its markets, she watched the night sky, even while giving it her own colouring of stripped and melancholic beauty:

Moon has set
and Pleiades: middle
night, the hour goes by,
alone I lie down to sleep.

In a world of voyaging and departures, absence was often at
the heart of the poetry. One loved woman, not named by
Sappho, had left her. She had been married away to a Lydian
prince and was now across the sea from Lesbos in the capital
of that empire at Sardis. She had been the most perfect of
singers. Aphrodite had loved her and another young woman in
Lesbos called Atthis had longed for her.

Now she stands out among the Lydian women
            as sometimes at sunset
                  the rosy-fingered moon

      surpasses all the stars. And her light
                  stretches equally
            over salt sea
                        and flowerdeep fields.

      And the beautiful dew is poured out
            and roses bloom and fail
                  chervil and flowering sweetclover.

      But she goes back and forth remembering
                  gentle Atthis and in longing [imerō]
            she bites her tender mind.

Love may have been Sappho's subject and her métier, but
courage was her mode. She often spoke of her own agedness,
or her longing for the time when she was young and a virgin.
But she was more worldly than these moments of despair might

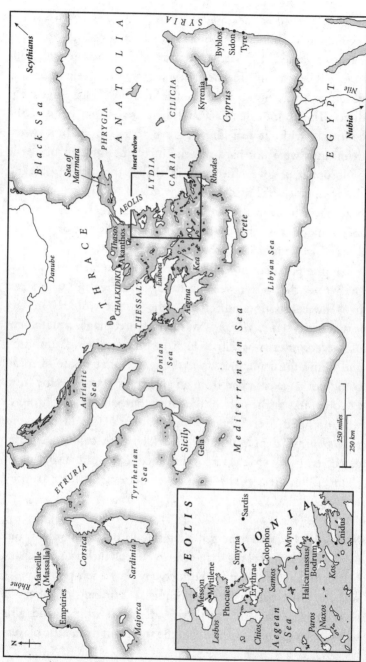

Lesbos and its sixth-century connections.

suggest. She could be tough-minded, angry, insistent on her own dignity and even nobility, disparaging wealth that was unaccompanied by virtue, reproachful, teasing and full-bloodedly roistering in the lyrics she sang, as well as loving, generous, sweet-minded and mournful of loss. Her language is direct. This is not café music and there are few grace notes. She confronts without fear the personal-actual. At a time when definitions were not hard-set, she might be thought of as the philosopher of love. The drive of desire, the loving gaze and the acceptance of loss define the world of her poetry in which nothing is more real than life as experienced by the person. 'Black night falls,' she says, but not on a landscape or a city or a sea. 'Black night falls', she says, 'on her eyes.'

Sappho paraded multiplicity. Eros was 'the melter of limbs', she wrote, the 'bittersweet unmanageable creature who steals in'. The compound adjective – the Greek word is in fact 'sweetbitter', *glukupikron* – was her own coinage, a statement of the complexity within which love and longing, ambition and desire must manoeuvre and engage. That frame of mind could not have emerged from an autocratic state. It came from the openness at the core of the Greek harbour city. Aphrodite, who presided over Sappho's life and work, was in her word *poikilophrōn*, 'dapple-minded', sparkled with colour, as variegated as a woven carpet or brindled cow, but also full of change, complex in the essence of herself, intricate, subtle, not-singular.

Sappho's lyric voice emerged alongside its male equivalent, but for the Greek men of the sixth-century Aegean the focus and channel for this new lyricism – both convivial and self-promoting – was the wine party, the symposium, a 'drinking together'. It was almost always for men, with attendant women and girls whose roles drifted up and down the spectrum from flute players and dancers to high-class 'companions' and straightforward prostitutes or *pornai*, a word that means quite starkly 'bought women' or 'females for sale'. Adolescent boys might have been there, as wine pourers or for sex, serving the symposiasts, who reclined on cushioned benches along the walls. The tone could vary widely, from high-minded conversation, music and versifying to drunken games and frolics. There are some rare depictions of all-women symposia, and it seems at times that the setting for Sappho's poetry are eroticized female gatherings of that kind. But nearly every text and object that survives suggests that the symposium was a theatre for the expression of male togetherness and citizenship, male individuality and male performance.

Lying down in luxury had long been a habit of the Mesopotamian elites. Already in about 750 BC, the Hebrew prophet Amos had anathematized the indulgence of the Babylonians, who thought nothing of the suffering of the Jews:

Ye that lie upon beds of ivory, and stretch themselves upon their couches, and eat the lambs out of the flock, and the calves out of the midst of the stall;

That chant to the sound of the viol, and invent to themselves instruments of musick, like David;

That drink wine in bowls, and anoint themselves with the chief ointments: but they are not grieved for the affliction of Joseph.

Therefore now shall they go captive with the first that go captive, and the banquet of them that stretched themselves shall be removed.

'The banquet of them that stretched themselves' – along with harp music, the pleasure in sweetmeats, the use of perfume – had slowly made its way across Mesopotamia and Anatolia to the Aegean, from the Babylonians to the Assyrians, from them to the Lydians and then on to the Greek cities on the coast and in the islands.

Scenes from a symposium: (left) from a sarcophagus in Akanthos in Chalkidiki and (right) furnished for the guests from a tomb in Thrace.

A Greek sarcophagus that was discovered in the 1990s at Akanthos in Chalkidiki shows a symposium under way. Little flasks stand ready on the side tables, easily reached for when oil or perfume was needed or wanted. Cockerels, a pet dog and a partridge walk among the legs of the tables. A girl plays the double flute. Boys offer wine. Some of the reclining symposiasts wear turbans of a Lydian type. The companion women lie back with the men on the luxury benches or *klinai*. It is an eastern scene in a Greek world, the elite setting for the first moments of Greek lyric poetry. The richest of these luxuriants were buried in tombs that were furnished with stone versions of the equipment needed for a symposium, even down to the dishes of sweetmeats arranged before them on the table.

An air of rule breaking and self-indulgence, of an elite celebrating itself away from the mass of the people, pervades the male symposium. The atmosphere is of excited enrichment. It is a place in which the wealthy do and have whatever they want. This elite might be either aristocratic or new-mercantile, or a fusion of the two, much like Sappho's brother Charaxos, a man from an ancient family who traded Lesbian wine to Egypt and made a fool of himself by falling in love with a high-class courtesan, a Thracian slave taken to Egypt by a trader from

Samos. Songs and stories swung around the room. All who were admitted were equal here. Appetite was king and the symposium was a part-collegiate, part-competitive celebration of dominance.

Lesbos itself was a place on the frontier. The cultures to the east were as close as anything in mainland Greece – the Lydians just across the straits from Lesbos, the Phrygians and Carians a little further afield but linked by ancient trade routes that made their way deep into Anatolia and on beyond to Mesopotamia. People, objects and ideas travelled between them: shields and helmets made by the Carians were matched with swords made on the island of Euboea or even in Egypt. Lesbian soldiers went to fight alongside the pharaoh in Nubia and alongside the Babylonians in Palestine. The luxury habits of the non-Greeks entranced them: cloths dyed with Tyrian purple were the foundation of long and 'trailing' gowns. Elaborate hairstyles with false curls and decorated slippers, 'covering the feet with

East Greek archaic perfume bottles for the symposium.

spangled straps', came from the east. Purple handcloths were sent over from Phocaea, headdresses from Sardis. From the north came glamorous Scythian cloaks and from there or Lydia embroidered turbans. People, bodies, rooms – all were scented and perfumed in ways that had been learned and imported from Asia. In the sixth-century layers in Lesbos, archaeologists have found hundreds of small flasks for perfume, little more than 4 inches high, of Lydian form, known simply as *lydia* – the Lydian things.

Essence of roses came from southern Italy, saffron and the crocus scent of *baccaris* from Cilicia in south-eastern Anatolia, the headiness of spikenard from many sources, traded in from the east, sweet marjoram and apple blossom from the island of Cos, another aromatic from the dark roots of Cypirus in Syria and lily scents from Lydia. There were specialist suppliers: the famous *parfumiers* of Ephesus, the medicinal scent-agents in Egypt. As gums and oils, soaps and unguents, the perfumes floated through this luxury world. Perfumed oil was spread on the chests of guests as they arrived at dinner. In the most indulgent of houses, the host would scent the wings of tame doves with perfumes collected from across the eastern Mediterranean and release them in the room where his friends gathered, sprinkling the sweetness around them.

The equipment for these parties emphasized or dramatized their meaning. Wine jugs were used in the form of slaves' heads. A two-headed drinking cup or *kantharos*, now in Boston, perhaps represented a slave from the north and a slave from the south.

These *kantharoi* were high-handled cups that could be safely passed from hand to hand, always to the right, circulating to each diner in turn who on receiving it was expected to say his piece or make a joke. One *kantharos* preserved in the British Museum shows the moment Odysseus emerges from his hiding place on the shore of Scheria, stark naked and shaggy from his

A wine jug in the form of an African head and a two-headed
drinking cup, both for use at a symposium.

storm-broken voyage, confronting the young and alarmed
Nausicaa who is there with her entourage of girls to do the
laundry at the river mouth.

It is a graphic object, both a high-culture reference to the
great epic and a straight-up male joke. Every diner would have
had in mind Homer's verses describing Odysseus' emergence
from the bushes:

A fifth-century *kantharos* from Attica now in the British Museum.
A naked Odysseus terrifies Nausicaa. It is twin-handled so that it
can be passed easily from reclining diner to reclining diner.

He stepped out like a mountain-fed lion, trusting to his
strength, which makes its way through rain and wind.
Inwardly his eyes are burning. He walks among the cattle

and sheep or in pursuit of wild deer. His belly urges him to make an attack on the flocks and to make his way into a stoutly built fold. So Odysseus was on the verge of mingling with the fair-haired girls, naked though he was, as the need was on him.

The word translated here as 'mingling with', *mixesthai*, can also mean both 'join in battle' and 'have sex with'. Homer's dark-comic description of Odysseus as a lion ready to consume his prey as he approached the girls toys with the ambiguity. He is hungry after his travails but he is also hungry for sex. It is a predatory scene that would add laughter and sexual excitement to the symposium in which the trader-adventurers had gathered to celebrate their own potency and their ability to command the delights the world might offer.

Drunkenness was certainly part of the pleasure. The wine was dilute, perhaps to the strength of modern beer, and the usual provision was about a pint and three-quarters of that mixture per symposiast for every *krater*, or mixing bowl, that was produced. But the *kraters* could keep coming. 'Three kraters only do I mix for the temperate,' Bacchus says in one poem:

one to health, which they empty first, the second to love and pleasure, the third to sleep. When this is drunk up the wise guests go home. The fourth is ours no longer, but belongs to hubris; the fifth to uproar, the sixth to drunken dancing, the seventh to fights. The eighth brings the police, the ninth vomit, the tenth madness and breaking up the furniture.

The atmosphere is rough and masculine. The outer surface of a *skyphos*, a form of deep wine cup almost like a soup bowl, from which a symposiast could drink an enormous draft, always offered the chance of a laugh. A *skyphos* from the Milesian colony of Olbia on the Black Sea, one of the slave ports from which Scythians were transported south, and where blunt arrow-heads were used as a form of currency, carries an invitation. Neatly scratched into the black glaze on one side is the sentence: 'Whoever wants to have sex must pay ten arrowheads and he will fuck . . .' On the other side is the name of the boy: 'Hephaistodoros', inscribed more crudely than the invitation. The historian Marek Węcowski considers this:

> a pre-ordered symposium joke only to be 'personalized' at the appropriate moment . . . When given the cup, a diner was supposed to read the inscription on one side of the vase and then turn it around to discover who among his fellow-drinkers (present or absent) was targeted by this brutal joke. Or else, he could read the first part aloud and then pass the cup to the next diner . . . to finish off the joke.

Another *skyphos* of the same kind and date from the Greek city of Gela in southern Sicily puts it more blankly: 'He who has written [this] will bugger the reader.' Presumably writer gave it to reader as a kind of chat-up line.

Socrates would remind a young boy just what this atmos-phere meant: 'You must realize, my child, that a lover's friendship does not carry any good will. No, it is a kind of food: to satisfy their appetites, lovers love a boy in the same way that wolves love sheep.' The symposium was a theatre for a combination of contradictory impulses: an establishment of social unity combined with the assertion of superiority in a striving and competitive culture. To be a symposiast was reas-surance that you were included in the dominant party, with quantities of wine, music, food, games and beautiful and available bodies to confirm your standing. Everyone here would have been a success of some kind – economically, politically, socially – and so to be a symposiast was both a mark of that status and a consolidation of it. These men were citizens of their world. They owned what they saw and consumed what they owned. It was here that the owner class celebrated its existence. Wine, perfumes, boys, girls, harpists, musicians: all were commodified.

And yet there was an expectation of good manners, of evidence that you deserved to belong, a presumption Aristophanes would ridicule in *The Wasps*. A man-of-the-world is instructing an ingénu in the ways to behave.

Bdelycleon: Recline there, and practise the position that is appropriate to drinking in society.
Philocleon: How must I recline? Tell me, quickly!
Bdelycleon: In an elegant style.
Philocleon: *lying on the ground* Like this?
Bdelycleon: No, no, not at all.
Philocleon: How then?
Bdelycleon: Spread your knees on the rugs and give your body the most easy curves, like those taught in the gymnasium. Then praise some bronze vase, survey the ceiling, admire the awning stretched over the courtyard. Water will be poured over our hands; the tables are laid; we dine and, after washing, we now offer libations to the gods.

The atmosphere of Sappho's poetry seems to be missing. The hesitancy and the self-awareness, the sense of spiritual longing which is the fabric out of which Sappho makes her poetry is scarcely to be found in the more harshly defined atmosphere of the male symposium.

It may be tempting to see this as no more than a gender difference – men from Mars, women from Venus – but a contemporary, equally sophisticated and essentially un-Greek Mediterranean culture should make one pause. The Etruscans in central Italy had also taken up the custom of the symposium, perhaps from the Greeks, perhaps from the Phoenicians, and made use of all its ingredients – music, benches, cushions, wine, companionship, anointing with scents. But unlike the Greeks, free and equal Etruscan women were included in these parties and in Rome there is one moving survival of this Etruscan practice of companionship between the sexes, a sarcophagus in which a woman and her husband were probably buried and which, in the figures that adorn and form its lid, memorializes their lives as companionate people.

Even if the form of the two figures is Greek-like, both of them originally holding jars of scented oil, and even if she wears the pointed slippers that her equivalents in Ionia wore, and even if their hair is braided like that of their Greek contemporaries, nothing in the Greek world has been found to match it. Lovingness, for all the adoration of Aphrodite, is one of the qualities that seems largely to be missing from the Greek symposium.

The Etruscan Sarcophagus of the Spouses.

The roots of that difference are scarcely discoverable, but for whatever reason the male Greek atmosphere, in which every attitude from ribaldry to elegy, love songs to grief songs and beauty to comedy could be played, did not admit of female companionship. It is another instance of this early Greek world disturbingly combining opposites: deep civilization with a kind of barbarity, how-to-be with how-not-to-be, the graceful with the brutal.

Among the first of the male poets to compose these symposium lyrics was Archilochus. His dates are not precisely known, but he lived at some time after 650 BC, a professional soldier, from the Aegean island of Paros in the Cyclades. His own circumstances – his name means 'Regimental Commander' – are almost emblematically uncertain: his father was probably an aristocrat, an adventurer and leader of men, founding a town on the metal-rich island of Thasos, 'an island crowned with forests and lying in the sea like the backbone of an ass', as Archilochus described it. The lead and silver mines there were worked by armies of Thracian slaves and Archilochus may have been the son of one of them, his status hovering all his life between nobility and servitude.

He became a freelance warrior-poet and the fragments of his poetry that have survived reveal him as a hard, proud, tender, melancholy, longing, funny, lustful and vulgar man. Meleager, a Hellenistic poet from Gadara in what is now north-west Jordan, called him 'a thistle with graceful leaves' for his bitter and brilliant descriptions of those he hated. It was said when he died that wasps hovered around his grave.

He was no respecter of status:

> I have no liking for a general who is tall, walks with a
>   swagger, takes pride in his curls, and is super-clean-
>   shaven.
> Let my commander be bowlegged, standing upright, and
>   his hair woolly on his shins.

He could run himself down, confessing that he threw away his shield in escaping a battle with the Thracians, mourning the way his prospective father-in-law disliked him and prevented his marrying a girl he loved. He embraced his standing as the underdog:

The fox knows many tricks, the hedgehog only one.
  One good one.

Archaic Greece was replete with foxes. It was a world that
encouraged them. But Archilochus could love unaffectedly:

  O that I might but touch
    Neoboule's hand

which is a fragment of the first European love poem. And
just as openly despise:

  How can I like the way she makes love?
  Give me sweet figs before sour wild pears.

Or embrace the vividly vulgar:

  His prick swelled up like a donkey from Priēnē that was
  hung like an oat-fed stallion.

And perform all the characters of a man who was carving
his own path through life:

  I do not care for the riches of golden Gyges [the tyrant of
  Lydia], nor ever have I envied him; I am not jealous of the
  works of the gods, and I have no desire to be some great
  tyrant; anything like that is far beyond my ken.

He could play the knowing tease, addressing a girl first with
the oblique:

  I shall be tame, I shall behave
  And reach, if I reach, with a civil hand.
  I shall climb the wall and come to the gate,

slipping towards the not-quite-said:

> I shall come no farther than the garden grass,

drifting for a moment into Sappho-like romance:

> I said no more, but took her hand,
> Laid her down in a thousand flowers,
> And put a soft wool cloak around her.

Before finishing with the brutally direct:

> I caressed the beauty of all her body
> And came in a sudden white spurt
> While I was stroking her hair.

The audience for this is the male symposium. Unlike Sappho's sense of glimmer and delicacy, there is nothing private here. The tale is being told for a party of admiring men. Its man-vigour lies in registering the shifting tones of the seducer's experience, the canny-charming-apparently-modest-actually-exploitative-funny-erotic-nifty progress, as if each version of himself were coming round on a carousel, each window with a story to tell, before finishing in front of his friends with the undeniably and arrestingly conclusive.

He could be the warmest of companions:

> Charilaus, son of Erasmon,
>   By a long chalk the best of my friends,
> I shall tell you something funny,
>   And you will *love* it.

And the bitterest of enemies. A man called Lycambes had sat at dinner with Archilochus. They had talked and thought themselves the closest of allies. But Lycambes later betrayed him. He had broken the bond of the symposium and the tiny fragment that remains of the poem addressed to him is a shard of pure loathing:

> You have turned your back on salt and table
> By which you swore a solemn oath

But there is grace in Archilochus. The sea, with its Odyssean dignities and cruelties, is never far from his mind:

> How many times
> How many times,
> On the grey sea,
> The sea combed
> By the wind
> Like a wilderness
> Of woman's hair,
> Have we longed
> Lost in longing,
> For the sweetness of
> Of homecoming.

And he can mourn as richly and poignantly as Homer:

> Why should the sea be fat
> With my drowned friends?
> Why, why should the fire dance
> On this handsome face
> And feast on the legs of a runner
> That Poseidon killed?
> This lovely body wrapped in white
> We give to the ecstatic fire.
> He was once the lover of enchanted women,
> Once the companion of Ares, War.

Or address the enemy in bitterness:

> In the hospitality of war
> We left them their dead
> As a gift to remember us by.

It remains a miracle that from the rest of Europe at this moment we might have objects – jewellery, weapons, pottery – and structures – forts, ramparts, the marks in the ground where buildings stood – but from this corner of the eastern Mediterranean these insights survive, giving us a glimpse into the human sensibility of 2,500 years ago. Preserved on papyrus that was later used as waste paper to wrap the bodies of those in Greek Egypt who were too poor, as Guy Davenport said, 'to await Resurrection Day in linen and gold', these words allow you to look beyond the crested helmet and the gaze of a goddess to a form of humanity that is vividly and almost mysteriously present. Crudity and elegance are interfused in it, privacy and sociability, honour and appetite, threat and courtesy, love and abuse, cruelty and brilliance, as alive now as they were 2,600 years ago.

A third poet, Alcaeus, also from Lesbos, mingles the tonalities of Archilochus and Sappho. He was of distinguished lineage, proud of what his father and grandfather had been – although never specifying it – and was embroiled in the difficult and violent politics of Lesbos. In ways that are not quite clear, he plotted as a member of the city elite in Mytilene to depose those who were his rivals and install those who were sympathetic to him, sometimes in alliance with the Lydians 10 miles away on the mainland, sometimes with others in Mytilene, sometimes betrayed by them and sent into exile.

He was capable of ribaldry to equal Archilochus in the wild and intemperate versions of the symposium – 'Wine, beloved boy, and truth' one of his declamatory fragments says. Another:

Let's drink! Why do we wait for the lamps? There is only a finger-thickness of daylight left. Take down the cups. Dionysus gave men wine to forget their sorrows. One part water to two of wine [much stronger than the usual mixture of one part of wine to three of water] right up to the brim and keep it coming.

But the symposium was an elastic organism and Alcaeus could be more serious than this. Wine, after all, was 'a window into men's souls'. His watchword was moderation, not gluttony, a commitment to the social organism of the city and to the sense of the shared middle. 'Observe Alcaeus's nobility,' one later critic wrote, 'his conciseness and sweetness combined with forcefulness.' He could loathe and condemn his rivals but the essence of his life-view was to be 'a steward of yourself', a steward of your household, a steward of your city, believing in what the Athenians would come to call *aristokratia*, a term that havers significantly between the 'rule of the best' and the 'rule of the rich'.

Like many of the cities in archaic Greece, Mytilene oscillated between an oligarchy of the leading families (who would undoubtedly have described themselves as 'the best') and rule by a single man who had emerged or been chosen from among them. Alcaeus is the first person known to have used the word *monarchia*, the 'rule of one' – something he fiercely disliked and disparaged. Here and elsewhere these 'monarchs', coming up out of the ranks of the oligarchs, took a Lydian word as their title: *tyrannos*. It had negative connotations only for those oligarchs who were excluded from power by the *tyrannos*'s assumption of it. For the *tyrannoi* themselves, the title was as attractive as the scents, the trailing gowns, the turbans and the reclining benches of the symposium that had come from Lydia with it.

These politics were central to the oligarchic-mercantile exist- ence of Lesbos and it is no surprise that the great and repeated metaphor that Alcaeus uses for his political poetry, to be sung with ferocity, regret or rage at one symposium after another, was the vehicle at the heart of their harbour lives: the ship at sea. Alcaeus is the first person ever to have used the metaphor of the ship of state, easily assuming among his sailor-captain friends that the language of the sea could express without hesitation the meanings of the state. 'This wave comes on in turn,' he began one lyric, whose subject migrates from ship to city and back,

> climbing up on the one before and it will be hard baling for us when it rolls aboard. Get the ship in good order as soon as we can and we can make for a strong, safe harbour. Don't let fear or weakness grab hold of us now. A great ordeal is standing clear before us. Remember how hard it was the last time; now every man must summon up his courage and do his duty. Let us not disgrace our noble fathers lying beneath the earth . . .

The Homeric echoes were surely deliberate but here the papyrus, found like so many in the sands of Oxyrhynchus, breaks into fragmentary poetry:

> . . . from fathers . . .
> . . . our spirit . . .
> . . . is like . . .
> swift . . . heart
> . . . us . . .
> . . . wait . . .
> . . . monarchy . . .
> . . . and let us not accept . . .

It is not difficult to imagine how stirring this would have been late one evening in a symposium room near the harbour in sixth-century Mytilene, Alcaeus' friends and allies around him, shipmates and co-conspirators against anyone in Lesbos who nurtured dreams of dominance.

He and his friends were not confined to summer sailing. One of his poems describes how on one voyage, trusting to a newly made ship either late or early in the year, he must pull a warm cloak around him as the migratory cranes, which fly north in March, south in September, pass overhead to their own destinations.

He can summon an image of his ship at night, as he sails home from the southern Aegean. They are in a winter wind, the sea is cold, and he prays to be accompanied by the bright stars of Castor and Pollux, the divine twins at the heart of the constellation of Gemini, which appear high above the masthead only in the early months of the year and then can sometimes seem to flare, in the electrical storm known as St Elmo's fire, from the rigging itself:

> As we leave the Peloponnese,
> Come here, strong sons of Zeus and Leda;
> appear with kindly heart,
> Castor and Pollux,
> who travel on swift horses
> over the broad earth and all the sea,
> and easily draw men to themselves
> from chilling death,
> leaping up on to the rigging of their well-benched ships,
> brilliant from afar as you run up the fore-stays,
> bringing light to the black ship
> in the night of trouble.

When the wind rises, Alcaeus confesses his inadequacy:

> I cannot understand where the winds are coming from: one wave rolls in from this side, another from that, and we in

the middle are carried along in the arms of our black ship,
thrown this way and that by the great storm. The bilge-water
is up over the mast-step; the whole of the sail is torn to
shreds and patches; the anchors are dragging; the rudders . . .
my feet are caught in the ropes: but this is what [saves] me;
the cargo . . . [is carried off] above . . .

And then the ship itself begins to speak:

. . . the whole cargo . . . as much as possible by the surf
[?] . . . she says she has no wish to be struck by a . . . wave
and to fight against the wave and the wild storm and to be
broken and battered by a hidden reef . . .

In the frame of this poetry, which is both political and
personal, lyric and epic, the crew of the ship at sea, the men
drinking together in the symposium and the ruling party in the
city, all anxious about the storm that threatens to overwhelm
them, are one.

A fragment preserved on a flake of Egyptian papyrus poignantly and laconically describes Alcaeus' world:

. . . the North wind
. . . city . . .
. . . lyre . . .
Under the roof . . .
. . . share . . .

The grand sea imagery rolls through their lives, but what of the
voyages these men undertook? They are not to be thought of
as latter-day Odysseuses. There is daring and adventure here,
but also a steadier, larger and more organized enterprise.
According to Herodotus, a Greek merchant called Sostratos
from Aegina was so rich it was 'impossible for anybody to

compete with him'. He exported Greek pots (and their contents) from the Aegean to Etruria and until the last few decades was merely a name with a reputation attached. Slowly an archaeological reality gathered around his name. Many wine jars were found bearing an *SO*-mark, which a little tentatively were identified as his, and in 1970 a stone anchor was found at Gravisca, the port of the rich Etruscan city of Tarquinia north of Rome, that bore the inscription: 'I belong to Aeginetan Apollo. Sostratos had me made.'

Sappho's brother Charaxos, the wine-dealing lover of Rhodopis, the beautiful Thracian slave from Egypt, would have been part of that world of highly capitalized ship-trading venturers, a man with a lineage of which he was proud but which did not prevent him from engaging in commerce of this kind.

It was a connected world which those gathered in the symposium would have considered their own. A woven web of goods crossed these seas: sponges from Rhodes, millstones from the hard rocks of Erythrae, marbles from Naxos and Paros, painted pottery from Corinth, resin from the pines inland at Colophon, mastic for gums from Chios, and even perishables needing a swift voyage: freshwater fish from Myus near Miletus, salt fish from Thessaly, raisins from Rhodes, herbs fresh and dried from Cnidus, figs and honey from Caria in the Anatolian mainland, prawns from Smyrna, apples from Euboea, dates from Tyre and Sidon.

The world of the symposium scarcely makes sense without these luxuries made available by sea journeys. At one level, a deep connection exists between the cultivation of desire that the symposium celebrated and the *eros* of the voyage itself. Longing for what is not to hand is the fuel for this culture – to acquire, to use, to have, to enjoy, to preside over and perhaps also to know. It may be that the exploration of the self so urgently alive in early Greek lyrics and the philosophical desire to understand the structure of the world in its entirety were both outcomes of this voyaging hunger, to hold what was beyond the horizon and to know it, to set out on the sea and bring back the riches it held. And in this it is clear that Sappho's sensibility was centrally connected to this world. Among the girls she mentions, most memorably she thinks of Anaktoria (her name means 'the palace girl') 'who is gone':

> I would rather see her lovely step
> And the movement of light on her face
> Than chariots of Lydians or ranks
> Of footsoldiers in arms.

What were armies or troops of horsemen next to the object of longing? More than the glories of the world, the best thing on earth was 'what you passionately desire'.

Small trading vessels shipping wine and olive oil to tiny local quays survived until the age of photography. Left: Port Sigri on Lesbos; right: amphorae from Sifnos in the Cyclades being landed at Port Sigri.

The ships themselves were various. Many of the wrecks that have been found were clearly engaged on small local journeys, calling in at beaches, selling to one place what another might have had in excess. Most of them would have employed the ancient technology by which the planks were sewn together with withies, caulked with linen or wool soaked in tar, and the hull waterproofed with an overall tar coating – 'the black ships' that the poetry repeatedly describes. The capacity of these shore-visiting ships was not inconsiderable: one off the coast of modern Turkey at Pabuç Burnu, east of Bodrum, carried about 260 amphorae, all made in the eastern Aegean, some for wine, some for oil, each able to hold about 4 gallons. The ship itself, as well as any cargoes that have since rotted, would have carried about 5 tons of the precious liquids.

Other vessels were already graduating to a larger and more hi-tech level. Increasingly, the strakes – the boards of which the hulls were made – were joined with a mortice-and-tenon system that is stronger in a heavy sea and may have been derived from the Phoenicians. Matting has been found in some wrecks in which the pottery jars were packed against breakage. One large wreck off the Sicilian city of Gela, a vessel about 60 feet long and almost 20 in the beam, had its hull sheathed in lead against the boring of marine worms.

The wine cups in the Pointe Lequin wreck were carefully stacked inside large amphorae.

Technology was already in pursuit of the gains the Mediterranean exchange system could provide. Of all the sixth-century BC wrecks that have been found, none reveals more about the world of the symposium than one that went down not far from the coast of southern France, off Pointe Lequin, on the northern shore of a small island to the south-east of the Greek colony of Massalia, the beginnings of Marseille. It had been founded by the intrepid mercantile sailors of Phocaea, the seal city, and already by 600 had become a trading hub for the western Mediterranean. Tin and slaves reached them down the Rhône/Seine corridor from the north. The harbour at Massalia was one of the best on what is now the French coast, where both wide-hulled trading ships of the kind found at Gela and the narrower, faster *pentekonters* which Herodotus said the Phocaean traders used could find shelter from all winds.

The wreck was discovered in 1985 and as it was slowly exca-vated over the following decade it proved a reorientating window into the trading practices of the archaic Greek world. Five tons of material were brought up from the seabed: amphorae and other commercial containers, loom weights and merchants' weights, terracotta and bronze statuettes and above all more than 2,400 pieces of fine ceramics dedicated to the drinking of wine: 1,700 individual wine cups, all made of the same clay, some larger, 6½ inches across at the bowl, some smaller, about half that, all covered in reddish-brown slip, and all clearly the product of a standardized workshop.

They had been carefully packed and transported inside large amphorae, which is the reason they survived the sinking. The modern divers found the cups still nestled at the bottom of the protective amphorae.

A chemical comparison of these cups with others found in excavations in Marseille, in the Phocaean settlement at Empúries further round on the Catalan coast (the name is from *emporion*,

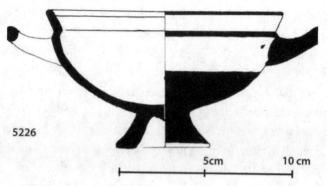

5226

5cm   10 cm

The standardized wine cups from the Pointe Lequin wreck.

'trading station' in Greek) and from a wreck off the coast of Majorca showed that they all had a common origin, perhaps in southern Italy or Sicily.

It is a suddenly modern picture of life in the decades after 600 BC: not a small-scale, amateur, have-a-go business, but a highly organized and regularized supply chain from a large-scale workshop transporting fine ceramics in large batches to distant markets in the western Mediterranean where demand had been sufficiently established to make this a risk worth taking. It is impossible to know what proportion of marine traffic remains on the seafloor to be seen today as wrecks, but it is certainly a small fraction of a percentage point. To gain a true picture of what was happening in the archaic Mediterranean, the elegant tableware of Pointe Lequin needs to be multiplied by a factor of many hundreds. Extensive suites of rooms must be imagined in which the drinking parties were held, not only by Greek settlers but by the multiethnic, mercantile populations of their cities and trading stops.

Increasingly, the messages sent between these connected places have been rediscovered. Most that might have been written on perishable materials have disappeared but those inscribed on lead tablets, which were delivered to their recipients folded or rolled up, preserve the quality of communication across the distances of the archaic Mediterranean. Lead letters of the sixth century have been found in Olbia, the Black Sea colony of Miletus, written in the Ionian dialect, asking about goods that had been seized, as well as about iron tools and valuable plate from Lydia. Others deal with the trade in slaves or relations between members of the same family living and working in remote harbours. One lead letter was written from a master to his slave in Attica, ordering new couches for his house and some baskets and leather straps to be fitted to his donkey, Phalias.

The most graphic of all was discovered in 1985 in the ruins of a house in the Phocaean settlement at Empúries in Catalonia. The lead tablet, which was rolled up, was roughly rectangular, about 4 inches high and 6 wide, weighing a highly portable 3 ounces. The text has fourteen readable lines in which the letters are scratched into the lead with a fine point, using the archaic Ionian alphabet and dialect. Almost certainly, it was written by a merchant from Phocaea, either from the mother city itself or now living in the Phocaean colony at Marseille.

The lead letter from the Phocaean merchant to his man in Empúries.

The text is fragmentary – the lead has rotted – but the life it represents is vivid enough. The merchant is giving his correspondent instructions:

[You must take care] to be in Saguntum [a settlement near Valencia], and if . . .

. . . for [the citizens of Empúries], but not for passengers . . .

. . . more than twenty, and wine not for . . .

. . . [that] the cargo that was in Saguntum and bought by Baspedas [the name of a local trader]

. . . launched to transport goods also in . . .

. . . to . . . what are we to make of all this . . .

. . . and invite Baspedas to tow you

. . . [ask] if there is someone doing the towing to . . .

. . . of our [cargo? vessel?]; and, if there were two, let him send two . . .

. . . but that he is the [man responsible?]; and, if on his part, he wants . . .

. . . which he shares in half; but if he disagrees . . .

. . . stay there and send me a letter saying how much . . .

. . . as soon as possible for him . . .

. . . Here are my commissions. Hail and farewell.

This is the world of the harbour mind: dealing, fixing, needing information, expecting communication to run back and forth, striking bargains, with relationships that are both competitive and cooperative. Profits are to be made and benefits shared. Wine is playing its part.

It was said even in antiquity that the Phocaeans brought the cultivation of the vine to France and Iberia. Both the elegant cups from Pointe Lequin and the Empúries letter are surely associated with that beginning. These vessels from the heartland of Hellas were symbolic of what might be considered the real thing, the symposium in which culture, poetry, warmth and even Greekness might be drunk in with the magic of the vine. There is an intriguing implication: was the symposium, its poetry and games, its luxuries and half-anxious assertion of male dominance, not only a symptom of this culture, but one of its motors, generating trade as much as celebrating it, a shared ritual of triumphant, self-heroizing, sea-straddling togetherness which could in itself be exported and draw riches in its wake?

There is one revelatory connection: the practice of the symposium, the way it made its way across the tides and currents of an evening, was conceived of as a voyage. To embark on a symposium was to sail out on to a sea that could bring you happiness and wellbeing, just as the sea could; or leave you sick and distraught, on the verge of being wrecked, as the sea could. The sea of wine held both promises and dangers.

The number of people at a symposium, perhaps six or eight, was not very different from the number in the crew of a sailing ship, as estimated from the domestic equipment found in wrecks. One wreck discovered at Kyrenia in Cyprus carried enough for four: four dishes, four wooden spoons, four *kantharoi*, four oil jugs. It may be that sailors shared plates and spoons but modern experimental voyages have shown that ships could be sailed with crews as small as that. The sails did most of the work. When large oars or sweeps were needed to take a ship out of a wind-bound harbour, no more than two or four men could do the work. An owner or a travelling merchant could make up the numbers.

Imagine this: a crew have been far out on a trading voyage. Profits have been made and they have come home. The hull is laden with the riches of Egypt or Tyre. The ship sails into the harbour at Mytilene and ties up at the quay. Without transition that crew walk up into the city and become the companion drinkers of the symposium, summoning the wine and the women, music and garlands, boys and poetry. Symposium and voyage map each other.

Bacchylides, a late sixth-century poet from the island of Keos in the Cyclades, understood the symposium to be a swooning voyage of conquest and riches:

> As the cups go quickly round, a sweet subduing power warms the heart . . . That power sends a man's thoughts soaring . . . straight away he is stripping cities of their diadem of towers – he dreams that he shall be king of all the world; – his halls gleam with gold and ivory – over the sunlit sea his wheat-ships bring wealth untold from Egypt: such are the raptures of the drinker's soul.

It is then, as Pindar, the fifth-century eulogist of the successful and the powerful, said, that 'the wearisome cares of men vanish from their breasts, and, on a wide sea that is rich in gold, we are all together voyaging to some imagined shore . . .' He echoed Sappho's famous lines: 'He that is penniless is then rich, and even they that are rich find their hearts expanding, overcome by the darts of the vine.'

What, if anything, can we take from this distant world of buccaneer merchants and men on the make, poets and adventurers, merchants and oligarchs? Their lives were an amalgam of harsh vigour, careless dominance, courage, subtlety, wit, ingenuity, an expansive attitude to the world, a hunger for the vivid and a concern for the wellbeing of their city as much as for themselves. They seem at times to be pirate-citizens and, if it is possible to feel irredeemably removed from them and their uncompromising demand on others, occasionally an object has a way of bridging that time and culture chasm.

One of the most famous images of Dionysus the god of wine, on a wide, shallow cup now in Munich, shows him as the heart-expanding king of his own symposium, lying back as a symposiast would, with a wine horn in his hand, his torso naked, as a symposiast's would be, happily sailing through a dolphin-rich sea, a sea that is alive with the verve of the voyaging animal, in a ship that has a dolphin prow and dolphins painted on its hull, while overhead, climbing the mast, the vine offers bunches of pendulous grapes.

It is a picture of liquid fluency, running on the broadest of reaches, contentedness afloat, a life achieved and rewards taken, the image slowly emerging to the diners as they drank the

Dionysus sails on his dolphin-voyage, with his drinking horn in hand and grapes sprouting from the mast above his head.

contents and found revealed in front of them an archaic Greek vision of heaven on earth. Perhaps that is also the sensation to take away from Alcaeus and his friends: look into this bowl and find a capacity for happiness that comes, in the end, from a life of adventure and openness to any wind that might blow.

5

IS POLITENESS A VIRTUE?

XENOPHANES
COLOPHON, IONIA, 560–470 BC

Xenophanes, born in the small Ionian city of Colophon in about 570 BC, is the heir to Alcaeus. Everything Xenophanes wrote feels like politeness itself. He was the first true advocate of the middle ground, the first thinker to leave behind any hint of the piratical and to embrace the warm pullover of companionable life, the first anti-romantic. Sceptical, post-heroic, profoundly civic, quasi-puritan, intrigued by actuality, prepared to face down inherited shibboleths and with no interest in violent domination, Xenophanes exudes a kind of mannerly wisdom.

There is nothing shamanic or anarchic about him. Where the focus of the thinkers in Miletus had been otherworldly – Thales fell into the well because he did not know his way around the streets – and the Aegean poets had largely attended to themselves, Xenophanes looked to the city. He appeared to love the *seemly* above all, taking his place at the symposium with a kind of reasonable discretion, expecting the other symposiasts to be decorously there beside him, equally polite, equally well oiled, equally quiet and equally unconvinced by the egotists at the party. He was the first sage of urban normality.

He is said to have lived and written until he was over 100 years old, but in 545 BC when he was about twenty-five, the Persians had invaded and conquered Colophon along with other Greek cities in Ionia. Xenophanes left home and travelled

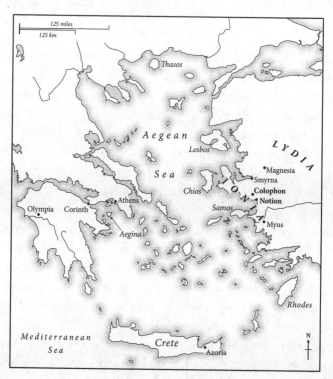

Colophon and its connections.

throughout the Greek diaspora, first to the island of Paros in the Cyclades, to the mainland of Greece, then on to southern Italy and Sicily, teaching, writing and dispensing his version of wisdom to any who would hear it. Through him, perhaps, Ionian ideas first began to spread through the wider Greek world.

The city of his birth was uniquely close to the Lydians at Sardis, so that the life of Colophon fused Greek and non-Greek. It had a fleet, built from the timber of its pinewoods, based at Notion, Colophon's harbour at the sea end of its valley, but its focus was landwards, towards all the glamour the Lydian world could provide. Lydian lushness flowed through Colophon so that its citizens became indistinguishable from their rivals to the east. Like them, these Greeks wore earrings – both men and women – used silver mirrors and ivory combs, loved no one more than a coiffeur and sported spools of beaten gold twisted through the ringlets of their hair, wore long flowing robes and embroidered headbands, both of exquisite workmanship and value, were drenched in perfume, clouds of which filled the streets behind them, carried parasols against the midday sun (both men and women) and lived in a fog of sensuality.

Or so at least the later Greek historians would write of them. Was it true? Most of the accounts of the Lydians and their effects on the Greeks come from the historians who wrote after the traumatic wars with the Persian empire at the beginning of the fifth century, for whom an unalloyed Greekness had become central to their idea of themselves and of the meaning of virtue. For those later writers, Colophon's Graeco-Lydian identity raised a mixture of suspicion and contempt, as a culture whose luxuriant non-austerity the Greeks were both drawn to and repelled by.

One story lies at the foundation levels of this ambiguous relationship. Long before, in the first half of the seventh century, Colophon had been the only Greek city, along with Magnesia, to fall to Lydian attack, largely, it was said, because their resolve and strength had been dissipated by a love of Lydian luxury. Lydianness meant they had forgotten how to act like men.

Herodotus, the fifth-century champion of a unitary Greekness, set against the corruptions of the east and the barbarities of the north, began his great and famous histories with the story of how a man called Gyges had come to the Lydian throne. It is an emblematic tale. Gyges was an officer in the royal bodyguard and high servant to Candaules, king of the Lydians (his name means 'Dog-Throttler'), who was so much in love with his own wife that he thought her the most beautiful woman in the world. But he worried that Gyges did not agree. The only way he could convince his servant of her beauty was for him to see her naked. He devised a plan:

I will put you behind the open door of the room in which we sleep. When I go in to rest she will follow me. There is a chair close to the door, on which she will put her clothes one by one as she takes them off. You will be able in that way to look at her body slowly and carefully. When she is moving from the chair to the bed, and her back is turned, make sure she does not see you as you leave through the door.

Gyges, reluctantly, did as he was asked, saw the queen undress and 'gazed at her', but as he crept out she spotted him and realized what her husband had done. Saying nothing, she plotted her revenge and the next day summoned Gyges: 'Take your choice. Murder Candaules and become my lord, and so obtain the Lydian throne. Or die now here in this room.' Gyges chose to kill his king. The queen required him to do it as Candaules slept, in the room where she had been seen naked the night before. She gave him a dagger and hid him behind the same door. When Candaules fell asleep, Gyges stabbed him in the bed and so laid claim to the throne. Civil war erupted, but the oracle at Delphi sided with Gyges against Candaules' followers and in that way Gyges founded a great dynasty of Lydian kings. It would end only with the death of Croesus four generations later, finally defeated by the power of the Persian empire that conquered Lydia and all the Greek cities on the east side of the Aegean in 546 BC.

True or not, it scarcely matters. This is a tale to define the difference between Greek and non-Greek. The sense of Lydian transgression is palpable: a world of betrayal and desperation, thick with the erotic charge of voyeurism and violence. The men in it are unmanly: Candaules cannot control his infatuated lust – Greeks did not, on the whole, lust after their wives; he must derive his pleasure from displaying his wife's nakedness; Gyges must hide to win the throne; his victim is asleep when he kills him. Only the queen – never named in the story – has the (for Greeks, implicitly manly) self-control to exact her revenge.

It is also a dramatization of the alluringly wicked. Moral disgust is envy in disguise. Herodotus allows his readers to share Gyges' delighted-horrified gaze, to shudder at the indulgence and then be thankful they do not live in such a world. Modern anthropologists doubt that Herodotus was telling the truth in these stories, but his histories repeatedly and even obsessively describe the libertine and un-Greek sexual habits of peoples in Scythia, Babylonia and Egypt. In Lydia itself, he claimed: 'All the daughters of the common people prostitute themselves, gathering together a dowry and they do this to contract a marriage. Moreover, the women give themselves in marriage.' No idea could have been more socially disturbing to the Greeks, for whom the role of men was to control the lives of women and daughters. For female sexuality to become a way of achieving a price in the market, by which those women could decide on their choice of husband, would have felt like social anarchy. Men in a society where they allowed it to happen could hardly have called themselves men at all.

According to this late Greek vision, the Lydians were emasculated, lacking moral strength, made hopeless in battle by their self-indulgence, and nothing but *abrotatoi* – most delicate, pretty and dainty creatures. Is all of this an anachronism? Can one pick any truths out of the propaganda? Were manly Greekness and effeminate Lydianness really as polarized as Herodotus and the other fifth-century Greek writers liked to say?

The reality seems to have been less sharply defined. For all the assertions of effeminacy, the Colophonian cavalry was said to be so effective that it was decisive in any battle. 'To put the Colophon on it', at least according to the later Greek geographer Strabo, meant to settle a question once and for all. Heroic defence of a city and the enjoyment of the deliciousness of life were thought in the sixth century to be quite compatible. Rooms in which the symposiasts celebrated their cushioned and mattressed comfort, with wine from large mixing vessels on high stands, beautiful boys serving them and elegant women dispensing perfumes, were decorated not only with mirrors but with martial helmets and battle shields hung on the walls around them.

It seems as if the Colophonians had achieved in their own city culture a balance between sophistication and vigour, a delight in the pleasures of life and the civic virtue to sustain it, and this culture of accommodation lies behind the civilized, middle-ground thinking of Xenophanes.

He began embedded in the riches of this Graeco-Lydian world. His love of grace and discretion may be symptomatic of precisely this encounter between Greek assurance and Lydian *luxe*. His description of a Colophonian symposium is decorousness itself:

> For now the floor is swept clean; clean are the hands of every man, clean are their cups. A servant sets fresh-woven garlands around everyone's head, another hands around sweet-scented unguent in a saucer. A mixing-bowl stands waiting, brimful of good cheer. And another wine is ready, which promises never to run out – a soft-tasting one, redolent of its flower-bouquet in the jars.
>
> In the middle of the room the frankincense sends forth its pure and holy scent, and there is water, cold and sweet and pure. Ready at hand are the brown loaves and the table filled with cheese and thick honey. The altar in the centre is covered in flowers; and singing and happiness fill the room.

Interestingly, though, Xenophanes' account of the symposium also carries a note of restraint, as if, even as a young man in the 540s, he was disenchanted with the sybaritic indulgences and tendency to violence of other Greek symposiasts:

It is the right thing for men of good cheer first of all to sing a hymn to the god [perhaps Dionysus] with reverent tales and pure words, after pouring libations and praying for strength to do the right (for this is indeed a more obvious thing to pray for, not acts of violence). Then it is proper to drink as much as you can take and still get home without the help of a slave boy, unless you are very old.

Riotous parties, with drunken violence at their heart, are not what Xenophanes wants. The communality of the city is the prize, to be held and celebrated by those who are lucky enough to have been invited to the party. He speaks with the voice of a responsible oligarch. When men sing songs or tell stories at these feasts, they should describe noble actions and think of what in the past has demonstrated moral excellence, but they should avoid violent legends – 'the fights of Titans or Giants or Centaurs' which are no more than the 'fantasies of our ancestors' – the word he uses, *plasmata*, means anything artificially formed or moulded, of wax or dough, figments or idols of 'those who came before us'. Few things are more destructive of the good life than reheated ancient fables. Above all, the symposiasts are not to deal in stories of the kind of civil strife to which these oligarchic, part-mercantile, part-aristocratic cities were chronically vulnerable. 'There is no good, wholesome use for such tales,' Xenophanes told his audience.

A political adjustment has appeared – from the glory of big men to the stability of the community; from individual excess to cooperative welfare; from ancient illusions to modern practicality; from a kind of individualist self-seeking, for which violence was one means of expression, to a conformity with the wellbeing of your peers.

Modern men are to forget the ancient stories. Homeric Gods and their amoral, disconnected existence have nothing to do with us. We are here, in this city, evolving and devising a life for ourselves. Almost visibly, the past is being left behind in a set of changing attitudes. This is not the invention of democracy – there is nothing approaching universal suffrage – but it does look like the invention of the political.

What can it have been like to be in these streets, to have met these rich, comfortable people and their luxury accoutrements, with these ideas of civility surfacing within them? Next to nothing can be seen of the archaic city of Colophon now, save a few stretches of overgrown wall among the olive trees and, in the pastures, the crumbling excavations left by the archaeologists. It is a place of butterflies and dragonflies dancing between the thistle-heads. Everywhere sherds of ancient pottery prod out through the soil. The situation is welcoming, about 10 miles in from the Aegean, up the little valley of the River Ales, surrounded by a rim of hills and almost disconnected from any sense of the sea. Tang-scented pinewoods come close on each side, that pelt of wood rolling up and over the peaks and ridges of the hills. All the bony clarity of the coast is absent.

Aerial view of Azoria from the west.

Colophon and Değirmendere, the Turkish village that now half occupies its site, is a fruity place, full of running water, lemon and orange orchards, with plane trees along its trunk roads and a street market in which hens in cages, little chicks and breeding cocks, peppers, grapes and marrows, pickaxes and mattocks, baulks of timber from the pinewoods, coffee stalls and tea shacks all crowd out the traffic.

From the seventh century onwards, it was a place of fertility and riches, famous for its horses and hounds, but too little of what was here then remains for anyone to be able to rekindle the buildings and spaces of the archaic city. One must look elsewhere to see the physical forms of a Greek community as it first decided to become a city and embark on its political career. Across the Aegean, a long and brilliant archaeological campaign has been conducted by Donald Haggis and his team from the University of North Carolina to reveal the nature of a small Greek settlement in the sixth century BC, exactly contemporary with Xenophanes and exactly at the point it became a city.

The site of Azoria – its ancient name is lost – is a virtually untouched capsule of this archaic world. Here, physically, you can walk through the life spaces of these first Greek urbanists. It sits high on the slopes of the dry, almost treeless mountains overlooking the coastal plain in north-east Crete. In late summer, dust blows down its narrow streets, across the farmland far below, to the shore of the deep gulf of Mirabello about 2 miles away and on to the sea beyond.

Colophon is two or three days' sail away from here, as is Corinth or Athens. The coast of Egypt perhaps twice as far. Wine jugs and oil lamps from Attica, a round-bellied cooking pot from the slave-trading island of Aegina in the Saronic Gulf, wine amphorae from Chios and a deep drinking cup from Thasos in the northern Aegean have all been found in the ruins of the city, as well as vast storage *pithoi*, made somewhere along the Cretan coast, decorated with wave patterns, centaurs and crane-like birds, all pressed into the clay. The biggest is capable of holding 200 gallons or more. If the essence of a city is its gathering of riches and the cultivation of connections, as the fuel of a social and economic acceleration, Azoria is a model of its kind.

It was for unknown reasons burned and abandoned early in the fifth century and, unlike almost every other city site, hardly ever reoccupied or built upon. As a result Azoria is an almost unencumbered window into the making of a sixth-century city. There are many local variations across the Greek world – the long and narrow Cretan houses are arranged very differently from the courtyard model in Ionia or mainland Greece – but, for all that, Azoria is a map of the genesis of the Greek city, a physical key to the shaping of a frame of mind and way of life. Social, political and psychological impulses are all apparent in the decisions taken by its sixth-century citizens.

Before about 600 BC, there had been a cluster of dispersed villages around Azoria, with about ten or twenty houses in each of them, pursuing stable, agricultural lives for generation after generation. Some of the houses had been occupied and slowly

One of the giant storage *pithoi* under reconstruction.

added to by their families over 400 or 500 years. In about 600
BC, this pre-city life was abandoned. The villages in which the
people had lived for half a millennium were deserted and all
moved to the site of Azoria. The new city was enormous by
comparison, the buildings spreading over more than 40 acres.
Intriguingly the people brought many of their heirlooms with
them: a ceramic *pithos* that was at least 600 years old when it
was carried to the new city, a legacy from the Bronze Age; tiny
ivory votive figurines perhaps from Phoenicia; wine-mixing
bowls that would have belonged to distant ancestors but had
been treasured over the generations.

This was no chaotic resettlement of people in trouble. Nor was
it the work of a dominant overlord. Communal decisions are
apparent at every turn. The old centre of Azoria was completely
rebuilt to house the families that were gathering there. All earlier
buildings and the plan of the streets between them were obliter-
ated and a new physical form provided for their shared lives. It
was a redefinition of who these people were. No longer were they
to be scattered in self-sufficient house clusters; now they were
gathered in a series of city blocks hinged to huge-stoned spine-
walls built in terraced, concentric rings around the hilltop. The
centre of the town was then provided with three or four extraordinary communal structures, well beyond any previous household
use: a large hall, more than 60 feet long, roofed in olive-wood
beams, with a stone bench around all sides. Dr Haggis's team
found two pots here that held the remains of stews – one of
lamb, with chickpeas, onions and oregano, the other a broth of
wheat grains, broad beans and grapes. Below that was a vast
multi-roomed warehouse full of food and drink, with a storage
capacity of at least 9,000 gallons of wine or oil set out in banks
of jars, to service the great hall. Nearby was a large olive-oil press
and store, and on the other side a set of kitchens in which the
feasts must have been prepared, with traces everywhere of pulses,
cereals, lentils, grapes, olives, almonds, figs and pomegranates.

Above that, on a set of four terraces, a complex of four or five dining rooms, each capable of housing a party of up to twenty, with their associated kitchens, storerooms and a shared sanctuary or chapel in which meat offerings were prepared and burned and – judging from the grape pips sunk into the floor – in which libations were made and the lees poured out.

These different rooms were arranged in three or four suites, where fruit stands from Rhodes and pots from the Ionian cities were found stacked and smashed in the final fire. Part of the boss from a bronze shield and the curved crest of a helmet, both of which would have decorated the walls of the dining room, were found in the rubbish. There was plenty of food here too, crushed into the clay of the floors: bones of pig, sheep and goat that had been cut up into individual joints; stands for the large wine-mixing and wine-cooling bowls from which the drinks would be distributed. The wine cups were of a standard size and shape, often with a plain black glaze that might suggest elegance, civility, uniformity and a sense of equality in the standing of all those who were there.

The equipment of a kitchen in Azoria.

This was not life on the edge of viability. One of the communal kitchens was well provided for – and preserved – with more than sixty vessels, for carrying, storing and boiling liquids, a bucket, some settling dishes, a ceramic sieve, spouted jugs, many cups and other tableware, a mortar for grinding herbs, lamps for work in the evenings, water jugs and many cookpots.

These rooms and their contents are all the marks of the civic: life not based on a war band, nor on a single regal power source, nor separated into isolated families but framed around a regulated and careful coexistence, to which each producer contributed, taking in the goods of the land, allowing for large communal gatherings, perhaps decision-making meetings, and for subsidiary groups to come together in rooms that look as if they were designed for the kind of bond-forming drinking party we know as the symposium.

It looks on the ground like the recognition that community requires structure, that jointness is viable and that a group of people can come together to make provision for shared wellbeing. As a unique survival of a preserved city from the sixth century BC, Azoria can be taken as the physical equivalent of the psychological and social shape of the cities in which these early Greeks lived. It was clearly oligarchic. The cluster of expensive dining rooms with their heroic equipment from ancient wars (the helmet crest is thought to be up to a hundred years older than the building in which it was found) could only have been for the select few. Even the large meeting hall could have accommodated only the leaders of the city. Azoria looks, in short, like a city designed for the governing few, among whom there was a determination to share power and policy. The quality of *isonomia* – equality before the law – may have been treasured here but only by an elite. Azoria is the equivalent in stone of the world of Xenophanes' mind.

He shared with the other philosophers a certain arrogance. 'Most things', he thought, 'are inferior to mind.' He did not like competitive sports and disparaged the Olympic heroes on whose shoulders every city liked to heap praise and reward. If a man won a victory by his pace on the track, Xenophanes wrote,

> or in the pentathlon at Olympia, in wrestling or boxing, or in that dreadful contest which they call *pankration* [a kind of all-in fighting in which no holds were barred]: in the eyes of his fellow-citizens, he becomes more glorious to look at. He will be given the best first-row seats at the public games, bread from the public stores, a trophy as an heirloom. Even if he won in a chariot – by the horse's effort rather than his own – he would be given all of this, but he is not as worthy of such rewards as I am. For our *sophiē* [to be understood as art or skill or learning or wisdom, as these qualities were not yet distinct] is better than the strength of men and horses.

This is the first championing of intellectual skill over bodily strength. Brain now matters more than brawn and the reason is clear: this excellence at sports is politically useless. If a man is a good runner or fighter or charioteer, 'the city would not enjoy any better government'. The source of joy for a city that comes from having a victorious athlete at Olympia is a 'small' and passing pleasure. 'For those things do not enrich the innermost stores and granaries of the city.'

For Xenophanes, the old world, of which this cult of athletic prowess was a descendant, could not have been more misguided. Previous generations had failed to see the world as it is. Homer attributed to the gods everything that is shameful and reproachful – stealing, adultery and lying among them. But why had previous generations seen gods in this way? Because of a failure of the imagination. To have imagined gods like this was only a kind of human dreaming. People, ridiculously, have a way of imagining that gods are just like them, that they are born, they wear clothes, walk and talk and have bodies just like ours. Xenophanes pointed out that the Ethiopians thought their gods had black skins and flat noses; for the Thracians gods had grey eyes and yellow-red hair (the word Xenophanes used is also used for the colour of egg yolk).

But think, he suggested, 'if cattle or horses or lions had hands and were able to draw, they would make their gods' bodies like their own: horses would have horse gods and cows cow gods'. The God that Xenophanes imagines is not like that. God is abstract. Nothing about him resembles anything mortal. Whatever God is 'rests always in the same state, moving not at all, as it is not fitting or seemly for him to come and go, now rushing here, now skittering there.' God, supremely, is a great and universal stillness, both infinitely present and infinitely capable, with no need of action in order to be. 'All of him sees, all of him thinks and all of him hears.' He is the great intelligent consciousness of Being whose mind creates reality: 'Without toil he shapes all things by thought alone.'

Xenophanes, in other words, embraces eternity. Although Zeus in the *Iliad* had occasionally been able to make things happen by thinking about them, the magnificent immanence of Xenophanes' God stands far beyond the busy squabbles and rivalries of the other Olympians. It may be, although this is not quite clear, that Xenophanes thought God was the same as the world. Whatever is, is God and the majesty of that conception is allied in his view of the world to a deep scepticism about the power of the human mind.

No man knows or will ever know the truth about the gods and about everything I speak of. For even if one chanced to say the complete truth, he would not know it for the truth. Seeming spreads its net over everything.

God sees, thinks and hears, but human understanding is limited. There is no quasi-divine power in us. Our condition is communal ignorance and every form of understanding must accommodate that sense of limitation. 'If God had not made yellow honey, they would say that figs are much sweeter.'

We might make our judgements on what we have known, but that is no guarantee that what we guess is true. Nonetheless, the thinking mind should constantly be applied to the material world. The rainbow is not a goddess called Iris but a cloud that is 'purple, red and yellow to the eye'. If you are not sure whether a woman who has died was human or divine, make your choices: if divine, don't mourn; if human, don't sacrifice to her. Look at rocks and you will find the impressions of shells and fish in them. What more evidence could you need that the earth was once covered in mud and that one day it will be carried down into mud again?

The general world-view of the Ionian ruling class in the sixth century BC was polarized between an adulation of the young, athletic and desirable and an appreciation of the old, comfortable and fat. The stone sculptures in which they invested, and which they set up in public shrines and burial grounds, were divided along those lines, a double vision of handsome, elegant young men and women, conventionally called the *kouroi* and the *korai*, and very different representations of the middle-aged ruling class, in whose statues a soft doughy fullness flows from breast to belly, to buttock, thigh, calf and even feet.

The *kouroi* and *korai* clearly derive from Egyptian models. For more than 2,000 years Egypt had celebrated its pharaohs, their queens, chief priests and officials with tall, forward-facing human figures, carved from stone blocks to which they were still attached, almost always with one foot placed in front of the other, but with the weight on the back foot, leaning slightly away from the viewer. They were only ever meant to be seen from the front.

That basic stance was imported by the Greeks but subtly altered. The Egyptians were usually clothed, if only with a light kilt, but the Greek hero was almost always shown naked (the women were clothed). He was released from the stone block out of which he was carved and his stance, still with one foot in front of the other, given more of a forward movement so that his weight fell on his front foot. The human being is mobilized. His arms and hands, still by his side, were also set free of the stone. His musculature was more pronounced and he was also intended to be seen from all sides, so that his back and buttocks were as carefully and subtly carved as any part of him. An unexaggerated fullness of muscle had come to inhabit the stone.

About 200 of these wonderful figures survive, the earliest from Ionia and the Aegean islands, later moving to the mainland of Greece. In a culture that so consistently celebrated the beauty and attractiveness of the young male body, there is clearly an erotic charge to them, but they are no mere lust objects. They have no individuality and are not portraits. There is nothing lascivious in pose or portrayal. They represent an ideal of imagined male beauty, with a serenity and clarity that are embodied in their naked dignity. They have nothing to hide and know no shame but are astonishingly present and, in their original painted condition, when their flesh was reddened and warmed, their hair yellowed, would have been disarmingly *there*, a near-magical simulacrum of a living person.

All the desire for clarification and realization of the human that is apparent in the philosophy and poetry of this culture is also in these marble bodies, as much in the female as in the male. The *korai* are dressed in fine, figure-hugging cloth, sometimes overwrapped with a shawl, tightly belted, and are often wearing a kind of embroidered and ruffled headband of the sort Sappho describes. Many are portrayed holding a bird or a flower in front of them with one hand, the other down by their side.

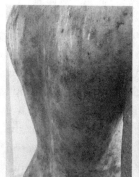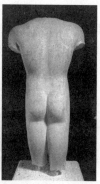

The marble flesh of *kouroi* in Izmir and London.

Some are shown with their lips open and their tongue almost protruding, caught in mid-song.

Even in their abstraction, these first Greek sculptures of the body have embarked on a path that is different from the Egyptian or the Mesopotamian. Those river cultures had represented

A kore in mid song, once at Colophon's shrine to Apollo at Klaros, now in Izmir, wearing what is perhaps 'a decorated headband from Sardis', as Sappho describes her dancing girls; another now in the Louvre with a mantle over the tight-fitting chiton, who once held a bird or flower to her breast.

people in stone as embodiments of power. These *kouroi* and *korai* describe a simple but perfect humanity. They have no status beyond their own beauty, come with no instruments of authority, and there is no hankering in them after the divine or metaphysical. As much as the thinkers and poets this book has pursued, the *kouroi* and *korai*, examples of which are still to be seen in Miletus, Ephesus and Izmir, steer away from the fatally bifurcated world of powerless mortals and all-powerful gods to one in which human beings occupy the centre ground. They represent human beauty.

Reconstruction of the Geneleos group near the entrance to the Heraion of Samos, with plaster casts.

A slightly battered group of sculptures set up along the Sacred Way to the great shrine of Hera in Samos in about 560 BC has two of these young women standing in the centre. To the left is a slightly older woman in a chair and at the right-hand end a figure lounging like a seal on a thick folded-over cushion. All are damaged and headless, and two are missing from the group – perhaps further young women – but together they depict a social universe. The *korai* are as we have come to expect, elegant, perfect, their ruched dresses just hitched up above one ankle for ease of movement. The figure to the right is different. The folds of his clothes, as the great British archaeologist Sir John Boardman wrote, gather beneath his belly 'like poured chocolate sauce'. The figure seems to be full-breasted, the lovely contours visible beneath the cloth, but this is the depiction not of a great matron of Samos but of a prosperous and happily well-fed man: his pillow, which is made of a stuffed and folded wineskin, has inscribed on it the last part of a name, -*archēs*, an ending usually given to a member of the male elite.

The front and rear view of the reclining and satisfactorily fat figure in the Geneleos group.

His statue was also intended to be seen from all sides. From behind, his shawl or *himation*, arranged under the hair or wig, is allowed to fall from shoulder to waist and buttock in the single, relaxed curve of supreme ease.

Herodotus several times referred to the wealthy of Ionia simply as 'the fat'. Solon, the great Athenian lawmaker and poet, thought 'luxury in belly, sides and feet' was a signal of wealth, and, to embody this love of the chubby, a statue from the tiny abandoned city of Myus near Miletus and now in Berlin has preserved the feet of a diner, delicately plump, settled into the softness of the marble mattress, as a poignant memory of a moment of comfort 2,500 years ago. Another symposiast from Myus, also in Berlin, allows the contented diner to relax with his knees slightly drawn up, his right hand, like those of the others, resting easily on his thigh and knee and in his left hand holding what looks for all the world like a frothing pint of beer.

One hardly dares describe these figures as having a physique; there is scarcely a bone to be sensed or seen. Sinuosity and the semi-liquid bulk that comes with wellbeing are portrayed as the sign of a good life. These people are not athletes or warriors. This is the kind of archaic Greek relaxedness in relation to life and other citizens that Xenophanes celebrated, an idea of perfection which is more about accommodation than hard-edged excellence, more the celebration of a life that has escaped from the everlasting contest of existence.

Symposiasts from Myus, contentedly relaxed in cushioned comfort.

The middle-aged have never been more lovingly portrayed. But these figures mean what they do only because, in these sculptural groupings, they are set against their opposites. Each means what it does in contradistinction to the other. First, the naked *kouros* seems more naked in the context of the clothed *kore*. Together, the abstracted and restrained perfection of those two figures is made more perfect by the fleshy co-presence of their indulged elders, who do not stand but sit or lie with their clothes pooling around them. Those luxurious figures can be seen to have benefited from a life of success and reward. But both states are forms of perfection, one the promise of youth, the other the fulfilment of age, one an ideal beginning, the other a consummation. In a way that Xenophanes would have acknowledged, this multiple and encompassing vision of the passage of human beings through life, in which one kind of marvellousness – contentment – takes the place of another – beauty – is a form of social wisdom, of a city culture that celebrated wholeness.

When, under the warrior-emperor Cyrus the Great, the Persians conquered Lydia and the Greek states in 546 BC, Xenophanes fled from Colophon. It was a symbolic moment: the free-thinker escaping imperial tyranny. You can follow his last unhappy route down to the sea past the shrine of Apollo at Claros to what was once the city and harbour beach at Notion from where he would have left for the still-free Greek world.

It is one of the beaches that Strabo, the later Greek geographer and historian, called good for 'launching' – the word he used means 'wetting'. There is still a wonderful fish lunch to be had in the taverna there. You must wait for it: a man in a skiff with the Turkish ensign at the stern rows his small boat around the bay, drawing his net into the enclosing circle, the hills of Samos grey behind him, dark-eyed dogs half-asleep on the sand, before in time he delivers his catch to the waiting coals.

It is a seductive place. Nowhere does Herodotus' famous statement seem truer:

These Ionians had the fortune to build their cities in the most favourable position for climate and seasons of any men we know: for neither the regions above Ionia nor those below, neither those towards the East nor those towards the West, produce the same results as Ionia itself, those in the one direction being oppressed by cold and moisture, and those in the other by heat and drought.

This is the perfect middle. The acropolis stands high above the beach. Beside it the narrow channel of the River Ales runs out to the Aegean, filled with little 16-footers, tethered to the bank, some with fringed canopies for picnics down the coast, their men on a sunny morning tinkering with outboards that refuse to start. Frescos of party boats, accompanied by leaping dolphins, have been recovered from Bronze Age Akrotiri on Thera, decked in flags and bunting, dressed overall for a day out. Is it not just as likely, in such a rich, sea-familiar culture, that there would have been little canopied pleasure boats like these parked in this narrow channel 2,500 years ago, ready to take their lucky families out for a day at sea?

Left: boats dressed for a pleasure outing in Bronze Age Akrotiri; right: their modern descendants in the channel of the River Ales at Notion.

Climb to the top of the acropolis on the ancient, notched stone track, past the sage plants, the big wall of the city from which the figs grow between the stones. Any meeting held here, in the small banked seats of the council chamber, the *bouleuterion*, or on the steps of the temple of Athena Polias, would, between the fragments of conversation, have surveyed the beauty of this sea world out to the west. It is inconceivable that anyone born here would not have loved it for the rest of his life.

Fragments of Xenophanes' nostalgia have survived from his years of exile as a wandering scholar, remembering when he was very old the moment he left Colophon as a young man of twenty-five, driven away by those who the Greeks without distinction called Medes or Persians:

For sixty-seven years now my thoughts have been tossed [*blēstērizontes*, usually applied to a man on his sickbed] restlessly up and down Greece . . .

Beside the fire during the winter, having eaten one's fill, drinking sweet wine and nibbling chickpeas, one should ask this kind of question: Who are you, and where are you from my friend? How old are you? How old were you when the Medes invaded the country?

With bitterness equal to that longing, he recalled the indulgence of the Colophonians who had allowed themselves to soften into defeat:

While they were still free from the loathsome tyranny, having learned from the Lydians all kinds of useless luxury, they would come to the place of assembly [the agora] wearing cloaks made all of purple, no fewer than a thousand of them, as a rule, boastful, delighting in their elaborate coiffure, with their hair drenched in ointments of super-sophisticated perfume.

This sounds like all-too-simple a story: freedom-loving Greek philosopher escapes the tyrants from the east and retreats to a Greek world where he can mourn his loss. But there is one extraordinary archive that suggests something slightly different.

In the Ashmolean Museum in Oxford there is a rare hoard of more than 900 minuscule ancient Greek silver coins. They look more like lentils than money. Most of them weigh about 15/1,000ths of an ounce, the weight of a drop of rain, most of the others less than that. If you poured all 900 into a sack, it would come to about half a pound, a bag of metal rice, coinage sugar. No one is sure where this money came from (the coins arrived in the Ashmolean in 1953 as a gift from the great numismatist and collector Sir Stanley Robinson), but each is stamped on one side with the roughly sketched, big-eyed and bobble-haired image of what is taken for an archaic Apollo. The best guess is that they came from Colophon, which had in its territory at Claros the great oracle and temple of that god. His head would remain the visual signature of Colophon for centuries to come. These are almost certainly its earliest coins; some of the same form have been found by metal detectors on the acropolis at Notion.

A Colophon coin (life-size).   Colophon Apollo (6× life-size).

They were minted in the late sixth century, after the Persians had taken over the city and its territory, and installed their ruling satrap in Sardis. Specialists who have pored over the minor differences in the heads of the god and in the shapes stamped into the reverse have made an astonishing discovery: the 900-odd coins were made with a total of more than 800 separate stamps or 'dies'. It can be estimated that each die would have been used between 1,000 and 5,000 times before it wore out. This was minting on a spectacular scale. The coins are hardly rubbed or used: they would have been buried when they were almost new, made at one moment or over a very short period when in a single impulse the city governors of Colophon decided to strike hundreds of thousands if not millions of very low-value coins.

This was money not as the valued treasure of a small and confined elite, let alone of a single tyrannical power source, but more like money as we know it: currency, the corpuscles of exchangeable value running through the veins of a city, the bloodstream itself, not intended for foreign trade – very few of these coins have been found beyond Colophon or Notion; they were for internal exchange – but there to facilitate the enormously shared connectedness of a city in the sixth century BC. What was going on?

This common currency, of tiny individual value, was coinage whose function, as the numismatists Henry Kim and John Kroll have said, was 'restricted to the modest, quotidian exchange needs of the agora and the general population at large'. It was usable by all but the very poorest of the people, including all the local traders, the market-stall holders, the small makers of pottery and metal goods, those working in the boatyard at Notion, the fishermen, the wine makers, the oil pressers, on whom the entire economy relied. It was not quite a democratic gesture – there was no suggestion that voting rights came with the use of the city's money – but it was an act of inclusion, a sign of the agora at Colophon teeming as it is now with small producers and manufacturers, buyers and sellers exchanging silver coins in the smallest conceivable denominations, and recognized to be doing that as an essential function of a coherent city.

Minuscule coinage was an act of civic inclusion so that these coins, more than the fragmentary stone remains, become the spirit of the city. The governors of Colophon and Notion, even in their perfumes and their purples, cared to make the life of almost everyone there engaged with the identity of their small state. The coins are curiously intimate objects. Characters in ancient Greek comedy, particularly if they are idiotic, tend to carry their small change in their mouths and swallow it when they fall over. For years, this was thought to be an easy joke until a skeleton was found in 2002 by archaeologists excavating in the Lydian capital of Sardis. The man, who was armed, a soldier, had been killed in the mid-sixth century fighting: a tiny silver coin was found inside his skeletal mouth. He must have had it tucked inside his cheek.

And so these tiny morsels of silver might also have lived for a while in the cheeks of the Colophonians. Petty cash was made part of the life of the entire community. They would have tasted it as they went about their mornings. It is the most Greek of gestures performed under Persian rule. Was it Persian or was it Greek? Or does that distinction even make sense? The categories are not closed. Under a Persian satrapy, in the still-Greek city he had left behind, is surely something of which Xenophanes would have approved: a way of extending the high-minded courtesy and inclusiveness of the symposium, its overriding belief in the joint and corporate coexistence of the attendees, to the city as a whole. Everyone in Colophon and Notion could be equally fat. A Persian–Greek world, in contrast to all the later fifth-century xenophobic accounts of it, could embody civilization.

6

IS LIFE A FIRE?

HERACLITUS
EPHESUS, IONIA, 540–480 BC

Heraclitus was the mirror opposite of Xenophanes, not offering the consolations of civilized calm but seeing strife and tension at the heart of existence. Life for him was a transforming blaze. Most of us cannot see it because our time-window is too short and our perspective limited, but for Heraclitus, with the long-distance gaze of the philosopher, the essence of being was a becoming and withdrawing, a restlessness, the emerging and disappearing of things as they are, every phenomenon of life no more than the tongues of a burning fire.

He can be seen as the first systems theorist, understanding that reality consists not of things in stable, isolated existence but of the often ferocious interaction of many opposites. Dynamic networks in time and space define reality more than the objects that are connected by those networks. It is a trader's vision: the coming and going is what matters, more than the particular things that come and go.

Xenophanes, with all his focus on the fixed and proper thing, had based his ideas on the necessary coherence of civic relations; Heraclitus founded his on the dynamic co-presence of multiplicities. Apparent identities are in the process of transformation. Nothing remains as it is. Nothing now is what it once was. Opposites are only different aspects of the same one process in

175

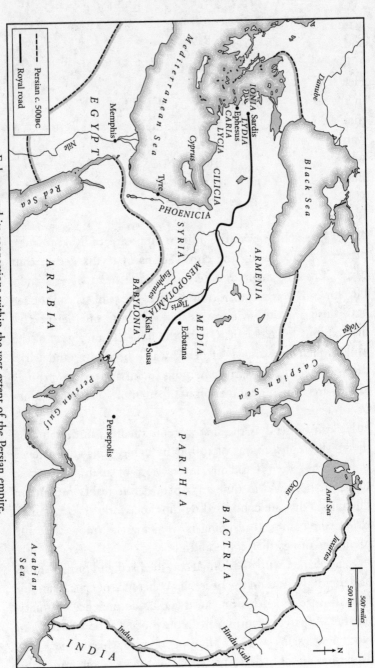

Ephesus and its connections within the vast extent of the Persian empire.

action. Accept this fire of transformation as the underlying fact and a deeper understanding will come.

One brief and apparently insignificant ancient story encapsulates Heraclitus' vision. Some visitors were looking for him everywhere in the streets of Ephesus, which was his city. He was nowhere they might have expected. Finally, they found him in a kitchen, warming himself by the oven. They stopped at the door and waited, surprised to find the great man in such a humble corner. But he called out to them: 'Come in, the gods are here too.'

It was the most ordinary place in which to find a genius. No Rodinesque heroism but a man huddling close to the warmth of a fire, claiming that the oven in the kitchen was as much a place for the divine as any temple. So ordinariness could conceal the extraordinary. And in this place all the ingredients of the Heraclitean vision are to hand: the oven itself, its transformation at the heart of life, the dough becoming bread, the actions of the heat; the unreliable nature of appearances – the kitchen might as well be a temple – and the unity of life despite our endless categorization of it, the intimacy of opposites: philosopher/kitchen, gods/oven, thinking/cooking, cold flesh/radical mind.

A much later bronze head of a philosopher, found in Ephesus and now in the museum there, was given the venerable, sceptical, disenchanted air that clings to Heraclitus' name.

Little is known of him. Several stories reiterate his hostility to the Ephesians, despicable for their vulgarity and incontinence. He hated their praying to images and their sexual excess: 'The waste of semen is a diminution of the self.' Like all of us, they found his philosophy difficult, and for them his reputation was simple: a man who liked to speak in riddles, 'Heraclitus the obscure'. 'The soul wants to be wet,' he said of them and their indulgences, 'but it is death for souls to become water.' A dry, strict integrity, with an austere attention to the underlying and scarcely accessible truth of things, was the only route to wisdom. 'A dry soul: wisest and best'.

The head of a philosopher. Bronze, Ephesus, AD 240.

He loathed the ancient gods and their often disgusting rituals, rejected Homer and other ancient poets for promulgating an absurdly anthropomorphic vision of the divine. He liked to spend his days with thieves, gamesters and other refugees from the law. He preferred playing knucklebones with children to any conversation with their parents. He was well-born, from an aristocratic family that pre-dated modern Ephesus and was eligible for an honorary and hereditary kingship-cum-priesthood, but he renounced it in favour of his brother. He refused to make a law code for the promiscuous people of a city without philosophy. Democracy was far from his mind. 'It would be a good idea if the citizens hanged themselves, every grown man, and leave the city to those who are still children,' he said. 'They have expelled the most excellent man among them, saying "Let not even one of us be excellent; or, if anyone is excellent, let him go elsewhere and live with others."'

Heraclitus did not lay out a guidebook for a complex world. Much of what he has to say is a denial of apparent truth. Nevertheless, three principles can be derived from the fragments that remain of his writings.

First, life as the fire of change.

Second, that change is not anarchic. We do not live in a lawless universe. Things are burning in the eternal conflagration of existence but they do so under control, systematically 'kindling by measures and going out by measures'.

And third the law that governs that process of change is straightforward: all opposites are merely different dimensions of the same one thing. However disparate things seem to be, fundamentally everything is one, even if that singular thing has discord or 'strife' deep within it.

One thing, what is wise: to know the thought that steers all things through all things.

After you have listened, not to me, but to the word [*logos*], it is wise to recognise that all things are one.

Different metaphors are folded into this vision. Apart from the fire, the Heraclitean reality we all encounter can be seen to be structured according to what the Oxford philosopher Jonathan Barnes has called 'the tension of incompatibles'. Heraclitus' model for the nature of reality is the bow or the lyre. The strings of the lyre pull against its frame; the string of the bow pulls against the upper and lower limbs of its body. If the tension is not maintained, if the strings spring free or the frame breaks, the integrity of the object is gone. There must be tension, but not too much or too little. Only because the bow or lyre is internally stressed to the right degree – 'being pulled apart it is brought together with itself' – does it maintain its wholeness. Unless they held those contradictory forces in tension, neither bow nor lyre would exist. Their identity exists in their opposition to themselves. It is symptomatic of this moment in Greek culture that Heraclitus chooses, as the model for the underlying structure of reality, the two attributes of the great archer-lyricist god Apollo, for whom bow and lyre were the instruments through which his glory shone in the world.

Anaximander in Miletus had thought that a kind of cosmic justice would emerge over time, as the claim of one part of reality would be compensated for by the claim of another, but Heraclitus makes the intuitive leap beyond that Tweedledum–Tweedledee vision, by recognizing that the relentlessly dynamic and equally relentlessly stressed relationship of parts is justice itself. 'Strife is justice; all things happen by strife and necessity.' Only when strife is done with, when the bow breaks or the string comes adrift, is there *in*justice, a form of dominance which does not allow an equal coexistence of opposites. Even, he says, the barley drink, the *kykeon*, a religious and ritual concoction made of wine, water and grated cheese, sometimes mixed with honey and herbs, 'falls apart if it is not stirred'. It is in the nature of a harbour city to mix opposites, and Heraclitus' discovery is that this yoking together of contradictories is the source of identity.

One has to go slowly with this, but the three underlying Heraclitean facts – the fire; the 'tension of incompatibles'; the oneness of things – makes for a tightly integrated system, a model for life, with ethical and political implications. Reality is essentially joined and the joining of opposites in tension is the just and harmonic condition. The meaning of goodness is indistinguishable from what is just and what is just allows the flourishing of all opposites in tension. Everything cycles through these conditions. Without strife there can be no goodness. The fire is goodness itself.

Ephesus was the rival of Miletus as the most dynamic of the Ionian ports, on the same shore, in its own silting estuary, a day's sail further north. Just as the River Meander at Miletus

The fragment of the star bowl in Ischia showing the constellation
Boötes, the Herdsman, by which Odysseus steered away from
Calypso's island (see p. 73).

The temple of Athena on the acropolis at Notion.

The ancient quay at Teos, one of the Ionian harbour cities, still in use for fishing boats. The bay is protected from the northerlies, with a sandy bottom and good holding, the foundations for the life of the harbour mind.

The ruins of Priēnē, raised above the valley of Meander, in whose muds and silts the site of its predecessor is permanently lost (see p. 95).

The rock-carved seats of the Panionion on the northern slopes of Mount Mycale, where representatives of all the cities of Ionia met to resolve disputes and discuss their common interests.

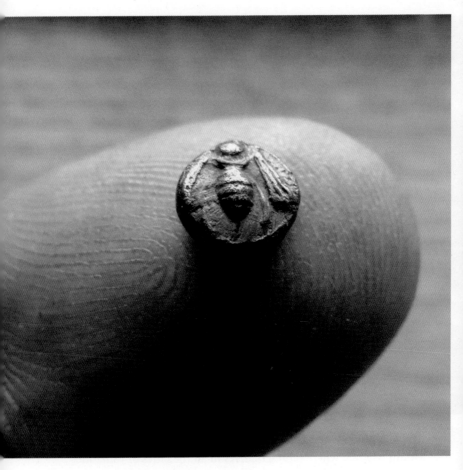

A silver obol from Ephesus, struck in about 550 BC,
bearing the bee symbol of the city (see p. 21).

Lion settled into the silt at the entrance of the harbour at Miletus (see p. 93).

From the top of the hill of Zeytintepe, once sacred to Aphrodite, the goddess of love, looking west over the silted-up gulf of Miletus (see pp. 85–93).

One of the archaic statues from the Sacred Way between Miletus and the oracle of Apollo at Didyma, of a full-bodied young man, made in about 580 BC, whose figure displays the luxuries and rewards enjoyed by the Milesians (see pp. 167–8).

A symposium scene from the Tomb of the Diver at
Paestum. The symposiasts lie back on cushioned benches.
A man and his beloved boy, lyre in hand, come near to
kissing. Another plays *kottabos*, a competitive game in
which the lees of the wine are thrown from the cups at a
target. Delight rules.

A man on his symposium couch holds out a *kylix* for
more wine, while a naked boy draws a jug of it from a
large *krater* in which the wine is mixed with water. A
young woman prepares scented oils. Helmet and shield
hang on the wall behind. Hound and partridge nose
among the furniture. From Thera about 470 BC
(see p. 120).

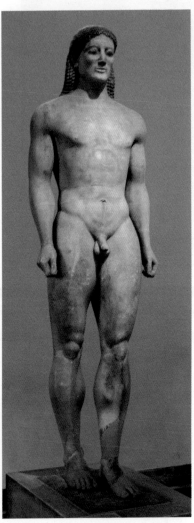

Left: An Egyptian limestone figure of a man from about 2400 BC. *Right:* The Kroisos Kouros found in Anavyssos, Attica, and made in about 530 BC of marble from Paros. The change in emphasis is from authority to beauty, from potency to human perfection (see p. 166).

A golden letter, left in the grave on the chest or mouth of the Pythagorean dead. Its words are a conversation in the afterlife:

[The dead Initiate]: I am parched with thirst and dying.

[The Source of life-giving water]: Then come drink of me, the Ever-Flowing Spring. On the right there is a pale cypress. Who are you? Where are you from?

[Initiate]: I am the son of Earth and Starry Heaven. But my race is heavenly.

(See p. 218.)

The diving boy from the sarcophagus at Paestum (see pp. 226–8).

Persephone, queen of the underworld,
the source of wisdom and understanding (see p. 244).

The rare survival of a richly coloured terracotta cornice from the Greek city of Metapontum. The lion is a spout head, in such good condition that it was probably never used. Whiteness was not a Greek ideal (see p. 275).

Ephesus.

had gradually destroyed the harbours there, the Caÿster at Ephesus would in time slowly clog its sea connection. The shore is now some 6 miles away from the remains of the city. Black-and-white cattle graze on the marshes where the sea once was. The ancient harbour – the last of a sequence of them, each one moved seawards through antiquity as the river made its predecessor unusable – is a tangled nest of rush and reed.

The Ephesus hubbub.

Behind it are tall limestone hills, in which the later Greeks built a famous theatre, and from there the great avenue of Ephesus drives down towards the harbour and far beyond it to the shore. Two million tourists a year now throng its Roman and Hellenistic streets, an urban hubbub that probably does more to rekindle the place as it was in the sixth century BC than any of the abandoned silences of Miletus.

It would become a large city, with 250,000 inhabitants, a place in which the cultural exchange between Greek and non-Greek ran deep and wide. It is not difficult in the mind's eye to fill its streets with the stalls and market tables of a modern commercial city, the shopkeepers shouting their wares, the interweaving of coming and going, the concourse of civility, canaries in cages hung from the stall roofs overhead, fried falafels on wide metal dishes, the street hummus, the hawkers of pots and baskets, the well-heeled perfumiers, the goldsmiths, the jewellers,

The street atmosphere of archaic Ephesus lives on in any number of modern east Mediterranean cities.

all of them embedded in the unending multicultural chatter of our species.

The surviving objects from sixth-century Ephesus mark it out as the most sophisticated place in Ionia: carved ivories that fuse Egyptian, Greek, Phoenician and Anatolian models, inlays for furniture or the arms of a lyre. Both men and women in Ephesus wore boat-shaped or horn-shaped golden earrings, not too large, with lines of golden pinheads creased into their golden cushions; other earrings of rare rock crystal were cut into plain discs, perhaps to be fixed in the lobe of the ear; ivory and golden plaques were sewn on to fabrics; fat drum-, dome- and pomegranate-headed pins adorned the hair or clothes; all in a world lit by marble hanging lamps suspended from gilded chains.

Jewellery from Ephesus.

Foreignness was the medium of this urbanity. It was a city without walls, dependent for its security on the power of its fleet and its connection to the Lydian empire in Sardis. The citizens were equally at home speaking Lydian and Phrygian as they were speaking Greek. Loanwords from those languages, as much as from the Semitic languages of the Near East, filled their poetry as they must have filled the talk of the sixth-century city. Textiles with Babylonian or Assyrian names, the wooden writing tablets on which a stylus could inscribe the letters in wax, certain kinds of jars, gold and semi-precious stones such as jasper, spices including frankincense and myrrh: words for these objects and materials entered Greek from Anatolia or the Levant. Even now some of the terms borrowed from the Levant by the archaic Greeks are in use in modern European languages: cinnamon, cumin, sesame and tympani all arrived and remained in these harbour cities as both things and words. When we call a rough-woven bag a sack, we are using the term that came to these Greeks as *sakkos*, probably from the Phoenicians. The Hebrews called it a *saq*.

Certainly, the Ephesian elite lived in luxury, in a world full of sauces and gravies, game meats and puddings. Grouse, hare, sesame pancakes, barley rolls and waffles dipped in honey swam through their lives. A fragment survives in which Hipponax, a scandalous Ephesian satirist exactly contemporary with Heraclitus, describes one well-fed diner relaxing after he has taken his fill: 'His stomach gurgled like a pot of soup.' Here the word used for that intestinal gurgling, *eborboruze* – the first intestinal onomatopoeia in European poetry – can stand as the background music to much of Ephesian life.

Hipponax was the poet of lushness, of gratified flesh. His poetry wallows in double entendres:

And one of them, dining in peace and lavishly on tuna and the rich garlic and cheese-based *mussōtos* sauce every day, like some eunuch from Lampsakos, devoured all he had, so that now he must dig the rocky mountains, chewing on humble figs and barley rolls, fodder fit for slaves.

This is richer than it seems, not merely the depiction of a man who has spent everything he has on luxury foods, but an elaborate, innuendo-thick joke at the expense of an ageing Ephesian. The lines contain the first known use of the word 'eunuch'. The characterization is sharpened by this character coming from Lampsakos, a colony of Miletus and Phocaea on the Hellespont – a place big in the tuna business – whose

presiding deity was Priapos, the huge-membered god of pene-
trative sex. The impotent man, Hipponax smirks, was reduced
to endless and voracious cunnilingus, but even that had now
come to a desiccated end: no more sumptuous *mussōtos* sauces;
instead, the grim labour of chewing on old figs and digging
dry and stony ground.

Exquisite, degenerate, fabulously rich, with powerful and
vivid connections to the other cultures of Asia and the
Mediterranean: it may be tempting to imagine a kind of mate-
rialist, dissolute modernity for this archaic city, full only of
traders and collectors, the ultra-sophisticated and their spoilt
bodies enmeshed in luxury – always enabled by the ever-present
underlay of slavery – but Heraclitus' Ephesus cannot be quite
so easily categorized. Ritual practices with deep roots still shaped
its life. If, for example, a famine or plague or some other
catastrophe struck the city, the cause, in Ephesus as it had been
for Homer, was known to be the rage of the gods. As remedy,
the Ephesus elders in the sixth century found the ugliest man they
could and led him out 'as if to sacrifice, to purify and cure the
city's ills'. He became the scapegoat.

> They set the victim in an appropriate place, put cheese, barley
> cake and dried figs in his hands, flogged him seven times on
> his penis with the long stems of the maritime squills that grow
> everywhere on the rough dry ground by the sea, with wild fig
> branches and other wild plants, and finally burned him on
> wood taken from wild trees. On the third day when the ashes
> of the man had grown cold, the heralds of the city scattered
> them on the sand of the sea, and into the sea itself and into
> the winds so that the city would be cleansed of its ills.

At the heart of this ritual world of the Ephesians, set slightly
outside the city then as now, was the great temple of Artemis.
Along with the rest of Ionia except Miletus, Ephesus had been

conquered – perhaps even peacefully taken over – in about 560 by King Croesus of the Lydians. It was a place the conqueror knew: as had long been the tradition, the families of the king of Lydia and the rulers of Ephesus had intermarried. His sister had been the wife of the ruler here and their son, Croesus' nephew, was now acting as tyrant. Before the takeover, the building of a new temple was already under way but with Croesus' intervention it became the most astonishing building in the ancient world, on an Egyptian scale, a vast rectangular structure in white marble, 350 feet long and 180 wide, larger than a football field, surrounded by a double row of enormous Ionic columns, 127 of them, 60 feet high, almost twice the height of the Parthenon in Athens. Croesus paid for them and had them inscribed, some in Greek, *Basileus Kroisos anethēken* – 'King Croesus dedicated this' – and some in Lydian, *Krowisis inl*, to mean the same.

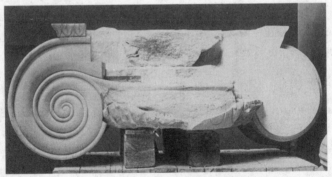

The capital from one of the Artemision's giant columns, now in London.

This Artemision was a cross-cultural shrine. There was another in the Lydian capital at Sardis dedicated to the same goddess and built by the Ephesians. Here in Ephesus Lydian priestesses officiated. The entire building was enriched with carvings, from which a few fragments were excavated in the nineteenth century and taken back to the British Museum. One mesmerizing marble face of a woman is to be found there now, not quite symmetrical, half smiling, with large hooded eyes and the nose and lips carved and rubbed into the soft and dreamlike contours of Ionian beauty.

An almost-smiling archaic face from the Artemision at Ephesus.

Later copies of the cult figure of Artemis from her temple at Ephesus.

She shares her enigmatic smile with many archaic Greek sculptures, but nothing can match for sheer impact the astonishing life-sized image of Artemis herself that stood inside the temple. Only later copies have survived but they continue to embody the vast and encompassing multiplicity of Ephesus. Artemis was the most promiscuous of goddesses; almost anything in the sphere of divinity could be claimed as hers. She fused the Greek hunter-goddess Artemis with the Anatolian and near-eastern fertility queen Kybele. This multiple figure was a water goddess, a deity of the margins, overseeing the menarche, a fertility goddess, a goddess of the crossroads, a defender of her city and her people, a goddess of the animals and the wilds, an earth goddess, a lover of virginity, a listener to people.

Her temple was an asylum throughout its history. Debtors could seek protection there; female slaves when accusing their masters of abuse could hide there in safety until the trial was heard. It was a place for tricksters and thieves, the heart of gambling in the city. As guardian of brides and wives she often, in thanks for a happy marriage or birth, was dressed in exquisite cloths. Her priests were eunuchs, unable to defile the virginity of the god they served, and perhaps both perfumed and dressed in women's clothes.

One can only stare at the astonishing image. Her architectural crown announces her as the defender of the city. Her skirts are alive with beetles and griffins. Lions guard her on each side as if she ran a pack of them. Horses and pomegranates, cats and bulls, winged harpies and griffins cling to her or emerge from her. Her eyes gaze before her in the stare of unassailable power. Around her neck all the elements of the world produce their boundary-crossing creatures: a crayfish out of water, a horse with a fish's tail, a man–horse centaur with a bow, many lions and many human figures, in procession around her chest above an unmatched grape cluster of what were later interpreted as the multiple breasts of the fertility goddess, but which may originally have been ornaments hung about the statue, perhaps the equally fertile testicles of bulls that had been sacrificed to her power.

The writings that Heraclitus left – he had them preserved in the Artemision – are gnomic, full of paradox and apparent contradiction, in statements devised so that the words seem to play games with each other, repeating syllables, constructed musically, so that his sentences can sound like the meaning he needs to convey. To write about the union of opposites he says: 'The name of the bow [*biós*] is life [*bíos*] but its work is death.'

In discussing wholeness and the co-presence of opposites, he talks of *sullapsies*, 'combinations':

> *hola kai ouch hola,*
> > wholes and not wholes,

sympheromenon diapheromenon,
      concurring differing,
synadon diadon;
      concordant discordant,
ek pantōn en
      from all things one
kai ex enos panta
      and from one all things.

For the famous thought that you cannot step into the same river twice, the words this poet visionary used are the words of a stream running over the pebbles in its bed:

Potamoisi toisin autoisin embainousin
Into the same rivers on those stepping in
Hetera kai hetera hudata epirrei
Different things and different waters flow.

This says more than its usual translation conveys and there is more here than the mere fluidity of things. The language is sculptural, re-enacting the reality of many rivers and many waters, of the many occasions and the many people who stepped into them, even while enacting the strange identity of multiplicity in singularity, of the unity of things – each of the rivers is only one river – despite their endless variation. The verbal form is a recognition of the rhyming complexity of reality: same-and-not-same, this-and-not-this, you-and-not-you, now-and-not-now, dramatizing our presence within that reality. Our apprehension of the world may be unreliable but we have a mysterious ability, even in sentences such as this, to step beyond that unreliability to a kind of understanding which is more than anything sensory perception can give us. These words enact a kind of meaning our senses cannot grasp and yet even that perception has its sensory, rhyming elements, the sibilants and diphthongs hissing in our ears. It is a micro-drama of the act of poetico-philosophical understanding.

Or take the sentence proclaiming the process of endless exchange at the heart of reality, the way in which everything is in constant reciprocal movement between the substances of which we are aware. The heart of reality is a vast process of change, the ever-burning fire to which Heraclitus repeatedly returns, not at the end of the world but in the daily reality of existence, just as in a mercantile city, the essence of things, their value, is in constant movement between different embodiments of it:

> *Puros te antamoibē ta panta*
> All things are an equal exchange for fire
> *kai pur hapantōn*
> and fire for all things
> *hokōsper*
> just as
> *chrusou chrēmata*
> goods are for gold
> *kai chrēmaton chrusos*
> and gold for goods.

Or take, finally, his insistence that the truth is scarcely available, that what is not apparent is more likely to be true than what is, presented in the simplest of all sentences, one that conceals more than it reveals:

> *Physis kruptesthai philei*
> Nature is usually hidden.

Those three Greek words perform something of what Heraclitus had recognized: *physis* can mean 'the process of things', things as they come to be what they are or merely 'things as they are'. And so the sentence can mean 'Whatever is is habitually hidden.' Or more troublingly, perhaps because of the endless nature of exchange, 'The underlying meaning of things is hidden' and so 'This sentence cannot mean what it says it means.' All surfaces deceive, you will never know whatever essentially is; it is impossible to know anything. 'If one does not expect the unexpected, one will not find it, for it cannot be searched out nor arrived at.'

That sense of unknowability or unsayability was not Heraclitus' last word. Some of his followers, including a man called Cratylus who appears in Aristotle's *Metaphysics*, took Heracliteanism to its ultimate – and distorted – end. The unsayability of a reality that was in constant flux meant for Cratylus 'that one need not say anything'. Silence was the only possible truth. His despairing conclusion was that one cannot enter the same river even once, because, if everything is in flux, as one enters it the previous river has become another. Cratylus drifted into a wordlessness in which his only response to reality was to point at it with his finger.

Cratylus' silent finger is not Heraclitus' position – there is more to his reality than endless change – but his depiction of the world is nevertheless one in which it is easy to be lost. So much concentrated paradox, so much strangeness, so much more implied than what is said all leave one with the feeling that here is a thinker with an understanding of the world who is not much interested in conveying it to others. He is too great for us to share in the greatness. Like nature, Heraclitus is usually hidden. 'Although *logos* [the structure of things] is common to all,' one of his fragments says, 'most people live as if they had a wisdom of their own.' That is scarcely an invitation to partake of the understanding Heraclitus perceives.

So what can be drawn from Heraclitus' fire?

> Vitality is dependent on exchange.
> Justice is a form of tension-in-action.
> Goodness is indistinguishable from flux.

Singularity is stultifying and stiffness wicked.
The nature of reality is not anarchic but runs
   according to the hidden laws of change.

In political cultures where an aristocratic or mercantile oligarchy usually prevailed, these were important ideas: a city government in which competing factions remained in cooperative tension could be productive and creative; one in which factional conflict broke out – a situation called in Greek *stasis* – would be the breakdown of civic order; the emergence of a tyrant from the mass would be the imposition of singularity which was inherently unjust. Only the first of these, a dynamic, harmonic and conflictual multiplicity in which solutions were never final, could guarantee wholeness. What seems to be wrong with politics – the chronic condition of disagreement – is in fact its virtue. The fire is the source of virtue.

It is a rich and subtle conceptual ecology. Strife, justice, the fire of endless change, the arrangement of the universe itself are all aspects of the same one thing. Any sense of goodness or wisdom in a city or a person can only be a reflection of that vast and endlessly churning cosmic reality. Like a harbour city, reality embraced change, was founded on openness, was essentially mobile, rich because dynamic, with no place for immobility. Everything there is tainted and flavoured with the materials by which it is surrounded: 'God: day dusk, winter summer, war peace, satiety famine; but he changes like olive oil which, when it is mixed with perfumes, acquires its identity from the scent of each.'

Heraclitus hated learning. Learning, of the kind other philosophers liked to accumulate, had nothing to do with the kind of knowing he urged on his compatriots. An openness to the dynamics of reality is the opposite of what we think of as philosophy: not the certainties of a sage, but a full-blooded embrace of cosmic doubt. Only a frame of mind that remains constantly aware of the presence of possibility, of new answers, can have any hope of being wise or good.

The Greek word for justice, *dikē*, comes from the verb that means 'to bring to light', to demonstrate and make clear. Justice is 'the indicated way', the way of things that the arrangement of the universe suggests. If the way of the universe is an ever-lasting fire of transformation, then in personal, social and political terms strife is justice. All is connected and Heraclitus might be seen as the first great poet of connectedness. His title for his own book is unknown. Ancient scholars guessed it might have been *On Nature* or *The Muses*. Some called it 'a true piece of helmsmanship to the line of life' and 'a guide of conduct, the keel of the whole world, for one and all alike'. For others, including reputedly Socrates, the text was so difficult that it would require one of the famous divers of Delos to penetrate its depths.

Heraclitus was a revolutionary, joining hands with another at the far end of western philosophy. On the opening pages of *Thus Spoke Zarathustra*, published in various forms through the 1880s and 1890s, Friedrich Nietzsche rolled back the millennia of western thought, welcoming the death of God and the end of conclusiveness. For him, suddenly, only the eternal Heraclitean sequence remained:

Everything goes, everything comes back; the wheel of Being rolls for ever. Everything dies, everything blossoms again. Eternally runs the year of Being.

Everything breaks, everything is joined anew; eternally the same house of Being is built. Everything parts, everything greets every other thing again; eternally the ring of Being remains true to itself.

In every Now, Being begins; round every Here rolls the sphere of There. The middle is everywhere. Bent is the path of eternity.

Many might have been filled with dread at the prospect – if God were dead, what meaning was left in the world? – but for others, the 'free spirits' among whom Nietzsche counted himself, even on the lip of madness, the news of a godless existence, without necessity, was an invitation to openness, filling him and them with 'amazement, premonitions, expectations':

> At long last, the horizon appears free to us again, even if it should not be bright; at long last, our ships may venture out again, venture out to face any danger; all the daring of the lover of knowledge is permitted again; the sea, our sea, lies open again; perhaps there has never yet been such an open sea.

Nietzsche had gone back to the world of Heraclitus, reimagining the harbour mind, finding life in openness and reconnecting to the prince of flux and fire.

The Ionian cities including Ephesus were under Lydian rule until Lydia itself was conquered by Persia in about 540 BC. A Persian satrap was installed in Sardis. The Persian king Cyrus the Great had sent messages to the Ionians asking them to come out in revolt against the Lydians, but they had refused. When Lydia succumbed, the Greeks asked to be subjects of the Persian empire on the same generous terms of self-government as Lydian Croesus had given them. Cyrus in turn refused and attacked the cities. Almost the entire population of Phocaea left for the western Mediterranean. Half of the people in the beautiful city of Teos also departed. But others, including the Ephesians, remained and were conquered.

With that conquest, Greekness now entered an intriguingly connected world. The habit of the Persian emperors was to draw in riches, beauty and wisdom from all parts of their astonishingly widespread domains. Cyrus had defeated the Medes in 550 and would take Babylon in 539. His son conquered Egypt in 525. The mountain provinces of Bactria and the Hindu Kush were added in 515. The Greek and Indian worlds were now in the late sixth century BC parts of the same highly interrelated empire. The Persians maintained a dazzlingly efficient road and postal system. Greek and Indian functionaries were to be found both at the Persian imperial courts in Ecbatan under Cyrus and at Susa under his successor Darius. Greek physicians, scholars, artists and sculptors all made their way there and could occasionally return to Ionia and the islands with a Persian retinue in train. Slaves from both ends of the empire were sold in Babylonian slave markets. Ivory, precious carnelians and rare teaks all came to the Persian Gulf from India and from there upriver into Mesopotamia. Indian elephants were at work in Babylonia. When the Ionian cities revolted against Persian rule in 499 and the Persians enacted savage revenge – the thin layer of grey ash which is all that was left of Miletus after the Persians burned and demolished it still appears in every trench opened there by an archaeologist's spade – large numbers of Greeks were sent in servitude to Susa and Bactria.

Greek inscriptions were carved into the walls of the quarries at Persepolis. Greek faces, identical to those seen on contemporary pots, have been found scratched into the unseen parts under the foot of a statue of Darius in Persia. A north Indian

Fragment of the foot of a statue of Darius, graffitied on its underside with Greek heads exactly as they appeared on contemporary pots in Greece itself.

woman called Busasa kept an inn at Kish, an ancient Sumerian city 50 miles south of Baghdad in Mesopotamia. Functionaries with Indian names, Karabba and Abbatema, were at work in Susa. The Greek physician Democedes was so admired that the Persian king gave him a huge house in that imperial city.

Greeks will have met Indians there. The court was a polyglot culture. A body of translators was constantly available for any visiting dignitary from distant parts of the empire. Letters from the imperial centre at Susa to the Greek cities were written in Greek by draughtsmen in that diplomatic office and there can be no doubt that these trans-Asian connections remained real for years. According to Aristoxenus, a disciple of Aristotle, an Indian yogi would meet Socrates in Athens and ask him what he was studying. Socrates replied that he was studying human life. The Indian laughed and asked him how he could study human life without studying the divine.

After the Persian conquest of Ephesus, the Persian–Aegean connection was full of mutual borrowings. Statues of Aphrodite were erected in the Persian capitals. The Ephesians took the Iranian term *Bagabuxša* meaning 'He who serves God', roughly semi-transliterated it into Greek as *Megabyxos* and used it as the title of the rich and powerful eunuch-priests who presided over the temple in Ephesus. A foreigner was always appointed to the role, perhaps because it was difficult to find Ephesians who would happily have themselves castrated for the job. Darius, who like other Persian kings could speak and read Greek, was said to have enjoyed a copy of Heraclitus' book. The emperor invited him to come to Persepolis. Needless to say, Heraclitus refused and remained at home among the children playing at the temple.

Intriguingly, though, it may be that Heraclitus drew some of his most important visions from Persia itself. The prophet and seer Zarathuṣtra, Zoroaster as the Greeks called him, was an almost equally hidden figure. He came from north-eastern Iran and his dates are uncertain, but the hymns and prayers he had written were certainly in play by the time of Heraclitus at the end of the sixth century. Even as the Persian armies were conquering Lydia and the Greek cities, aided by a Phoenician fleet stealing in between the islands, Darius had himself portrayed worshipping the great Zoroastrian figure of Ahura Mazdāh, the Lord of Wisdom, the uncreated and eternal spirit who stood as the eternal source of meaning. At Sardis, the seat of the Persian satrapy in Lydia, a temple was built to Ahura Mazdāh, and he was there recognized under the name of Zeus the Lawgiver.

Like the Hebrew prophets and Heraclitus himself, Zoroaster maintained his place outside the inherited forms of belief. He had little truck with the sources of worldly power. Like them, he despised the coarseness of everyday life, execrating drunkenness and sexual self-indulgence to the point of loathing. His religion was not cluttered with mystical or theological baggage. His ethics were plain and straightforward, with an emphasis on the need for a human understanding of the nature of god. It was rigorously and even disturbingly high-minded. Man's responsibility was simple enough: to make the choice between good and bad.

There is some kind of coming together in sixth-century Judaism, Zorastrianism and early Greek philosophy. All were beginning to dispense with the complex multi-headed pantheon of anthropomorphic gods, substituting for them something more austere: a singular almost unaddressable godhead, which might take the form of a philosophical principle, of the kind the Greeks in Ionia had been searching for, or one all-powerful god, with no image to represent him, that was slowly emerging for the Israelites.

All were puritan, deniers of the flesh, and that instinct may be a key to what was happening across west Asia. The boom in population, communications and the economy of these centuries, the era of this book, generated a double reaction: not only the appetite for riches that spread unprecedentedly wide across these cities (even if profoundly dependent on a large, enslaved labour force) but a counterforce, for a stricter, less materialistic and anthropomorphic way of understanding reality. Enriched pleasures fuelled the search for something beyond the things of this world. The very life of the dynamic trading city, the Tyres, the Ephesuses, the Susas, stimulated its own critique. Ezekiel, Heraclitus and Zoroaster were all symptoms of a swing of the pendulum away from the worldliness of the cultures that had given birth to them. The high-mindedness of philosophy might in that paradoxical way be seen as yet another symptom of luxury.

What connects Heraclitus with Zoroaster more closely is the central role played by fire. Zoroastrians also thought fire holy. To extinguish it was a sin. As it was for Heraclitus, fire was a Zoroastrian god. It could be prayed to under the name of Ātar. He was the son of Ahura Mazdāh, the Lord of Wisdom. The Greeks knew of this. Strabo says that Persians prayed to fire before any other god. Fire was the dwelling of the archangels. Three times every day, the archangels formed an assembly in the abode of fires, and good works and righteousness emerged from the flames.

Fire for Zoroaster, as for Heraclitus, was universal. It was in the rocks and in men and animals; it was responsible for the brightness in the human eye, the digestion of food and the warmth that the body exudes in sleep. Fire was in the earth and in plants, warming the roots, producing both flowers and their scents. Fire was in the clouds. And, for everyday use, it was in fire itself.

Heraclitus did not quite think like that. For him, the fire had gone out in the earth. But as the Oxford classicist Martin West said, for Heraclitus 'The parts of the world that are not fire nevertheless retain the vital forward flow of fire. Fire makes a link between apparently widely separate cosmic districts.'

As it was for Zoroaster, that vital forward flow of fire was for Heraclitus the source of universal, godlike justice. Justice is the god of the eternal fire. This connection between the ever-lasting burning in existence and the sense of what is right is so central to both Heraclitus' and Zoroaster's conception of the universe that it is possible this great Greek philosopher, burning with indignation in his overwhelmingly fleshy port city in the eastern Aegean, was speaking with the voice of Persia in his mind.

In 1951 the writer and publisher André Fraigneau held a series of radio interviews with his friend Jean Cocteau. They were discussing Cocteau's collection of works by the galaxy of artists who had been his friends and companions in pre-war Montparnasse: Léger, Miró, Modigliani, Brâncuşi, Duchamp, Matisse, Mondrian, Man Ray, Picasso among them. It was an unrivalled gathering of genius.

> Fraigneau: There must be some of these things that you are particularly attached to? If, for example, I don't know, well, if there was a fire at home, which is the object you would choose, the one you would take with you?
>
> Cocteau: If there was a fire at home?
>
> Fraigneau: Yes.
>
> Cocteau: I think I would take the fire.

7

IS THE WORLD
FULL OF SOULS?

PYTHAGORAS AND ORPHEUS
KROTON, CALABRIA, 570–490 BC

A deep change – very nearly a complete reversal – now comes over the pattern of thought that had first emerged in the trading cities of Ionia. It takes the form of a voyage to Italy, a shift westwards to a different atmosphere, a new geography and economy, and a transformed frame of mind.

Where the Ionian cities had been perched on their headlands crammed between the mountains of Anatolia and the sea, or on islands off the coast, dependent for their wealth on the connections they could establish with the rest of the Mediterranean, with no riches inherent in their own territories, the Greek cities of Sicily and southern Italy, collectively known as *Megale Hellas*, 'Great Greece', to which the thinkers started to migrate towards the end of the sixth century, were the opposite: settled in rich, wide agricultural plains of untold productivity; exuding a confidence in the appetite of the market beyond their shores for anything they could produce; with plenty of room in which to lay out generously conceived city plans; their territories carefully divided into regular and highly organized farms; peopled with settlers mostly from the farmer-warrior communities of the Peloponnese and occasionally from Crete; passionately athletic; subtle diplomats but also ferocious destroyers and enslavers of

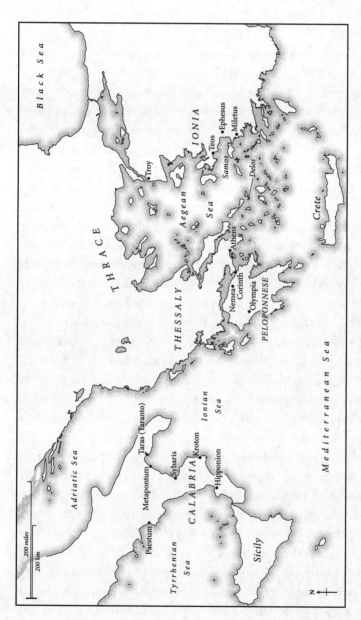

The Pythagorean seas.

the indigenous cultures of the Italian peninsula. Greek Italy and Sicily were imperial-minded and rich, a world dependent on slaves, in effect a new-found-land.

The pattern is not quite neat – the lyric poets of the Aegean are an exception to it and all these thinkers were interested in social justice – but the Ionian and the Italian realms represent two different, if connected dimensions of early Greek philosophy. They confront each other across the seas that separate them: the Ionian thinkers largely set at an angle to the universe, with nothing much of a coterie of followers around them, refusing the blandishments of religion and power, and instead basing their search for intelligibility on the physical world; the Italians, by contrast, gathering entire cities of followers, concentrating less on the physics of nature than on the nature of the ideal, the shape of mathematics and the qualities of the human self, the mysteries of the soul and its relationship to death.

In their hands, philosophy, which until then had been a critique of the world, came to assume authority within it.

Pythagoras stands at the head of this change. He became both a religious guru and a social reformer, capable of miracles, regarded as semi-divine, even the son of Apollo by a virgin birth, ascending to heaven on his death, teaching in parables, but also an adviser on the moral life, a governor of his adopted city and state. He seems to have been something of a proto-Christ figure combined with a Platonic philosopher-king, entranced by power, creating a school of followers that would persist for centuries, alienating many, who eventually persecuted him, and generating a long and complex tradition from which the person of the man himself is difficult to extract.

He was said to be tall and of aristocratic bearing. Before his birth, the oracle at Delphi had prophesied his beauty. He wore trousers in either the Persian or the Scythian fashion. He was the first person to be called a philosopher and was the only one of these thinkers to have been given his own verb – *pythagorizein* –

meaning 'to do Pythagoras', to follow in his footsteps, observing the rites and rituals that enshrined his thought. If you had met him, you would have thought him a wizard.

Tens of thousands joined the cult over the years. He was rarely referred to by name but almost always as 'The Man'. Others, including Heraclitus and Plato, thought him and the crowd of pythagorizers little but conmen and charlatans, seducing the citizens with the prospects of eternal bliss and backing their enticements with threats of damnation for those who failed to observe his rules. 'Wandering priests and prophets approaching the doors of the rich,' Plato called them in the *Republic*,

persuading them that they have a power from the gods conveyed through sacrifices and incantations, and [that] any wrong committed against someone either by an individual or his ancestors can be expiated with pleasure and feasting . . . They persuade not only individuals but cities that they really can have atonement and purification for their wrongdoing through sacrifices and playful delights while they are still alive, and the same after death.

Anything less like the subtle, ironical scepticism of Heraclitus or even the straight-up thinking of a Thales it would be difficult to imagine.

Significantly, the one fact we all know about Pythagoras is wrong. The theorem which recognizes that the square of the hypotenuse of a triangle is the sum of the squares of the other two sides has nothing to do with him, even if it carries his name. It had been known and understood in Babylon and Egypt for at least a thousand years before he was born, and in India and China perhaps as early. But it is symptomatic of this mysterious and alluring man that such an intriguing geometrical fact should have drifted towards him and been clamped to his reputation. Like many of the inspirational figures of history,

Pythagoras could attract and encompass almost everything: magic, mathematics, the stars and planets, music, geometry, the soul, mysticism, vegetarianism, the life in everything, the need to live well, the good city and the ability to remember a past from long before one's own birth. All played a role in his persona, which came to spread its influence across the cities of southern Italy.

His biography is to be understood as the story not of his life but, perhaps as importantly, of what his followers wanted to imagine his life had been. Like Christ and Socrates, Pythagoras never wrote a word. His teachings took the form either of *akousmata*, things that had been heard, the rumours and traditions of wisdom. Or, for the more sophisticated, *mathematika*, lessons that included all the details of his science and theory. And so, by one route or another, it was known he was born – and every one of these statements carries a silent caveat – in Samos, off the Ionian coast. His mother was a Greek but his father was Phoenician, a Syrian from Tyre, or maybe a 'Tyrrhenian', an Italian, perhaps from the Greek city of Kroton, to which Pythagoras would eventually go, or from an island in the northern Aegean, a rich merchant, or perhaps a gem carver, who sent him to be educated in Miletus, perhaps by Thales, perhaps Anaximander. He was, in other words, heir to all the interminglings and synthesizings of the eastern Mediterranean.

The young Pythagoras then wandered the Near East, immersing himself in the religions of Egypt, taught Egyptian by Amasis II, the pharaoh himself, before absorbing the mysticism and habits of secrecy of the priests of Egyptian Thebes. After a time in Babylonia, perhaps as a prisoner, and then in Persia, where he may have met and sat at the feet of Zoroaster/ Zarathuṣtra, and possibly have met some Indian wisemen, or Celts from Gaul, he returned to Samos, teaching the philosophy he had learned on his travels.

He had become the mouth of wisdom itself, living on Samos

even as it was in political and civil turmoil. A long rolling crisis engulfed the island and only broke in 540 when an aristocrat called Polycrates – the name means 'very powerful' – and various of his relatives took power. Those relatives were soon dispensed with and Polycrates became a fleet-wielding, monument-creating tyrant. He was self-indulgent and vain, but highly cultivated, in love with poetry and song, presiding over a luxury court of honey cakes and ivory parasols, where men and women were garlanded with myrtle and coriander and with flowers brought in from Egypt. He kept the poet Anacreon as his court bard, singing of rooms 'filled with the excited gaze' and 'thighs twined around thighs', girls walking ahead of him 'with hips swaying'. Anacreon liked to play his lyre all evening and on into the night, becoming famous to all Greeks for his sweet and elegant songs to lovers of both sexes:

> O boy with the girlish glance
> I want you
> But you do not notice,
> not knowing that I am your chariot
> And you hold the reins of my soul in your hands.

When asked why he wrote hymns to boys rather than to gods, Anacreon said 'Because they are my gods.' And to his patron, one tiny surviving fragment hints at the smart ironies of this sophisticated world:

> So you too, Polycrates, will one day enjoy undying fame,
> Perhaps not unlike my own.

Needless to say, Pythagoras was ill at ease under this tyranny de luxe and so left for Italy. He was later to be accused by his enemies there of tyrannical and domineering tendencies himself, and so this part of the life story may have been devised to counter the accusations. If he had fled from a tyrant, how could he consider exercising tyranny himself?

Whatever the truth of it, his sailing from Ionia to Italy is the hinge not only of his own life but of this whole story of early Greek thought. From now on, until the emergence in fifth-century Athens of Socrates, followed there by Plato and Aristotle – and even Plato visited Syracuse twice – the great Greek thinkers were in the west.

From Samos Pythagoras would have crossed the Aegean to Corinth, over the narrow isthmus and then re-embarking in the Gulf of Corinth. From there, he would have made for the Greek colonies in the instep of Italy, an often travelled route, connecting the mainland with the powerful and rivalrous cities of Taras (now Taranto), Metapontum, Sybaris and, the one in which Pythagoras would finally settle, Kroton. By the late sixth century, these cities had been in existence for 150 or 200 years and were now the enormously rich capitals of what the Greeks recognized as the most fecund lands they knew.

The Greek Italian cities shared a reputation for riches but, of them all, Sybaris came to represent everything the mainland Greeks and Ionians both envied and despised about this new moneyed paradise. According to Diodorus of Sicily, a Greek historian of the first century BC, the Sybarites were 'slaves to their belly and lovers of luxury'. They set up their colonies on the western coast of Italy and traded and intermarried with the Etruscans. The only people who could keep up with them were the pleasure-lovers of Miletus and Ephesus.

Proverbial stories clung to them. They banned noisy occupations such as blacksmithing, carpentry and chicken-raising from within the limits of the city. The roads that led out into the country were roofed over to keep travellers from too much sun. From the vineyards in their country estates, they piped wine to terminals on the sea shore from where it was carried to their city houses in seagoing wine ships. When a rich Sybarite heard from a friend that a man had suffered a rupture when seeing others at work, he told him not to be amazed. 'I have got a stitch simply from hearing you tell the story.' Its richest citizens could travel in private galleys rowed by fifty of their own slaves. One, Smindyrides, after sleeping on a bed of roses, complained when he woke in the morning that the roughness of the petals had raised blisters on his skin. Another had always wondered at the courage of the Spartans, but after going to Sparta and tasting the food decided that there was not an ounce of courage in them. 'The most cowardly Sybarite would choose to die three times a day before eating what the Spartans eat.' Another version has the Sybarite, after his Spartan dinner, realizing that their disgusting diet was the reason the Spartans were so ready to die. Public banquets in Sybaris were often held and the master chefs rewarded not only with golden crowns but with the copyright on their recipe for a full year afterwards. Most fatally, the city decided to teach its cavalry horses to dance as an accompaniment to the

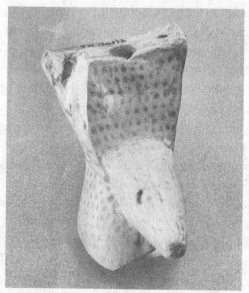

A Sybarite *aryballos* in the form of a penis.

banquets. It seemed like an embellishment of life, until one day, in battle, their enemies played the dance tunes on their trumpets and the Sybarite horses skipped away from their army into the ranks of the enemy.

Not much has been found of Sybaris, drowned in river silt and buried under two subsequent Graeco-Roman towns, but in the museum there, among the usual and expected objects of a rich Greek city, is one surprising object that hints at the atmosphere of the most extravagantly indulgent Sybaritic banquets: a tiny jug for perfumed oils in the form of a small penis, the pubic hair neatly stippled around the little pointed shaft.

This southern Italian Greek country remains deeply beguiling in the light of a southern spring, the woods dusted green with new leaf, the silvery olives pruned hard, the occasional strip of a cherry orchard in pink flower, the roadside stalls already selling artichokes and oranges, tomatoes and melons all grown in the surrounding fields. It is not a Greek landscape and there is no sign of the habitually sharp Greek meeting of rock and sea, or of the country as Plato described it, looking 'like the skeleton of a sick man, all the fat and soft earth having wasted away'. The flesh is still here in Italy. Vast green barley fields stretch towards the distant mountains. Swallows sweep over the cornlands, the chaffinches sing in the willows, bullfinches pick on the buds of the cherry orchards, goldfinches chirr like a running stream in the reeds that fill the marsh ditches. Candelabras of giant fennel stand along the roadside and the verges are polychrome with borage and mallows, asphodels and wonderful wine-red lupins. Now and then a hillside is covered in a sheet of giant golden southern bird's-foot trefoil, each flower the size of a sweet pea.

The medieval-cum-modern city of Crotone now occupies the site of archaic Kroton, spread across both sides of a shallow river valley where it comes to the sea. Careful keyhole archaeology, wherever a new building project has allowed, has revealed the highly developed condition of the city to which Pythagoras came. It was huge, covering 1,500 acres, with walls that were 10 miles round, organized in three large blocks, each aligned to the quays on the shores of the Ionian Sea, where famous, large and busy shipyards built merchant vessels and war triremes using the timber of the forests in the hills above.

Orderliness governed a place that attended carefully to civic coherence. The word 'colony' has long been applied to these cities in southern Italy, but it scarcely represents them. Kroton, like Metapontum, Sybaris and Taras, as much as the great cities in Greek Sicily, was the vibrant centre of its own life. There was no need to look with envy or anxiety to the Greek mainland or Ionia. This *was* Greece, as much as anywhere in the Peloponnese or Ionia. When Xenophanes said he left Colophon to spend his life 'tossed . . . restlessly up and down Greece', he meant Sicily and southern Italy as much as anywhere else. Of course, the whole bundle of Greekness had come with the migrants. Mixing bowls and drinking cups for the symposium, statuettes and personal adornments have all been found here, exactly as they were in Miletus or Ephesus.

Kroton's larger territory, with boundaries defined by temples to the gods, was also carefully orchestrated, subdivided into rectangular plots that were set out perpendicular to the coastline, and with farm steadings established where there was water. Small shrines were set up along the foot of the hills, and marked many crossroads and springs. To the north of the city, it was largely grass farms for beef and sheep as well as commercially worked forests. To the south, the ground was more fertile, and more than 130 separate sixth-century farms have been identified in a spread of country that oozed fertility, generating wealth for generation after generation.

It was a form of the blessed world. Kroton was known as the healthiest and most athletic of places – if only for its social and physical elite. At one Olympic Games, to which all the

The wide fruitful plain of Sybaris, the source of its riches.

cities of Greece sent competitors, the men who finished 1st, 2nd, 3rd, 4th, 5th, 6th and 7th in the 200-yard foot race in the stadium at Olympia all came from Kroton. Speed and strength were the city's specialities. Its greatest late sixth-century athlete, an aristocrat called Milon, who became a follower of Pythagoras, won the prize for wrestling at seven Olympics, first in the boys' competition in 540 BC, and then six in a row for men between 532 and 512. For these decades, he was all-conquering, with six victories in the Pythian games at Delphi, ten in the Isthmian at Corinth and nine in the Nemean games that were held first at Nemea and then in various other places in the Peloponnese, at every one proclaiming the triumphant name of Kroton to the Greek world.

A powerful religiosity governed these Italian city states. Successful athletes dedicated statues of themselves, marked with bronze plaques, in shrines to the gods high on hillsides. Temples stood on promontories in the Ionian Sea, as sea marks and to welcome visitors from abroad. Life was enmeshed in a religious frame. The cult of Dionysus as a deity who could cross the boundaries between the living and the dead was almost universal. And so Pythagoras may have found the atmosphere and expectations in Kroton more sympathetic than in Samos or elsewhere in Ionia. There was no tyrant to court or upset. The members of a rich elite had the ease in which to consider their own fate after death.

Pythagoras arrived from his sea voyage in this remarkable city surely not alone. He would have brought followers with him from Samos and may have picked up more on his passage across the isthmus at Corinth. He was soon teaching, both Greeks and foreigners. He was known to have a special relationship with those from the north, from Thessaly, Thrace and beyond.

A mysteriousness hung about him. Those he taught formed a secret society, bound by rules they were not allowed to divulge. Six hundred people would gather to hear him speak and afterwards 'wrote to their relatives as though something extraordinary had happened to them'. He was a charismatic, and life for his philosophical followers was to be a complete denial of everything around them.

Just as some people come to a festival to contend for the prizes, and others for the purposes of traffic, and the best as spectators; so also in life, the men of slavish dispositions are born hunters after glory and covetousness, but philosophers are seekers after truth.

They were never to think of their own interests, because men do not know what is good for them. Drunkenness was a form of ruin. All superfluity was wrong. And as for sex:

One ought to sacrifice to Aphrodite in the winter, not in the summer; and in autumn and spring in a lesser degree. But the practice is pernicious at every season, and is never good for the health.

Once, when asked when a man might indulge in the pleasures of love, he replied, 'Whenever you wish to be weaker than yourself.'

His house in Kroton became a temple to Demeter, the great earth mother goddess, as her name implies, presiding over the harvest, and the mother of Persephone, queen of the underworld. Pythagoras taught his followers the secrets of that underworld, often at night, in underground chambers away from the everyday business of the city.

It was here, the disciples believed, that Pythagoras himself made a descent into Hades:

He built a little underground room and instructed his mother to write down events as they happened, recording the time, and to keep passing the notes down to him until he came back up. His mother did this and after some time Pythagoras came up thin as a skeleton. He went into the assembly and announced he had just returned from Hades. What is more, he read off to them an account of what had happened during his absence. Taken in by his words, they wept and moaned and were sure that he was some kind of divinity; so that they even entrusted their wives to him, thinking they would learn something from him. And they were called *Pythagorikoi*.

Even down to that last sceptical phrase about the handing over of wives, this is clearly a hostile story of the behaviour of a mesmeric cult leader practising his tricks. A journey to the underworld? Not likely. But the great Greek scholar Walter Burkert saw echoes of something true in this late and antagonistic account. Pythagoras was said to have brought up with him from Hades 'the commands of the mother', *tēs mētros parangelmata* – not notes from his own mother (who was unlikely to have come with him to Kroton) but from *the* Mother, the great goddess Demeter herself. He had descended to the underworld and returned with meanings he would share with his followers. The shrinking away of his body in Hades is precisely the effect a guru likes to demonstrate to his cult, starving himself when away from his people as a signal of integrity and suffering. And so here is the Greek philosopher in the midst of all the luxuries and comforts and business of Kroton behaving as a priest and devotee of the great mother goddess in the Hades-like under-chambers of his house in the city. His aim was to demonstrate to those members of the Kroton elite that to follow him was to follow another way, to the discovery of hidden truths. With him they might descend into a transitional world where different disciplines applied and where the boundaries of illusion and revelation were as uncertain as in any moment of drunkenness at a symposium. In Hades he had encountered the punishments meted out to those of his predecessors who had followed the wrong path. 'Hesiod's soul was bound shrieking to a bronze column, and Homer's hung from a tree surrounded by snakes.' Pythagoras' promise to his followers was an escape from that torment.

Scepticism about a cult leader raises its head. Does one need the illusions of this other world? Why not attend to the realities by which we are surrounded? What is it with the theatricality of these performances? And the answer must be that a sense of otherness, of a presence beyond the tangible, is in all of us. Our ability to know, as Heraclitus made repeatedly clear, is limited. We live encased in the unknown. The more we know and the longer the perimeter of our knowledge becomes, the more we must be aware of what we do not know. Just as a questioning doubt is the grounds for understanding, ignorance is the condition of knowledge. And so the enquirer will necessarily head out into country he does not know and cannot understand, particularly if the mysteries of number have intrigued him. The patterns of mathematics seem to describe a world beyond the one we know. Can we enter it? Can we know it? The journey into the Pythagorean underworld is in that sense an extension of the questioning mind, beyond the boundaries of its own capacity, into places where questioning is the only attitude it can have.

In their everyday lives, the *Pythagorikoi* followed the road of austerity their leader had shown them. In a place of sheer abundance, they abstained from all luxury. All property was held in common. Mysterious taboos were applied: no eating of beans, nor even entering a field in which beans grew; none of his followers to go into sacred places when wearing wool or to be buried in it; no engagement to be had with white cockerels. Perhaps these arbitrary rules were effective as the boundary markers of the cult precisely because there was no rationale behind them.

In return, he could perform wonders for them. He was spotted in Kroton and Metapontum on the same day at the same hour. When he stood up among the spectators at Olympia, one of his thighs was seen to be made of gold. When a white eagle landed in the streets of Kroton, he stood beside it and stroked its back. As he crossed the River Casas near Metapontum, the river hailed him quite audibly, saying 'Greetings Pythagoras!' And he killed a poisonous snake by biting it to death.

The cloud of unreality thickens around Pythagoras and you begin to wonder: where is the vision in this? Was he any more than a miracle-monger or the 'prince of swindlers' that Heraclitus saw in him? Did he have anything more than a stock of learning and an equal supply of fraudulence?

He did, and, partly obscured by the theatrics and ritual of his practices, partly articulated by them, he had a vision of the human soul as something more than the breath of life that inhabits our bodies for a while when we are alive. The long

history of the soul in western culture begins with him, transmitted to Plato and on to the Christian world. Here in Kroton
was the first Greek moment in which anyone came to believe
that the soul that inhabits us when alive can survive the death
of the body and continue to experience a life after leaving this
one.

The earlier Greeks could never have conceived of such a thing:
souls after death in the Homeric poems are nothing more than
desiccated autumn leaves blown by the winds dragging across
the dark fields of Hades. When Odysseus encounters Achilles
there, the great swift-footed warrior weeps and tells him that it
is far better to be the meanest landless peasant on earth than
lord of all the lifeless dead. As he speaks, the dead rustle and
drift around him.

Pythagoras, in an extraordinary reconfiguration of the human
self, believed the opposite: the soul was imprisoned in the flesh
of the body when alive on earth. That belief was shared by the
followers of the cult of Orpheus, the great mythical singer from
Thrace in the far north, whose origins are obscurely tied up
with and roughly contemporary with the life and teaching of
Pythagoras in the late sixth century. Music, mysteries and a
relationship with the underworld are part of both sets of belief.
For both the Orphics and the Pythagoreans, the soul longed
for escape from physical existence and one way to guarantee
that path in the future was to lead an austere and honourable
life on earth. Indulgence in the flesh was only to thicken the
bars of the prison cage. Orphics and Pythagoreans all abstained
from animal blood-sacrifice.

Riches will always be the ground from which puritan movements arise. Intolerance and exclusiveness are inseparable from
them; they depend for their energy on a denial of the world
from which they come. But they can also enshrine, as the
Pythagorean–Orphic beliefs did, a careful vision of the human
being, not as a hard-dealing, manipulative, go-getting agent in

this world, but as a person who after death is likely to be lost and in need of guidance. The soul is something of a luxury product. The demands of the flesh have lessened for these people. Survival and shelter, food and drink, comfort and beauty are all givens for the rich citizens of Kroton. They figure in their own lives as the most significant players within it. No autocrat confines them, no poverty diminishes them. They are healthy and successful. Only one factor bites at the edges of this realm of contentment: death itself. Can it honestly be true that these marvellous selves will not last for ever?

For both cults, mystery ceremonies formed the core of the necessary connection to the otherworld. They were a source of some kind of infra-rational understanding, which gave the initiates a sense of fulfilment and of a mystery revealed. They were kept rigorously secret and what they were is still uncertain. Masks were worn and phrases uttered by the officiating priests. Something hidden was exposed by the opening of a chest. In the Dionysiac mysteries, a phallus was seen to rise from a winnowing basket filled with fruit.

What mattered more than these mechanics was the atmosphere of strangeness in which they were performed, a transitional experience for the initiates after which they could look forward to happiness in life and bliss after death. An epitaph for one priestess of the Dionysian rites in Miletus stated simply that, now she had undergone her initiation, 'she knows her share of the beautiful'.

It was the most wonderful of consolations: if you followed the right practices, bliss awaited you. The experience of the initiate was not trivial but, for those who underwent it, a transforming life event. Superficial learning gave no access to its wisdom, and to experience this transition to a kind of otherworldly understanding the initiate had to prepare: fasting, extreme thirst, sleeplessness, anxiety, sensory deprivation and a form of terrifying and overwhelming noise could all shake the foundations of the self, stripping away the normalities on which it had previously relied. The mystery required a voyage inwards and downwards. Loud, long and rhythmic dancing, with cymbals, clappers and instruments that could be whirled overhead, was all part of the way in which the consciousness of the initiate could be prepared. In many cases psychotropic drugs were administered. The moment of revelation seems to have been an out-of-body experience, a form of death-in-life, later described by Plutarch:

> At first there was wandering, and wearisome roaming and some fearful journeys through unending darkness . . . every sort of terror, shuddering and trembling and sweat and amazement . . . then marvellous light, and pure places and meadows follow after, with voices and dances and solemnities of sacred utterances.

It was in that condition, as Yulia Ustinova, the historian of Greek consciousness, has written, that 'every detail of one's surroundings may take on incredible beauty and acquire supreme significance'. The state of mind might appear irrelevant or even ridiculous to anyone who had not known it, and its sense of revelation could seem indescribable. 'During altered states of consciousness normal language abilities are often inhibited,' Ustinova has written, and 'the feeling of ineffability accompanying mystic revelations may be one of the important reasons they were shrouded in secrecy'.

This engagement with the irrational sources of perception lies at the heart of the Pythagorean–Orphic vision. Its focus was the individual soul and its purpose to embrace every dimension of the soul's experience both before and after death.

Among the most enigmatic and evocative documents to have survived from the ancient world is a set of about forty small golden sheets, the texts hand-inscribed on the wafer-thin metal, little more than foil, left on the chests or mouths of the Pythagorean dead. The letters either give or ask for advice on what to do and how to behave when first entering the next world. The origins of this practice are unclear but they seem of a piece with Pythagoras' own descent into the halls of Demeter and Persephone. Golden letters have been found in Crete and northern Greece. Equivalents on bone have been recovered from Olbia, the Greek colony of Miletus on the Black Sea, but most of them, and those with the longest and fullest texts, come from southern Italy. None is quite as early as Pythagoras himself but their words seem to be spoken in a voice that comes from his world.

The golden letter in Vibo.

Find a golden letter in a museum today – there is one in California, one in London, several in southern Italy – and, beyond any miracle story, these brief messages from this life to the next summon the Pythagorean vision of a soul that is the locus of consciousness and selfhood and which remains even in death the vehicle for everything a person might be.

The oldest and longest is now in the museum in Vibo Valentia in southern Italy, a morning's drive from Crotone. It was found there in the necropolis of the Greek city of Hipponion, on the shores of the Tyrrhenian Sea.

'Down by the well-made house of Hades', the slightly wavering text instructs the dead woman on whose chest the golden letter was folded and laid,

> is a spring on the right side, and close to it stands a white cypress: descending to it the souls of the dead refresh themselves. Do not even go near this spring. Ahead you will find the lake of Memory from which cold water pours forth: There are guardians there: and they will ask you with careful and considered wisdom what you are looking for in the darkness of murky Hades. Say: 'I am a child of Earth and starry Sky: and I am parched with thirst and am dying: But quickly give me a drink of the cold water from the lake of Memory.' And they will announce you to the king of the Underworld: and give you a drink from the lake of Memory: And you too, when you have drunk, will walk on the holy path of the many, on which other famous *mystai* and *bakkhoi* also walk.

The *mystai* are the initiates, those who have learned the secret of the cult and so can enjoy this salvation; the *bakkhoi* are the followers of Bacchus or Dionysus, the god of transitions, the boundary crosser to whom the Orphic and Pythagorean rituals expressed eternal reverence. *Mystai* and *bakkhoi* may be two terms for the same people who have been released into happiness for the next life.

The letters are an expression of the longing for the denial of death, for a future unlike the drifting autumn leaves of Homer's Hades. They are a means by which death will have no sting. Others will drink from the wrong spring and are excluded from the happiness Dionysus can offer his followers. Orpheus, Dionysus, Demeter, Hades and Persephone all seem to cluster around this promise, of which Pythagoras is the purveyor. Memory is the key, because memory denies time and allows the soul to escape the destiny that forgetfulness imposes. The letter declares the initiate's humanity: she is the child of earth and of the starry sky, the two limits of a worldly existence. But it is not a one-stage process. Souls can migrate from body to body to body through time. Most forget who they have been before, but Pythagoras himself, perhaps because he had drunk from the waters of the lake of memory, was able to remember his previous selves. He had once been a son of Hermes, the traveller god, and he may even at some time have been Apollo. He had been a minor Trojan warrior at the siege of Troy and had been killed there by Menelaus. For a while he had been a fisherman on Delos and at another time a beautiful prostitute called Alco. Some of these previous lives may be jokes made at Pythagoras' expense by those who were hostile to the idea of the transmigration of souls, but for all the unlikelihood, and seen in the light of the golden letters, it seems possible these were the claims he made.

For him and his followers, this immortality of the soul and its movement from one living thing to the next, the recycling of souls called *metempsychosis*, was central to the ethical, personal, political and metaphysical complex by which they were entranced. It gave a new dignity to the self. It implied a kinship of all living things. Soul was everywhere, as much in the world as in the self, so that the universe was filled with spirit, not in the form of the old anthropomorphic gods, but in the plants and animals by which they were surrounded.

They say that once when passing by he saw a puppy being whipped, and took pity on him, and said: 'Stop, and do not beat him; for it is the soul of a friend that I recognized as he was crying.'

The mechanics of this are unclear. Did the wind carry souls from one living thing to the next? Was everyone caught in the whirlwind of metempsychosis? Or only some of the initiated?

Was there an everlasting recycling of souls? Or could one escape the endless return? Whatever the answers to these questions – and they were probably various – it meant that Pythagoreans were largely if not entirely vegetarian. No eating of the loins, the testicles, the genitals, bone marrow, feet or heads of animals. Nor, in another strange category, any animal wombs, red mullet or sea anemones. Athletes might be allowed a prime steak, discovering in meat 'a power that was much better for developing strength', but on the whole austerity and abstinence from the fleshly were part of their system of belief.

A longing for the purity of otherness and Pythagoras' 'daily praise of virtue' led to another dimension of this semi-religious, semi-philosophical life: a belief that essentially, underlying all the complex surface phenomena of the world, existence consisted of numbers. Through numbers, Pythagoras could 'hear the harmony of the whole, because he had understood the universal harmony of the spheres – something that we other people do not hear because of the smallness of our nature'. In a beatific and mystical way, if one could shed the noise of life as we perceive it, we would be ushered into the realm of number. Numbers, in the form of geometry or music or the harmony by which the seven planets moved through the heavens in an orderly, repeated pattern, reflected in their motions the music of the seven strings of the lyre.

All numbers were individual powers and all had their significance: 1 was mind, the single thing that spreads through all meaning; 2 was opinion because no argument can be had with less; 3 is the number of the Whole, perhaps because the triangle is balanced and anything generated from 2 will always be 3, with a beginning, a middle and an end; 4 is justice, because the number is in perfect balance, an even number multiplied by an even number, to make a square; 5 is marriage, as the first combination of odd and even, 3 and 2, male and female; 7 is *kairos*, the right time or 'opportunity', a prime number, the rich and fertile bringing together of disparate things, and also the number of Athena and of the sun; 10 is perfect because the first four numbers add up to it in a perfect geometrical form. It is the whole of everything. This four-layer way of laying out the first four numbers was known as the *tetraktys*. 'What is the oracle of Delphi?' a Pythagorean question-and-answer asked. 'The *tetraktys*, which is the harmony in which the Sirens sing.'

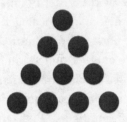

The *tetraktys*.

Can one empathize with this approach to the nature of existence? Walter Burkert saw in this a combination of doctrines, allying mystic underworld cults with an equally mystic approach to the questions of geometry, mathematics, music and astronomy, a vision which did much more than explain the idiosyncrasies of particular situations. A giant systematic mind was at work.

Past and present, pre-existence and life after death are comprehended in a single thought. And insofar as animals and plants are included in it, the unity and homogeneity of the universe are grasped. In the thought of the pre-existence and immortality of the soul lies an attempt at consistent thinking, a groping for something like an eternal, imperishable Being. Pythagoras . . . is not simply the prophet of old-fashioned piety, but at the same time, in his own way, a thinker leading, through ancient forms, to a new level of consciousness.

One can only imagine the mental and emotional excitement which this all-grasping portrayal of a harmonic universe, where death did not have the final word, must have created in sixth-century Kroton. Pythagoras seemed to convey a sense of meaning beyond the satisfactions to be derived from the symposium, the brothel, the marketplace, the barley harvest or the commercial voyage west and east. In the tradition begun three generations before by Thales in Miletus, and in forms despised by Heraclitus and his followers, Pythagoras was dreaming of a coherent universe thick with meaning in which all might share if only they followed the practices and rituals that his descent to the underworld had taught him.

It was certainly persuasive for the governing classes of Kroton. Pythagoras liked to give speeches to the people of the city, before the boys, youths, women and magistrates, guiding them into the paths of righteousness. He was said to gather 300 followers around him. None was allowed to speak nor see him in the flesh until they had proved themselves with five years of silent discipline. His authority and conviction, in a world of sceptical thought, the erosion of the old gods and endless antagonistic competition between cities, must have looked reassuring. Here was a sage who could guide the lost through this world and assure them that humanity's struggles were set within a cradle of harmony. The analogies with the growth of Christianity within the Roman empire are inescapable.

For most of his lifetime, a Pythagorean oligarchy ruled in Kroton. The city dominated its neighbours and, as evidence of its imperium, its coinage spread across wide swathes of southern Italy. In 510, this virtue-loving city, run by an ascetic and puritan elite, invaded its notorious neighbour Sybaris, and in an act of barbaric destruction diverted the river to flood the city, slaughtered the men, enslaved the women and left the site devastated and unoccupied for the next sixty years.

Milon, the great Krotonian athlete and Pythagorean champion, led the attack, wearing his Olympic crown, armed with a Herculean club and wrapped in a Herculean lion's skin. Returning from his savage triumph, he walked the streets of Kroton dressed in purple and with the Olympic crown on his head but now parading in a pair of pure white shoes to celebrate his victory.

As the leading Pythagorean, Milon met a proverbial end. Some time before, in one of the Herculean acts for which he was famous, he had been sitting with Pythagoras and his other followers, talking together in the eating hall in his house in Kroton, the centre of the cult, 'when a pillar began to give way. Milon slipped in under the burden and saved them all, and then drew himself from under it and escaped'. But his estimation of his own strength later killed him.

> Once, when he was travelling through a deep forest, he strayed rather far from the road, and then, on finding a large log cleft with wedges, thrust his hands and feet at the same time into the cleft and strained to split the log completely asunder; but he was only strong enough to make the wedges fall out, whereon the two parts of the log instantly squeezed together; and caught in a trap like that, he became food for wild beasts.

This was the punishment of hubris, and no more than a metaphor for what finally happened to the Pythagoreans of Kroton. Arguments erupted over the repartitioning and distribution of the lands taken from Sybaris. Milon and the Pythagoreans wanted too much for themselves. Years of resentment erupted in a populist movement against the self-serving, self-satisfied elite. Both Pythagoras' and Milon's houses were burned down, with many deaths. Pythagoras was expelled to Metapontum. The dates are a little uncertain but it may be that a tyrant named Kleinias, a man of culture who played the lyre and when taken by anger liked to be soothed by the music he

Chains and shackles from Kroton.

made, was responsible for the coup and the removal of the Pythagorean regime.

A set of extraordinary and poignant testimonials to that moment has been found in the ruins of a shrine just outside the walls of old Kroton at Vigna Nuova. The small temple there was dedicated to Hera, the goddess of liberation, and in it the archaeologists discovered a bronze cauldron from about 500 BC. It contained a set of heavy iron chains, alongside snapped shackles and other instruments of slavery, all of which had been dedicated to the goddess. The assumption is that they were left here by those slaves who were freed by Kleinias when the power of the Pythagorean elite was broken.

Ambivalence hangs around this story. The beauty and high-mindedness of the Pythagorean world-view had exclusivity at its core. Only the *mystai* were to be admitted to the inner circle of salvation. As a philosophy, it was deeply oligarchic and could scarcely have been interested in the emancipation of slaves. Just as the Thracian slave girl had laughed at Thales falling into his well, one can imagine the men and women who had been wearing these chains and shackles laughing at the sight of Pythagoras and his followers making their final, humiliated way out of the city to exile in Metapontum.

Not that the story of the Pythagorean discovery of the soul, with all its possibilities of liberty and self-realization, should end with that ignominious defeat of its worldly ambitions. There is another extraordinary image with which to remember it.

Sybaris had relied for its enormous riches, at least in part, on a route overland from its harbours on the Ionian Sea to all the opportunities on the west coast of Italy. In the seventh century, on that far shore, just south of Naples, it had set up a sub-colony called Poseidonia (later to be called Paestum by the Romans, its name today). It became a rich city itself, with close connections not only to the Greeks of Sybaris but to the Etruscans in Campania to the north. A fused Graeco-Etrurian culture developed and there are signs that the Bacchic complex – wine, the symposium, a fascination with Dionysus as the boundary-crossing god – became the grounds on which Greeks and Etruscans met in Poseidonia.

In 1968, a tomb was discovered about a mile south of the walls of the city which seemed to embody this cross-cultural world of Italic Pythagoreanism. In it was a plain but rich black *lekythos*, a bottle for perfumed oils from Attica, accompanied by a small lyre whose soundbox was a complete tortoiseshell. This was a marker for the cult of Orpheus, the great singer from the north, whose identity was entangled with Pythagoras' from the start and whose Thracian lyre was made of a tortoiseshell.

Like many Etruscan tombs but no Greek ones, this stone box, which is scarcely larger than a simple stone sarcophagus, was decorated inside with frescos. Most of these frescos are essentially Greek: a homoerotic symposium on the four walls, filled with all the usual scenes of drinking, music and flirtation that appear on cup after cup and vase after vase across the Greek world. But on the ceiling of the tomb is an image that is different.

On a plain pale ground, bordered by a dark line with palmettes in the four corners, a naked man dives through space into a rippled pool of grey-blue water below him. Some kind of tower stands beside the water, and on its far bank there is a conventionally represented olive tree. Another sprouts from the cliff behind him.

No one can be sure what this calm and beautiful image means, nor exactly what connection it has to the symposium

The coastal plain at Paestum.

shown below and around it, but echoes reverberate throughout its pale and refined spaces of the hopes portrayed in the golden letters: from the Bacchic worldliness of the symposium, the realm of transition, a young man is now diving towards the blessed water; a building like the house of Hades stands nearby; a tree grows there, if not of the prescribed kind (an olive, rather than the strange and unknown white cypress).

Above all, an air of liberation fills the picture. The young soul is diving from life into the afterlife, in flight towards the waters of memory, in a place from which all noise and trouble, the detail and complexity of the world, has been washed away, leaving only the prospect of clarity and bliss. He will be cleansed in those waters and his nakedness in mid-air is an image of the rewards that philosophy might bring to the enlightened soul, a perfect ease aloft in a heaven that is beyond any delights even the joys of the symposium might bring, diving free and clear towards an eternity of happiness.

This image is an answer to all the Heraclitean questions. Is the ultimate reality a life of fire? Yes, if all you can imagine is this life on this earth. But the Orphic and Pythagorean suggestion – a thought that has rippled on for the last twenty-five centuries – is that another life exists beyond it, beyond the fire of mutability, a life whose medium is a gathering of blue-grey waters.

The Orphic dive is an act of longing, not unlike the moments of perceived wholeness to which we all can be granted access now and then. And so the question remains: is the essence of life a Heraclitean blaze? Or a pool of Orphic calm? Or both? Is the Orphic dream somehow there, *within* the fire?

8

CAN I LIVE IN
MULTIPLE REALITIES?

PARMENIDES AND ZENO
ELEA, CAMPANIA, 510–410 BC

Pythagoras had made a fundamental change to Greek consciousness: thanks to him, and the Orphic movement of which he was a part, it seemed that the individual person, via the soul, might encounter and even inhabit a version of eternity. The unbridgeable gap between this mortal life and any other, which haunts the Homeric poems, had been crossed – and the bringing together of those realms had worked in two

The Tyrrhenian shore from the acropolis at Elea.

directions. Not only was it possible for the human soul to enter a world of everlasting bliss; souls could re-enter this world and inhabit all the many forms that life can take.

Optimism about the nature of the cosmos colours the Pythagorean vision. But it assumes as much as it reveals and the old question rears its head. How can these dimensions relate? And where does the final reality lie: here on earth or in some other sphere, to be imagined or known only by the thinking mind?

That is the question addressed by the great figure of Parmenides, Pythagoras' successor in southern Italy, who would in time become an inspiration for Socrates and Plato. He lived in the small harbour city of Elea, on the quiet shore of the Tyrrhenian Sea south of Naples. It had been a late foundation, by the seal city of Phocaea in Ionia, no earlier than 540 BC, and so was squeezed into one of the last remaining spots, not one of the giant productive plains which the great cities of Calabria had already colonized but a small and entirely beautiful pair of river valleys leading down to the sea on either side of a rocky ridge that formed the acropolis of the new city.

For all its ordinariness and slightness, Elea had an unforgettable origin story, of battle, exile, deracination and new beginnings, all of which would feed directly into the thinking of Parmenides himself.

When in 545 the Persians decided to attack and subjugate the Greek cities on the coast of Ionia, the people of Phocaea made a radical response. They had a proud history as the greatest of all the Greek merchant navigators. The site of their city in Ionia has no fertile hinterland but several deep and capacious harbours, protected against all winds, rimmed now with fishing boats and restaurants. Of all the harbours on that coast, it is the one that feels safest against all weathers. For centuries the Phocaeans had been sailing west, up into the Adriatic, and along the whole northern and western coastline of the Mediterranean as far as the silver-rich kingdom of Tartessus on the fringes of the Atlantic, 'not in round freight-ships but in fifty-oared vessels' – or warships. They had been the most dynamic of settlers, founding the cities of Marseille (Massalia) at the mouth of the Rhône and Empúries (Emporion) in Catalonia, entirely at home in the distant reaches of the sea.

Foça, one of the deep and accommodating harbours of Phocaea today.

When the Persians laid siege to the city, they tempted the Phocaeans with an offer: pull down only one tower of the defences and allow one building only in the city to be given over to the conquerors. The rest would remain in Phocaean hands.

The citizens asked the Persians for a day's leave to consider the idea, and for that day requested that they withdraw from around the city. The Phocaeans had already decided that 'the inevitable servitude' would be intolerable and spent their day of grace, as Herodotus wrote, in preparation for collective exile, putting on shipboard their wives and children as well as their furniture and the movable decorations of their temples. They then set sail for Chios, leaving to the conqueror a deserted town for the occupation of a Persian garrison.

It was the most magnificent gesture a Greek city could make. What mattered was not the sticks and stones, the physical thing, but the spirit embodied in the people, their freedoms and their precious sacred possessions. *Polis* was *dēmos*. Of course Phocaea could move. What was a harbour compared to a people?

They attempted to settle elsewhere on the coast of Ionia but nowhere would have them and so they decided to look further afield. Twenty years earlier they had founded a colony at Alalia in Corsica, 1,100 miles away, a way station en route to their kinsmen at Massalia and Emporion. The captains of the city fleet now decided to take their people there, a voyage to the other end of the Mediterranean. Before finally leaving, they returned to their home city, surprised the Persian garrison and slaughtered every one of them.

Some could not bear to leave and returned to Phocaea, but the rest of the fleet set out to sea, not via the isthmus at Corinth, but running south, around the stormy southern capes of the Peloponnese. With a wind from the right direction, either astern or at least abaft the beam, a speed of between 4½ and 6 knots could be achieved by ancient ships, even the smaller merchant craft, with a length overall of about 45 feet and a beam of about 14 or 15 feet. A modern cruising yacht might hope for 7 knots on average but in the end usually finds it is less. Xenophon described the voyage of a pirate ship covering the 400 miles from Rhodes to Ephesus in four days, at an average of 4 knots, sailing night and day, with no pausing for the dark. When Cicero sailed from Athens to Ephesus, he took two weeks, but the wind must have been against him, and his crew must have

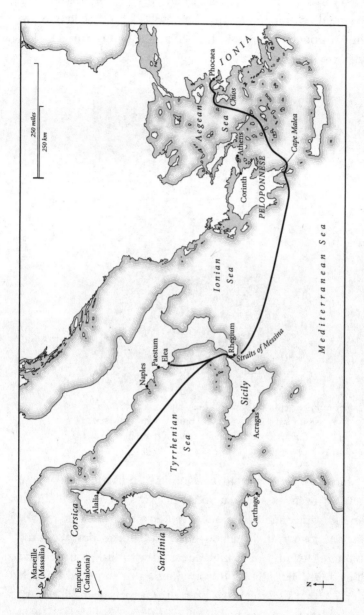

The Phocaean connection from Ionia to Italy.

waited out storms in safe island harbours. A hundred miles a day would be good going then as now and achievable only by sailing through the night. Half that could be expected for daylight sailing alone.

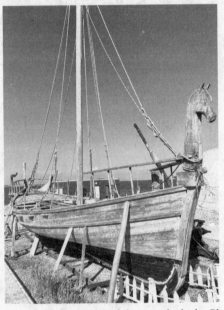

A modern replica of the kind of ship in which the Phocaeans would have sailed to Italy. Built by the University of Ankara, now at Clazomenae in western Turkey.

Chios to Cape Malea at the southern tip of the Peloponnese can have been no unusual route in archaic Greece, but that corner is windy and dangerous. Even now the winds are spooky there. Sudden cold katabatic gusts can hurtle down off the mountains, winds can change direction with little warning and sailing boats are advised to stay 5 miles or more offshore. It was there that Odysseus had been driven back from his voyage home to Ithaca, and pushed further south and away from Greece towards the land of the lotus eaters and his years of trouble.

'When you round Cape Malea,' the Greek geographer Strabo would write, 'forget the home you left behind you.'

But pass it they did, and from there the Phocaeans would have sailed directly across the Ionian Sea to the Straits of Messina between Italy and Sicily, before making their way north, perhaps directly again across the Tyrrhenian Sea to Alalia in Corsica. Their captains had made this enormous journey before. It might

Aléria in Corsica, on the site of the Phocaean city of Alalia.

have taken them a month. There they arrived with their double identity intact: adventurers and fugitives, exhausted and expansive, lost and found.

For five or ten years they set themselves up there, living as pirates, plundering the narrow seas between Corsica and the mainland of Italy, picking off the shipping en route between the Greek, Etruscan and Carthaginian harbour cities of the western Mediterranean. This sea was no empty tract but as full and contested as any of the trading zones of the late sixth century. In time, the Etruscans from the Italian mainland and Carthaginians from Sardinia could tolerate the piracy no longer and made an alliance to destroy the Phocaeans of Alalia. The sea battle was ferocious, two-thirds of the Phocaean ships were sunk and Alalia was lost. Again the refugees took to their remaining ships and headed first to Rhegium, Reggio Calabria, on the toe of Italy, and then onwards to a small territory up the coast, once called Hyele but in Phocaean hands to become Elea.

The valley of Elea from its acropolis.

It remains an entrancing place, scarcely visited, exuding settledness. There is nothing large about it. The good ground of the city is no more than 5,000 acres, rising up into a bowl of hills above the alluvial valleys of two little rivers. Olives and vines are scattered across it. This is not the wide rich buffalo-mozzarella country further north but something subtler and smaller, with willows and alders marking the courses of the streams, a soft and well-watered place where *frutte e verdure tipici* feel like the foundations of life. Red admirals cruise past the giant fennels on the heights of the acropolis, and the air is filled with the sound of sheep bells and the baby-roar of the Vespas burning up and down the beachside esplanade far below.

A cooling wind comes off the sea. Old seadogs in Roman times came to Elea to retire, and were remembered like Caius Nervilius Iustus who chose to be buried here, his gravestone recording that he was once in his glory days captain of the imperial fleet at Misenum on the bay of Naples. The emperor Augustus' doctor, Antonius Musa, advised both Cicero and Horace to come and take a cure at the waters. Horace certainly thought this little seaside town might be a good substitute for the hubbub and gossip of the hot-spring resort at Baiae near Naples where he usually spent his holidays. Cicero's friend Gaius Trebatius had a villa here, in 'a retired, healthy, and pretty spot' where the great orator used to drop in when en route to Greece, or needing to get away from the outrages and violence of life in the city.

There are no harbour works to be seen here now; the shore has thickened and almost the only sign of a connection with the outside world is the little red Naples-to-Reggio train that from time to time rumbles along its seaside viaduct.

The city of Parmenides is invisible, 15 feet down in the silt below the Roman streets. Only excavation has revealed it: stone footings and mudbrick walls, exactly as you would have found in the Ionian cities. Small stone houses clung to the slopes of the acropolis, with roofs of clay tiles and some of them, perhaps the temples, with lion spouts to the gutters and Hermes-faced terminals to the roof ridges.

Riches would come to Elea in time but this was, at the beginning, a refugee city, with no formal rectilinear planning to match the vast riches of the great Greek colonies to the south and east. Recent excavations have found two sixth-century bronze helmets here, one Greek in style, one Etruscan, which were probably dedicated in the early temple and would have been testimonials to victory in battle, and perhaps to suffering and escape.

Of all the places from which these philosophers came, Elea, where Parmenides was born perhaps soon after the Phocaeans arrived, perhaps a decade or so later, is the most modest. The Phocaeans did not make anything themselves in the early days. Their wine cups came from Poseidonia, cooking pots from Calabria and Corinth, other pottery from Sicily and even north Africa. Their religious memorials are touching evidence of an all-pervasive sense of vulnerability. The sea was full of enemies and the southern coasts of Italy were not beyond the reach of the Persian empire. Armed Persian squadrons, using Phoenician triremes, could cruise the Italian coast as far as Taras and Kroton.

Perhaps as a result, the Phocaeans' memorials seem to come from a people looking for comfort and shelter. A small stone shrine, bruised and blurred but similar to those found in Miletus, was probably dedicated to Kybele, the Anatolian goddess of fertility. She may have come here in a ship from Phocaea,

The little shrine to Kybele carried from Phocaea
to Alalia and on to Elea, where it still is.

reverently carried from the eastern Aegean all the way to Corsica and on to her final destination in Italy. A cup and jug found on the acropolis are crudely inscribed with the three Greek letters *IPH*, meaning 'holy', in the Ionic form of Greek used in the eastern Aegean. In Athens, the word would have been *IEPH*, but for these people Ionia was home and Athens a foreign country.

IPH: the simple word for 'holy' in the Ionic form of Greek spoken by the Phocaean founders of Elea.

As it had been in Phocaea itself, the main temple in Elea was dedicated to Athena. Other tributes were given to specific gods: to Zeus *Ourios*, the sender of fair winds, or even Zeus *in the form of* a following wind; to Poseidon *Asphaleios*, not the terror god of storm and earthquake but Poseidon the Securer, the Protector *from* storm and earthqake; and to both Athena *Hellenia* and Zeus *Hellenios* – *Greek* Athena, *Greek* Zeus.

These Phocaeans were now perched on the edge of the Italian peninsula, driven away from home after home, but they were Greeks and they prayed to Greek gods. The journey had been a long one but it had not diluted or eroded what they were. It may have enhanced and emphasized it. Their gods had come with them and they were as self-assertively

Greek as any Greek had ever been. Even later, when the whole of Italy had become Roman, the people of Elea continued to insist that they were Greek and spoke Greek rather than Latin to arriving travellers.

This was the background for the radical turn in philosophy now taken by Parmenides: a newish city, with the memory of trauma, far from central to its own culture, in need of consolation and certainty, to deny the mutability of the world, in recovery from a history of displacement and loss. He was of the first generation to be brought up here and so was the child of exile, heir to people in flight. Life had been broken and unity had acquired a premium. Nothing could seem more valuable than coherence in a world shaped by uprootedness. Extinction had been threatened and so indestructibility was now inseparable from goodness and truth. When faced with the prospect of

Parmenides.

nothing, the assertion of a great and perfect something might be a cure for trauma. Parmenides' revolutionary and difficult philosophical poem, which in one sense is a vision of everlasting fixity, might be seen, in the words of the poet and translator David Spitzer, as 'an official narrative of the city [of Elea], its injuries and survivals', a hymn to being, when being had very nearly been denied.

Parmenides would in time, perhaps at the end of his life, become a hero in Elea. According to Plutarch, writing in the first century AD,

he beautified and adorned his native country with most excellent laws which he there established, so that even to this day the officers every year, when they enter first on the exercise of their charges, are obliged to swear that they will observe the laws and ordinances of Parmenides.

It may be that he lived and worked in the city as a healer. A swirled marble pillar or *stēlē*, inscribed with his name and supporting a handsome and idealized portrait bust, both from the first century AD, were discovered in excavations in the city. His name on the *stēlē* is followed by the phrase 'OULIADĒS PHUSIKOS', meaning something like 'Healing Philosopher of Nature'. Other *stēlai* excavated in the same place down by the old harbour are all dedicated to the memory of doctors, in an underground chamber, a *hypogeum*, with statues and portrait busts of Asclepius and his daughter Hygieia, the healing gods. Some surgical instruments and strigils for cleaning the body were found alongside them. It might have been a Pythagorean-style therapeutic centre. Body and soul could both be cured there.

In a scene of strange and reorientating modernity, with its assumption of voyages across the Ionian Sea as a commonplace reality, Plato tells the story of Parmenides and Zeno his pupil (who, he says, may also once have been his beloved boy) coming to Athens at the time of the festival of the Great Panathenaea, perhaps in June 450. The two Graeco-Italians found the Athenians keen to hear what arguments they were making. Both were staying together in the part of Kerameikos, the potters' district, that was just outside the city wall, and the young Socrates was among the crowd of those who came to hear them. Others were there from Clazomenae in Ionia. Parmenides was then about sixty-five years old, grey with age, but handsome. Zeno was twenty-five years younger, tall and graceful. It is as if two foreign intellectuals had hopped on a jet to be lionized in the salons of London or Paris, with other scholars gathered there from elsewhere in the world they shared. Plato thought the Greeks lived scattered around the sea in little hollows, 'like ants or frogs around a pond'. Here they were now more like water boatmen, skittering across its surface, clustering for wisdom.

By the time of this meeting, Parmenides had long since composed his great work in which he appears as a *kouros*, a young man. It is a single long poem of which only parts survive, written in the hexameters which had been used by Homer and Hesiod, and which carried with them the atmosphere of the heroic that Parmenides required. Everything about it is on a vast and universal scale. Nothing domestic or trivial plays a part. Its subject is the greatness of the conceiving mind, which alone can grasp the singular truth of existence. Its title is lost but may have been, like many others, *On Being* or *On Nature*.

It is not philosophy dressed up in verse but a strange and transitional, semi-mystical performance, in part a vision of a revelatory journey deep into the halls of the dead, where the epic verses ring out their incantatory and otherworldly music; in part a closely argued and complex demonstration of the relationship between what is true and untrue; and in part a now fragmentary account of the way people have guessed the universe might be, of how it came into being, of how human beings and animals are born, of the qualities of matter and the nature of the stars.

The poem is in that way a universal text: an introduction to the unexpected world of the deepest conceivable understanding; a display of the strange truths that can be revealed there; and finally a long and detailed description of the world as we know it, one in which the final truth cannot be grasped, but where many and various opinions hold sway.

Parmenides was the beneficiary of all that had come before, but his emphasis is certainly more Italian than Ionian. He had no time for the double-headed paradoxes of Heraclitus, nor for the stories of the history of the cosmos dreamed up by the Milesians. From Xenophanes, his predecessor as an Ionian exile finding his home in Italy, Parmenides seems to have absorbed the idea of a single, everlasting and immobile non-human divine presence. Xenophanes may also have lived in Elea for a time and is said to have written a long poem about the founding of the city, which is lost, but, more significantly for Parmenides, he was the first to think that the gods were not as the ancient poets had imagined them, but the polar opposite: not many but one, not unpredictable but permanent, not quasi-human but abstract and immovable. The world that we know might be confused and animated, full of change and injury, but for Xenophanes God was not like that. For him constancy was the heart of the divine, a principle of unchangingness at the root of things that Parmenides would make the foundation of all existence.

From Pythagoras and the Orphic mysteries, representing the other side of his inheritance, Parmenides took the opposite – a belief in the revelatory power of a pilgrimage into a world beyond the one known only in the light of the everyday. His poem starts with such a Pythagorean or Orphic journey, dropping into the dark and the depths, looking for truth. He is himself the initiate, the *mystēs,* who begins not in calm contemplation, but filled with desire. In a whirl of energy and an almost anarchic, blazing hunger for strangeness, he plunges down 'the far-fabled path of the divinity', drawn in a chariot by a team of mares and guided by the daughters of Helios, the sun god. The mares, which are the horses of the night and the dark, carry him 'as far as my heart may reach', down the famous road which, as it did for the Orphic initiates, leads to the palace of Persephone, queen of the underworld.

Strangeness and power crowd about him as he hurtles for the depths. It seems for a moment as if the poem is a journey to all cities of the world. He is being taken to the edge of his own mind. The chariot is straining, its axle squealing and shrieking beneath him as the wheels spin onwards and downwards. This is no calm and rational introduction to the nature of truth but a hectic, phantasmagoric, self-obliterating, trancelike dive for it.

The young Parmenides comes without warning to the gates of the Palace of Night. Justice herself, the great and fearful goddess, described as *polupoinos,* either 'savagely punishing' or 'much punishing', holds the keys to the gates. But the daughters of the sun do their work and sweetly persuade the terrifying figure of Judgement to open the gates for him. As she draws the bolt, a blood-chilling sight greets them. This is the house-of-death-and-revelation and within the gates appears nothing but a vast and yawning *chasm* – the Greek word is the same as ours; it can be applied to the wide-open mouth of a lion – which is the dark gulf of unknowability.

The sun's daughters and their mares are fearless and on they drive, straight down the famous road, to the divine and majestic presence of the goddess Persephone herself. One might expect terror but the young initiate is welcome there. She is kind to him and takes his right hand in hers and he is now face to face with the goddess of truth and understanding.

Persephone, young, regal and perfect, from Acragas
c. 500 BC. An outer, golden crown may once have been
fixed above her braided and gathered hair.

Here, in the stillness of her presence, and the sense of awe
that accompanies it, the rhythm slows. He has arrived at the
otherworld of the mind. Anything from the life we know is
suspended. There is nothing to be seen or heard. In the house-
of-death-and-understanding mundane considerations do not
apply. The goddess, in an impassioned, chanted and fugue-like
statement, introduces him to the great and virtually unapproach-
able concept of the oneness of truth, reciting to her young
pilgrim-initiate a hymn to the unity of existence.

There are, she begins, two roads, one of Being and one of
non-Being. 'Come now, I shall tell you,'

>   – and you must take home the tale once you
>   have heard it –
> Just which ways of inquiry there are for understanding:
> The one, of what-is-and-must-be,
> Is the path of conviction, for it attends upon true
>   reality,
> But the other, what-is-not-and-cannot-be,

This, I tell you, is a path that is wholly unreliable:
For you can neither grasp what-is-not,
Nor could you point it out.
For it is the same to think also to be.

What-is-and-must-be can be known; what-is-not-and-cannot-be will never be known and is not conceivable – you cannot, as we might say, think of a round square – and so the second way of enquiry, into what-is-not, is literally impossible. We cannot ever ask or know about it.

Only the what-is can be known. But it is not to be confused with the material world known to the senses. The what-is does not need to have a material existence. It can exist and probably must exist only as an idea. Forget the information given to you by the senses: only what can be thought can be the same as what is. The world, the universe, centaurs, a perfect sphere, unicorns, the five-year-old Prime Minister of the United Kingdom, King Charles the 5,000th, goodness: all must exist as much as you or I or Alpha Centauri exist. What is conceivable is possible and as such exists. Only the inconceivable cannot exist. And an absolute distinction needs to be applied between those two categories. Anything either is or is not. Nothing can half-be.

Leave behind the sensuous world. The eyes have nothing to guide them, they are 'aimless', the ears hear nothing but echoes and the tongue does nothing but repeat other men's gossip. The goddess tells the young Parmenides to use his mind, to 'judge by reason'. Reason alone will show him the true reality of what-is. The world of the senses cannot be trusted. What-is can be accessible only to the mind. What-is-thought *is* what-is.

The goddess then embarks on philosophy's earliest piece of extended metaphysical reasoning. It is difficult, dense and hieratic. In a step of world-shaping importance, she makes a repeated and rhythmic assertion of the Idea as the reality underlying the muddled phenomena of the mundane world. Plato, for whom the insubstantial, pure and conceptual world was more real than the material world around us, took that notion from Parmenides. And from Plato descends our long tradition of the primacy of the conceptual, the rejection of the actual in favour of the ideal. 'By thinking', the goddess says, 'gaze unshaken on things which, though absent, are present.'

This is not a description of the world as we perceive it, the place we know full of beginnings and endings, comings and goings. The goddess's reality of what-is stands beyond and outside that perceived world. We have access to it only through the mind, and through that fleshless, abstract grasp we can know that what-is exists outside place and outside time.

> . . . what-is is unborn and imperishable, entire, alone of its kind, unshaken and complete. It did not exist once nor will it come to be in the future, since it IS now, all together, single and continuous.

There can be no change in the everlasting Isness of that being. The Is merely is. What-is can have no beginning and will have no end, but merely be, still and continuous. It must stand outside all mutability. If it were changeable it would not be what-is but would either decline or evolve away from what-is into what-is-not, an impossibility. Because if something exists, it can of course change its form, but it cannot either suddenly or gradually *not* be. If it exists, it will always exist. And if it exists, it cannot have come from nothing. Being is necessarily eternal, unchanged by time past or future.

Nor can it be many, since any one part of it would not be what-is but only an aspect of what-is. Isness can only be one whole thing, one whole everything. The forms it assumes might be multiple but those forms are not what-is. And so the goddess's Isness is one eternal thing, constant, unchanging and unmoving.

The core suggestion that Parmenides makes is something Plato would take from him. Knowledge cannot depend on the limitless multiplicity of the world that the senses deliver to us. Only if we hold on to the idea, for example, of a table can we identify the very many various things around us that have four legs and a flat top as 'tables'. Otherwise, we would be living in an ungraspable anarchy of the multiple, the endless chaotic actuality of the things we perceive. Only because the idea of the table stands outside the material world can we have any knowledge of 'tables'. Knowledge and language both require an ideal being that is not susceptible to change. If all we had was the endlessly mutable world, nothing could be known. We would be living in a sea of 'this' and 'that'. Knowledge of being can only be the knowledge of an unchanging, eternal idea.

In that way, this extraordinary poem, conceived in this small Italian town, with the sea breaking gently on its beaches, stands at the root of the idea that the intelligible, immaterial world of the thinkable is more real than the bodily world of the per- ceptible.

'Birth has been extinguished', the goddess tells her disciple,

> And death made inconceivable. What-is stays in the
> same state and in the same place, resting by itself,
> And so it stays firmly as it is, for mighty Necessity
> Holds it in the bonds of a limit which restrains it on all
> sides.
> There is no lack in it; for if there were, it would lack
> everything.
> The same thing can be thought and is that which
> enables thinking,
> For you will not find thinking apart from what-is, on
> which it depends for its expression.
> All those things which mortal men,

Trusting in their true reality, have proposed, are no
    more than names,
Both birth and perishing, both being and not being,
Movement between places and the flickering of bright
    colours.

Nothing we see and hear around us is real. Only Isness is real, which persists like a great and perfect sphere, everywhere the same, entirely connected to itself.

'Everything is one to me', the goddess says, 'Where I am to begin; for I shall return there again.' In her end is her beginning. Being is always whole, always perfect, always to be grasped by the thinking mind, always distinct from what-is-not. She despises those who think they can blur the distinction between what-is and what-is-not, calling them 'mortals who know nothing' who 'wander two-headed' through the world,

borne along deaf and blind at once, bedazzled,
undiscriminating hordes, who have supposed what-is
and what-is-not is the same and not the same; but the
path of all these turns back on itself.

Those phrases sound like a hostile description of the Ionian world-view and the ideas in particular of Heraclitus, for whom the tension within things, the lyre and bow that turn back on themselves, and the coexistence within single phenomena of multiple identities, was a description of the vitality at the heart of being. For Heraclitus, a river was both a river and not the same river. Its riverness was dependent on its not being one thing. It both was and wasn't at the same time.

For Persephone, the goddess of night encountered by Parmenides in his dream vision, that paradoxical view of reality is absurd. What anarchy of understanding must result from a principle by which what-is and what-is-not are considered the same? For her, and for

Parmenides as her initiate, there can only be a form of deep and trustworthy actuality beyond the kind of Heraclitean flux in which human beings are usually lost, adrift in the deceptive multiplicity of the world around them. 'It can never be made manageable', she tells Parmenides, 'that things-that-are-not are.' Even if a lifetime of habit had led him to think in that way, he must resist it and instead follow her on the path to truth and understanding.

This is a magnificent vision of the eternally true, but do you find yourself protesting against it? Does it not generate a sense of vertigo, as you stare past the phenomenal world to this other characterless and everlasting place of eternal changeless being which is somehow proclaimed as the only true thing? There may be a logic at work here but everything we feel we know, perhaps because our frame of mind is so relentlessly evolutionary – what-is surely came from what-was; and what-will-be must come from what-is? – contradicts it.

What could be more real, after all, than the world we see and feel around us? And how different could that multiform, various and dynamic cavalcade be from the still, silent, ever-lasting, continuous, disembodied wholeness of being that the goddess describes, a vision Parmenides apparently endorses, enlightened by his journey to her dark halls?

Some of the Greeks agreed. One of Socrates' followers, Antisthenes, told Plato that when he looked at a horse he saw a horse, not 'horseness'. For Aristotle, to suggest that what exists 'is one and immobile . . . is very similar to madness. For no madman is so insane as to think that fire and ice are the same thing.' A thousand years later, the Alexandrian Neoplatonist Simplicius of Cilicia thought Parmenides was at least in part deluding himself. 'He was not unaware that he himself had come to be, just as he was not unaware that he had two feet, even though he said that being is one.' Colotes, a bitter, brilliant and much despised Hellenistic thinker and follower of Epicurus, wrote a famous treatise called *That One Cannot Live According to the Doctrines of Other Philosophers.* He thought Parmenides laughable. If the whole of reality was 'ungenerated, indestructible, of a single kind, one and continuous', as Parmenides had maintained, what did exist? Did fire exist? Or water? Did 'the inhabited cities in Europe and Asia' exist? Did your toenails grow? And if you accepted Parmenides' propositions, what was there to stop you walking off a cliff, as there was no such thing? In essence, Colotes decided, 'Parmenides abolishes everything by suggesting that being is one.'

Intriguingly, though, Parmenides did not conclude his poem with this earth-shattering conception. The goddess quite suddenly pauses in her disquisition on eternal truth.

> Here I end what I have to tell you of trustworthy arguments and thinking about reality. From this point onwards, learn mortal beliefs, listening to words which, though composed, will be lies.

Parmenides' description of the – apparently entirely misguided – ideas that human beings have of the complex nature of the reality around them was no brief excursion into idiocy but a worked-out account of the material world. 'The unshaken heart of well-rounded truth' may have been to one side and un-informed mortal opinion on the other, but neither half was to be neglected. The heavens, the sun, which is a fire, and 'the wandering works of the round-eyed moon', whose light is reflected and circles the earth, the nature of light and dark themselves, hot and cold, the coming into being of men, the nature of male and female, the garlands of fire wrapped around the universe, the process of human thought – all this appeared in the second part of the poem, but is now preserved in such fragmentary form that little more can be said of his system.

A conundrum remains though. If only one thing – Isness – exists, and the world of our ordinary daily experience does not exist; and if our normal beliefs in the process of change and the multiplicity of things, and even our own coming into being, is completely wrong, and human opinion of the world is so misguided, why bother laying it out at such length?

That question has troubled people throughout the ages, but John Palmer, from the University of Florida, has recently suggested that this very division into what can be grasped by the mind and what can be perceived by the senses is precisely the point that Parmenides wants to convey. The two parts of the goddess's revelation are present in the poem as two parts of the way in which the world can be known.

Parmenides does not abolish the world of flesh and colour but sets it alongside the world of the mind. Both are real. Both exist but neither interrupts the other. The ever-changing world perceived by the senses and the never-changing character of what is understood by the mind are both permanently present for us. There are two levels of reality: the single immutable intelligible realm (the world of what-permanently-is) and the plural and ever-changing realm open to our perceptions. The two forms of reality have the same boundaries in space and time but are not made of the same stuff. They lie alongside and within each other but somehow remain distinct. This understanding of Parmenides suddenly enlarges the meaning of his strange and difficult poem. It is a dual account of the universe. The conceptual world and the sensuous world are both here, we know them both, but neither has anything to do with the other.

That bidimensional picture of Parmenides allows one to grasp something of the impact he must have had on those who first heard him. Otherworldliness is not something to be experienced only during a visitation from a god, or in terror and anxiety after death, or even during a trancelike journey to the underworld, but is a powerful presence here and now, graspable by the thinking mind. Eternity and truth can be known in thought, and the reality of that knowledge is more secure and trustworthy than any knowledge derived from the fallible human senses.

We live in two worlds which, in John Palmer's terms, are both here and completely distinct from each other. One is bright, rich and colourful. The other is everlasting. One is vivid, the other secure. It is Parmenides' great gift to us to have recognized that the imagined, the purely known and the reliably true are everywhere to hand as much as or even more than the sand of the beach, the waves of the sea or the light of the wandering moon. His poem is an act of grand consolation. Human beings do not need to reject either mode of being. Wholeness, in fact, embraces them both and to conceive of existence in that way gives credit to both aspects of the human organism where a thinking mind occupies a sensing body. How easy it is to let one overwhelm the other, but to allow that to happen is a route to one of two sterile ends: either desiccated intellectualism or the stupidity of pure sensuousness. Happiness has a foot in both camps.

The wisdom of Parmenides, drawing on a Xenophanean-cum-Pythagorean inheritance, was embracing and not exclusive. The Orphic journey into the earth, the singular vision of the goddess and life in the daylight all belonged together. His difficult and counterintuitive ideas of the eternal oneness of being were merely an aspect and not the whole of what he had to say. The poem itself suggests the answer: wholeness must understand both the eternity of the idea and the tangible realities and marvels of existence in the sublunary world. Neither is independently sufficient. Pythagoras had understood the revelations of the trance. Parmenides took that understanding further: journey into the otherworld, grasp the wisdom that will be given to you there, cultivate the thinking mind to understand the rationality of being and then apply yourself to all the phenomena, fallible as they might be, of the perceptible world. Fulfil the potential of these dimensions of existence and you will at least have a chance of being cured of its ills. That is the prescription handed out to the citizens by this philosopher-healer: drink up, think of eternity.

Parmenides had many followers, in Ionia and Athens as much as in southern Italy. Melissus of Samos articulated many of his ideas but in prose. Socrates and his pupil Plato at least began their philosophical careers entranced by the statements of Parmenides' goddess. In Elea itself, his most famous pupil was Zeno, whose career, as it has been preserved for us, consisted largely of defending the perceptions and reputation of the master.

The third-century AD biographer of the philosophers Diogenes Laërtius heard that Zeno:

> was a gallant man; and in particular he despised the great no less than Heraclitus. For example, his native place, the Phocaean colony once known as Hyele and afterwards as Elea, a city of moderate size, practised in nothing but rearing brave men, he preferred before all the splendour of Athens, hardly paying the Athenians a visit, but living all his life at home.

Clearly in one way, Parmenides' access to eternal truths meant that for Zeno worldly significance counted for nothing, even if that characterization is little but a re-running of the story of Thales falling backwards into a well: philosopher considers the stars and ignores the realities of life. But there may be something in it. According to Plato, Zeno had his book stolen and circulated before he could decide for himself whether to make his arguments public, implying at least that the substance of his truth mattered more than its reception. Another of Diogenes Laërtius' fragments suggests that Zeno did not care what anyone else thought. He would behave truly whatever the circumstances.

We are told that once when he was reviled he lost his temper, and, in reply to someone who blamed him for this, he said, 'If when I am abused I pretend that I am not, then neither shall I be aware of it if I am praised.'

The background to his own thought was the general mocking reception of Parmenides' suggestion that reality was one eternal, immobile and unchanging thing. According to common sense, that was clearly ludicrous. Was Parmenides the same person as his father? Or a frog? Were babies born? Did old men die? Were there not things in the world? And were they not constantly on the move?

Zeno's purpose, in the famous paradoxes that were preserved by Aristotle, was to show that the common sense of the world was just as full of absurdities and internal contradictions as anything Parmenides had suggested about the oneness of being. 'Many men had mocked Parmenides,' the Oxford philosopher Jonathan Barnes has written. 'Zeno mocked the mockers. His *logoi* were designed to reveal the inanities and ineptitudes inherent in the ordinary belief in a plural world; he wanted to startle, to amaze, to disconcert.'

In Greek, the meaning of *paradoxos* moves. To begin with it means 'something that is contrary to expectation or opinion'. Only subsequently did the word move to what paradox means for us, 'an apparently absurd or contradictory statement that turns out to be correct'. That transition from 'against received opinion' to 'actually true' is the focus of Zeno's disconcerting logical problems. He was clearly a brilliant man, and despite Diogenes' statement that he rarely left Elea, Socrates had heard that Athenian aristocrats paid him handsomely for lessons in skilled argument: 100 *minas* for the course. The number of lessons was not specified, but from each of his pupils Zeno collected, amazingly, a fee equivalent to the price of five slaves or thirty of the best purple robes, 100lb of silver or 25 tons of wheat, enough to feed sixty families for a year. No less than exquisitely decorated wine jugs and cups for the symposium, philosophy was expensive.

The paradoxes aim to show the absurdity of the familiar ideas of reality that we all share. First, the ludicrous notion that a fast runner will overtake a slow one.

A mid-fifth-century drinking cup discovered in the Etrurian city of Falerii shows Achilles and an enthusiastic tortoise. The painter of the cup may not have grasped Zeno's paradox: in this image Achilles skips happily ahead.

Zeno imagines a tortoise starting ahead of Achilles in a race – it is a sardonic play on the famous and tragic scene in the *Iliad* where Achilles pursues Hector around the walls of Troy. Obviously the tortoise will be overtaken by him, as Achilles is the fastest runner the Greeks have ever known. But he won't, because in the time it takes Achilles to reach the point from which the tortoise began, the tortoise will have made some progress itself. At that point, obviously, Achilles would still be behind. So once again the runner has to set off in pursuit. But by the time he reaches the point the tortoise had then reached, the tortoise will have moved even further ahead. However hard Achilles tries to reach the tortoise's new starting point, the tortoise will have moved on again. Nothing could be clearer:

the slowest conceivable runner in the world will never be overtaken by the fastest.

From everything we know of the world, that cannot be true, but it cannot be shown *not* to be true. The only possible conclusion is that our ideas of things in motion are deluded. The perceptible world, conveyed to us by our senses, is full of self-contradiction and cannot, under the strictest gaze of analytical logic, be shown to cohere. Parmenides was right: human perception is befuddled and the world of coherent truth can admit nothing of change or movement. Reality can only be a place of permanent stillness. All idea of motion is pure illusion.

Or take the question of the arrow. Everything that exists must exist in the now. As time passes, things exist in a whole series of nows. At any particular now, an object, whether still or moving, must be in the place where it is and it must occupy a place exactly equal to its own length. So it must be still and resting in the place where it is. If a man fires an arrow from a bow, the arrow seems to move through the air. But that is illusory because at every instant of its flight it can only be where it is and so it must be still. It can never be half in a place and half not. And so an arrow in flight never moves.

Or: if there are many things in the world, they must be distinct and separate from each other and so there must be something else in between each of them. But between each of the first things and the thing-in-between-them there must be something else to keep them apart, a thing in between a thing and the thing-in-between-a-thing. If there are many things, there must be an infinite number of things and so in a limited world, the things of which the world is made must be infinitely small.

But the infinitely small can have no existence. It is a nothing. If it is anything more than nothing, it cannot be infinitely small, as there will always be something smaller than it. For something to exist, it must have some size. But whatever is of a certain size has parts that can be distinguished from each other (if only its front and its back). Nothing can be the same as itself throughout. Each of those parts will also have parts (a back-of-front, say, or a front-of-back) and each of those part-parts will have parts (a front-of-back-of-front) and those parts will have parts (a back-of-front-of-back-of-front) and so on without limit. Everything must be made of an infinite number of parts. Each part will be of a certain size and so the size of anything is limitless. The things of which the world is made must be infinitely large. And so Zeno demonstrates the two opposite impossibilities: if there are many things, they must both be infinitely small and can only be infinitely large. That cannot be and so the idea that there are many things in the world must be wrong and Parmenides was right: existence can only be a single vast immobile thing.

'What you've said seems to be said in a way that's beyond the powers of the rest of us,' the young Socrates told Zeno in Plato's account of their meeting. Zeno replied that he was defending Parmenides against his detractors and:

> against those who say *the many are*, and it pays them back with the same results and worse, intending to show that their hypothesis that *many are* suffers even more ridiculous consequences than the hypothesis of there *being one*, if you pursue the issue far enough.

There is little in this of human experience, whether emotional, mystical or physical. It seems as if the fusions of the harbour mind have been abandoned in favour of a kind of heartless and logical brilliance which, taken seriously, delivers no more than an absurd and unknowable world. Zeno's contemporaries and successors accused him and his followers of that failing. Socrates thought that the philosopher from Elea was 'a god of refutation'. Aristotle thought Zeno 'a controversialist and paradox-monger'.

Much later, Plutarch recorded a memory that Pericles, the great statesman and orator of fifth-century Athens, had heard Zeno 'discoursing on nature in the manner of Parmenides and practising a kind of skill in cross-examination and in driving one's opponent into a corner by means of contradictory argument'.

That sort of lawyerly cleverness sounds more like sophistry than philosophy, of which the story has travelled a long way from its beginnings in Ionia. Humanity has been left behind and a nimble whip-smartness substituted for it. But that is not entirely fair to Zeno. These intellectual mazes are an act of loyalty to his mentor. The purpose of the mind games is not to demonstrate his own genius but to show how Parmenides' intuitive realization that the deep form of reality must be singular, immobile and eternal and that there is a great and permanent lastingness to existence is no more deranged than what the rest of us think anyway as we go about our daily business in the world of change and motion.

Zeno's paradoxes fulfil the requirements for a philosopher: a desire to know, an attention to what that knowing might be and finally a modesty, an *aporia* – meaning literally in Greek a pathlessness, no way through – a recognition that the answers are not to be had. The paradoxes deliver a paradoxical conclusion: the most penetrating thought can show only that the world is not anything even penetrating thought can understand.

9

DOES LOVE RULE
THE UNIVERSE?

EMPEDOCLES

ACRAGAS, SICILY, FL. 450 BC

The threads of this story finally meet and bind in the great figure of Empedocles, resolver of crises, unifier of visions, grand democrat and great sage of Acragas, the huge and powerful Greek city on the south-western coast of Sicily.

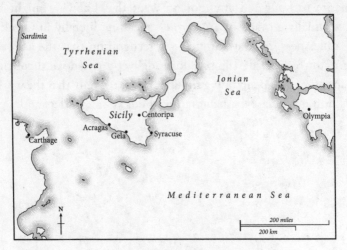

The Greek west.

The city that gave birth to him was everything you might expect of a great Greek colony in the west. Early in the sixth century, it was established a mile or two away from the shore in a wonderful position, between the sharp valleys of two rivers, occupying a high and wide but shallow basin, tipped towards the sea and surrounded on three sides by natural cliff defences that could easily be strengthened, either by quarrying those cliffs or by building walls above them. The colonists, from the Greek city of Gela along the coast, may at the beginning have been no more than a few thousand but embarked on plans with large ambitions. The walls of Acragas when completed were about 8 miles round, with nine gates, enclosing at least 1,000 acres, room for maybe 150,000 or even 200,000 inhabitants within them. The colonists made the harbour where the two rivers met the sea.

Skyline temples marked the city limits of Acragas.

The modern city of Agrigento is on the ridge at the inland heights, where one medieval church, dedicated to Santa Maria dei Greci, occupies the site of the temple of Athena. The hundreds of other acres of what was Acragas are now almost empty of anything more than an occasional ruin, the footings of the buildings revealed in the lionskin stone of the country. Sandy, dusty lanes make their way through the almond orchards and olive groves of a loose and easy landscape. Ships lie at anchor in the roads and further out the white shrimp fleet from Porto Empedocle is scattered dot by dot to the horizon. The city always commanded that wide stretch of water and could be seen from it in return; Acragas was always on display to its maritory. Inland, the hills have a relaxed, Arcadian elegance about them so that Acragas plays its own theme in relation to its place: not the hidden delicacy of Elea and its valley; nor the hardened, wall-to-wall productivity of Kroton or Metapontum; and not the edge-of-the-world sensation you find again and again in the cities of Ionia, but a sense of ease founded on the all-important substructure – the city's imperial brawn, the commercial drive of its merchants and the people-conquering potency of its assertive Greekness.

Olive and almond orchards now fill the urban spaces of the city.

Its early history is brutal, dominated by the figure of Phalaris, the tyrant who ruled Acragas in the central years of the sixth century. He was the archetypal monster, in whom command and cruelty enjoyed a complex relationship. The core Phalaris story concerns an Athenian bronzesmith, Perilaus, who claimed to know Phalaris' reputation for barbarity, and presented him with an ingenious bronze bull he had made. The tyrant was delighted with the beauty of what he saw. 'But how will you react,' Perilaus said to him, 'when you see the mechanism inside it, and learn the purpose for which it is designed?' He opened the back of the animal, and went on: 'When you want to punish anyone, shut him up in this container, apply these pipes to the nostrils of the bull, and order a fire to be lit underneath. The man will shriek and roar in unremitting agony; and his cries will come to you through these pipes as the tenderest, most pathetic, most melodious of bellowings. Your victim will be punished, and you will enjoy the music.'

When Phalaris heard this, he was filled with loathing.

'Come on then, Perilaus, why don't you be the first to show it off? Get in and pretend to roar and we will see if the pipes make the music you describe.'

As soon as Perilaus had crept in, to demonstrate, as he thought, the sound of the pipes, Phalaris closed up the back of the bull and lit a fire underneath it. 'Let the music-master be the first to play,' he told his listeners.

So that the man's death would not pollute the bronze creation, Phalaris had him taken out when half dead and thrown off the cliffs of the city.

Throughout the second half of the sixth century, Acragas grew and prospered, becoming a dazzling centre of luxury and sophistication, partly through trade, as it controlled the key commercial and strategic route across Sicily to the northern harbours on the Tyrrhenian shore, partly through conquest. Its population expanded, its huge walls coming to match any in the Greek world.

Vineyards spread up towards the hills. Olive groves produced an enormous harvest which was sold to Carthage, as there were still no olives grown in north Africa. Fortunes were amassed, monuments erected, sculptures made of choice racehorses and pet birds. When an athlete called Exaenetus won the stadium foot race at Olympia, 'he was conducted into the city in a chariot and in the procession there were, not to speak of the other things, three hundred chariots belonging to citizens of Acragas, each drawn by a pair of white horses'. The citizens' clothes were of the finest and lightest linens. The strigils and oil flasks used at the stadium or the baths were made of silver or gold. The richest of all of them was Tellias,

> who had several apartments for guests, with a number of servants whose job it was to invite all foreigners to come and stay with him. Several other citizens did much the same thing and received their guests with every kind of benevolence and liberty. Once when five hundred cavalry from their allied city at Gela arrived during a winter storm, Tellias entertained all of them himself and immediately provided every one of them with outer and under garments from his own stores.

His wine cellar had 300 vast casks cut out of the rock, each of them holding the equivalent of a hundred amphorae or almost 800 gallons. Beside them was a plastered wine vat, enough for a thousand amphorae (one and a half Olympic swimming pools) from which the wine could be allowed to flow into the casks. Wit came with the riches:

> Tellias was quite plain in appearance but wonderful in character. So once when he had been dispatched on an embassy to the people of Centoripa [an ancient rival city in Sicily] and came forward to speak before the Assembly, the multitude broke into insulting laughter as they saw how much he fell short of their expectation. Interrupting them, he said, 'Don't be surprised, for it is our practice to send to famous cities their most handsome citizens, but to insignificant and unimportant cities men of their own sort.'

When the grandest of brides was married,

> more than eight hundred chariots followed in her procession, the altars in all the sanctuaries and those in the courtyards throughout the city were provided with wood for celebratory fires, and to the shopkeepers the bride's father gave firewood and brush with orders that when a fire was kindled on the acropolis they should all do the same; and when they did as they were ordered, at the time when the bride was brought to her home, since there were many torch-bearers in the procession, the city was filled with light, and the main streets through which the procession was to pass could not contain the accompanying throng, all the inhabitants zealously emulating the man's grand manner.

The triton accompanies the crab on Acragas' coinage.

As ever, the riches came from the sea. The magistrates (who held military rank) could be addressed as the Tritons (the sons of Poseidon) and many of the coins, as well as the crab of Acragas, show an image of a triton blowing on his shell. It is from here that the most floridly roaring and howling account survives of the symposium-as-voyage. When a crew of young men from another city decided to have a party in the upper room of a house in Acragas,

> they became so wild when they had drunk themselves stupid that they thought that they were sailing in a trireme, and that a terrifying storm was overtaking them at sea. They were so off their heads that they threw all the furniture and bedding

out of the house as if into the sea, convinced that the captain had told them to lighten the ship in the ferocity of the storm. A crowd gathered and started to carry off the furniture, but even then the boys did not stop their madness.

The next day the authorities came to the house and soon saw that the young men were still all at sea. To the questions of the magistrates they answered that they had been hugely stressed by a storm and had been forced to throw into the sea any cargo they did not need.

When the magistrates said they were mad, one of the young men, though he seemed to be the eldest of the crew, said to them, 'You Tritons, I was so frightened that I crept down in the lowest possible place under the rowing benches and lay there.'

Seeing their unhinged state of mind, the officers told them not to fill up on more wine and sent them off. The young men all professed their gratitude . . . 'If we are delivered from such a storm and reach safe harbour, we will erect altars to you in our homeland together with the gods of the sea, as our manifest saviours, since you appeared to us at just the right time.' In this way, the house in Acragas came to be called Trireme.

The citizens of Acragas lived in such luxury that a little later, during a war against the Carthaginians when the city was under siege, the authorities were forced to pass a decree regulating the guards who were spending the night at their posts. None was to be allowed more than one mattress, one bedspread, one sheepskin and two pillows. Anything more was thought too comfortable.

In alliance with Syracuse and Gela, Acragas eventually defeated the Carthaginians. The victorious campaign was led by Theron, the city's rich and aristocratic tyrant. After the war, and under him, Acragas came to its peak of power. Greek historians used the word *megaloprepeia* to describe its citizens then, meaning that they exuded a magnificence or large-minded impressiveness, a sense of grandeur in their idea of themselves.

Fuelling that sense of its own greatness was an influx of slaves. In the streets of Acragas' ally, the city of Syracuse, it was said, 'such a multitude of captives arrived that it looked as if the island had made the whole of Libya [that is, north Africa] captive'. In Acragas too, thousands of Carthaginian prisoners were shipped in, so that the streets were 'crammed full of them'. They were put in chains and set to work.

There were so many prisoners that some private citizens took on 500 of them as slaves. The rest were handed over to the city authorities for whom they began cutting a system of underground water conduits, leading the natural springs in the city to a giant pool at the lowest point within the walls. That pool became an elegant lake, 'with a multitude of fish of every variety for public feastings, and, along with the fish, swans spent their time with vast flocks of every other kind of bird, so that the pool was an object of unalloyed pleasure for the citizens to look on'.

The *passeggiata* lake by which the people would stroll in the cool of the evening has been drained and is now a lush garden filled with olive trees and orange groves, but many of the conduits are still in use, driven into the rock to tap the aquifers and to bring the water down from the sources high under the northern ridge to the streets and piazzas of the city below them. The tunnels are capacious, 3 feet wide and almost 6 feet high, cut 30 or even 60 feet below the streets. Vertical shafts were pushed down to the required level, 3 feet wide with footholds notched into the two sides, and the connecting tunnels cut between them. The Greeks knew disease was spread by water or foul air and this huge and sophisticated slave-dug underground system was almost certainly designed to keep the water pure, untainted by pollution from the streets. Pillared reservoirs were built underground, roofed in heavy stone slabs, and the water was brought to the surface, by its own natural pressure, at fountains in the streets above. It was a communal resource; water was never piped to individual houses as there were slaves enough to carry it there.

Above ground, using the army of slaves, Theron began to build the largest temple in the Greek world, dedicated to Zeus. It was ruined by an earthquake in ancient history, probably in the fifth century before it was finished, but as you climb over its vast fragments it is easy enough to imagine its uncompromising vastness, built on a huge platform, 180 feet wide, 360 feet long, with the ridge of the roof rising 120 feet above the platform. The wall stones now lie among the olive trees as large as trucks, each capital the size of a small building.

A Doric capital in the wreckage of the enormous
temple of Zeus at Acragas.

An uncompromising, daunting and brutish presence was the temple's message. The body of a man could fit within each fluting of the columns. The pediments at each end portrayed 'The Battle between the Gods and the Giants' and 'The Capture of Troy', with entire cavalcades of colossus-limbed heroes in action. The scale was entirely Egyptian.

The colonnade was embedded in its walls and any sense of each column's independence from its neighbours was sacrificed for a statement of unremitting power. You could not negotiate with such a building. Most intriguingly of all, between the columns, the Temple of Zeus held a rank of giant embedded slaves, each one about 25 feet high, each made of twelve blocks of the sandy orange tufa, and of two different types, one a grown man, one a youth.

A reconstructed stone giant lies on the site of the Temple of Zeus in Acragas, with modern Agrigento behind.

This is a tyrannical version of the temple, probably begun in the late sixth century but still under construction after the defeat of the Carthaginians in 480 BC. There had been a long tradition in Assyria and Egypt of portraying one's broken enemy in stone and these figures, bearing on their shoulders the full weight of the temple of the king of the Greek gods, are a celebration, as unequivocal as the raped girl on the Thasos coin, of the enslavement and subjection of the enemy. Their arms are raised above them, partly to carry the burden, partly in the head-holding expression of grief that had appeared on Greek pots since the Bronze Age. The stone bodies of the defeated are the culmination of a slave landscape, dense with the brutality of compulsion, a humiliation immortalized in stone. The entire temple celebrates dominance and the acquisition of power. Here slaves could be used to create an image of slaves being used, a denial of civility in every stone.

A recumbent giant from the temple of Zeus.

The temple of Zeus represents everything Empedocles was not, the model of a tyranny which his philosophy would come to oppose.

Imagine the atmosphere of Acragas at the time of the tyranny in the early years of the fifth century: tens of thousands of north African slaves, housed at night in slave camps outside the walls of the city, driven into their work in chained gangs in the early-morning light. Then the works themselves, above and below ground, and the traffic and dust they generated. The draught animals, trains of oxen, the timber sleds on which the stones were drawn from quarry to site. The shops and arcades in which the Cypriot scents and Etruscan jewellery, the Athenian vases and

A cork model showing a possible arrangement in Theron's Temple of Zeus of Doric columns and giant slaves. The columns were about 80 feet high.

amber from the north were all sold alongside Indian pearls and onyx and lapis from Arabia. Everywhere sharp distinctions and juxtapositions, the elegant girls and posing boys, the wine amphorae carried on bare shoulders to the symposium houses, the sides of beef hanging in the shaded butchers' market, the saffron and cardamom in their open sacks, the wafts of baking bread, the grief, the luxury.

The war with the Carthaginians, which was pitiless and bloody and from which many mass graves of young warriors have been found, coincided with the attacks on mainland Greece by the Persians. In both spheres, the Greeks emerged victorious and changed. Theron, the tyrant of Acragas who presided over the building of the Temple of Zeus, was celebrated by Pindar, after he had won the chariot race at Olympia, as a man who had 'reached across the sea with his achievements and from his home grasps now the pillars of Heracles'. Acragas' largest temple is a monument to that world of dominance.

This was the imperial world from which Empedocles came

but which he does not represent. The reign of Theron the tyrant ended in 471, when his command of western Sicily ebbed and failed, and Empedocles, born in about 484, was in his teens. Some form of oligarchy may have taken over, but it did not last, and, perhaps under the guidance of Empedocles himself, Acragas turned to a form of democracy in which all 20,000 citizens could partake.

You can still walk through that change in political atmosphere. Leave behind the lumpen remains of the Temple of Zeus and make your way up on to the long ridge at the southern edge of the city where a great series of Doric temples for which Acragas became famous were built. They shared some qualities with the Temple of Zeus but they portray a very different world, and one that is much more suited to the thought of Empedocles. Standing out against the light, the sea and the hills behind, they frame the city itself as an act not of imperium but of monumental urbanity, a fusion of the religious and the civic, a political declaration of Acragas' identity to the city itself and to the world beyond.

Like mathematics and music, and the practice of philosophy itself, these Doric temples are not statements of worldly power but aim to represent a form of eternity, a removal from chance and the contingent. They are aligned with the rising and setting of the sun in spaces cleared around them to keep the noise and hubbub of the city at bay. Nothing connects them to any other structure so that the temples become prominent and perfect in themselves, images of self-government and of the power encapsulated in the distilled order of a just city.

Unlike, say, a medieval cathedral, whose inner space is the focus of its meaning for the religious, the Greeks worshipped at altars set outside the temples. The temple itself remained the preserve of the god and his servants. The stepped platform on which it was built was designed not to make an easy ascent for people but as a foundation in proportion to the temple itself, a form by which, it might be said, the temple stepped down towards the ordinariness of the earth. The temple was sanctity made civic.

The so-called Temple of Concordia, Acragas, in fact dedicated to an unidentified god.

At Acragas, they are still on their ridge, some tumbled and broken, others almost complete or restored. At the heart of each was the *cella*, meaning the 'room', a windowless stone box for the god, inaccessible to the mass of people. There are no openings beyond the door into that dark space and so the god resided there in the brazier-lit half-dark, its gold and ivory seen only in the glimmer of that semi-light, acknowledged and known by the city but scarcely encountered. We can guess at the form of these great hidden images of the gods from the clay statuettes found throughout the city. Many are of the presiding mother goddess Demeter, wearing her crown, some-times standing, more often installed on a throne in all her majesty, and like Artemis of the Ephesians hung about with fertility-holding vials.

Archaic clay figurines of Demeter found in Acragas.

Each Doric *cella* was ringed by – you might say dressed in – a colonnade on all four sides, the *peripteron*, meaning literally the 'around-wing', as though the more open pattern of stone and air in a colonnade gave a lightness to the building which the solid blocks of the *cella* could not match. Not that there is anything light or airy about the Doric columns. The massive and masculine lines of Doric columns, with their huge cushion capitals and naked, unelaborated style that allows them to stand unadorned on the temple platform, with no base, perform the role of honouring the god's shrine. They are a dignifying enclosure for what would otherwise be a plain stone box. There is an element to it of a guard of honour, shielding but not concealing the divine presence, not unlike a rank of hoplites standing in defence of a city, just as described in the instructions to the men of Sparta by their archaic poet Tyrtaios:

Stand near and take the enemy,
Strike with long spear or sword,
Set foot by foot,
Lean shield on shield,
Crest against crest,
Helmet against helmet.

That repetition of singular elements in each façade, unified without variation, is a statement of unity in multiplicity, precisely the central question around which early Greek ethics and philosophy turned. How do the one and the many inter-relate? What is the connection between the individual and the many? Here in a colonnade, far more than in a blank wall, or in the Temple of Zeus' embedded slaves, is a version of an answer: repeat the many within a controlling frame and they will become as one. Each column may be undeniably itself but each is just as clearly part of a larger unity. This is a form of solidarity but not solidity, togetherness without fusion, and the ethical and political implications are clear: the strong city will value each of its citizens and just as powerfully concentrate on the coherence of their world. In that sense, and perhaps intuitively, the Doric colonnade is an image of justice.

These buildings look like strange houses. They have a roof, gables, façades and elevations, but you are scarcely aware of them as enclosures. They are more sculptural than that, objects in space, originally glittering in a marble-chip stucco that coated the rough tufa, with the entablature and pediments painted in bright red and blue. They were glorious objects in themselves. As the Finnish architect and historian Tapio Prokkola has said, the Doric temple was 'the ultimate manifestation of the value-system of the *polis* in stone'. It was an ideal to which Empedocles dedicated his life.

In its service, many subtle adjustments were made to the architectural elements of the building. The stone drums were cut so that they were seen to bulge very slightly on all sides, the *entasis*, a word suggesting tension and strain, slightly more swollen than a purely vertical shaft, enhancing the sense of weight carried. The top step of the platform was given a very slight upward curve in the centre so that there could be no sense of it sagging. The spacing of the columns at the corners was closed up very slightly so that the building would seem to strengthen at its margins. The columns were given broad shallow flutings set between sharp and narrow ridges, so that in certain lights looking along the façades the rank of columns dissolves into a continuum of finely graded grey bands.

Much of what Empedocles stood for – the great civic virtues of integration – is on show in these buildings. They are a manifestation of the integrity and communality he valued above all else. In a way that is reflected in the architectural language of the Doric temple, his achievement was to understand the act of combination as central to the nature of existence – on a cosmic and fundamental level. Just as the Doric temples left behind the brutish assertions of the Temple of Zeus, the human philosophy of Empedocles left behind all the crudities and cruelties of tyranny.

He loved Acragas and was loved by the people in it. 'Friends, inhabitants of the great city by the golden river of Acragas', he began his long poem *On Nature*,

> Living on the high acropolis, filled with thoughts of
> good deeds,
> Compassionate harbours for strangers, with no
> knowledge of wickedness,
> I greet you!

It is near the heart of this book that this great philosopher could address his fellow citizens as *xeinōn aidoioi limenes*, 'harbours that are welcoming to foreigners', just as elsewhere he uses the same word *limēn* to mean the womb, the harbour in which life begins. The harbour mind finds its culmination in the thoughts of a figure for whom the welcome and absorption of the other constituted the essential structure of both goodness and reality.

He was a rich man, of long and aristocratic lineage, whose grandfather had been a victor at Olympia and had raised the finest horses in Sicily. As a grandee, Empedocles liked to walk the streets of Acragas dressed in purple with a golden sash, wearing bronze shoes and with flowers in his luxuriant hair. He was always accompanied by a retinue of young attendants, male and female. He gave money to them as acts of largesse or as dowries on marriage. The people of Acragas treated him as a kind of royalty and in response he glowed with a sense of his own marvellousness:

> For you I am an immortal god, no longer subject to death,
> I go among you honoured as I am seen,
> Crowned with ribbons and flowery garlands.
> When I arrive dressed like this in the busy cities,
> I am honoured by the men and women; they follow me,
> Thousands of them, asking for the way to life's rewards.

Some citizens were jealous, thinking him narcissistic and complacent, afloat on his own glory, absurd for his pretentious clothes and bogus theatricality, but most gave him the credit of his genius. He was 'free-spirited' and resisted any offer of political office, acting as a true democrat, helping to dissolve, in a way that is not quite clear, an 'Assembly of the Thousand' that had attempted to establish its oligarchic power over the city. He had an ancient aristocratic name but according to Diogenes Laërtius, the later biographer of the philosophers, he 'belonged not only to the Rich but to those who favoured the ordinary people'. There was in fact a modesty about him. 'But why do I insist on these things,' he asked himself,

> as though I were doing something great,
> To be superior to mortals,
> who are so weak and feeble in so many ways?

This large, sane embrace is the atmosphere of his philosophical poem, which is a work of vast, generous and systematic inclusion. More of his words survive than those of any other philosopher in this book, but he was acutely aware of how much he owed to the tradition that came before him. From Xenophanes and Parmenides he took the idea of an essential unity of being; from Heraclitus the dynamic interrelation of opposites; from Pythagoras a fascination with the nature and fate of the individual; and from Anaximander and the other Milesians an idea that the world is made of relatively few elements, and its form dependent on the transitions between them.

He valued no one more than Pythagoras. From him came the transmigration of souls and the strange taboos. Empedocles' followers, like Pythagoras', were to keep away from beans. To that he added a prohibition on bay leaves. Just as Pythagoras could recount his previous selves, Empedocles knew that at different times he had been 'both a youth and girl, a bush and a bird, and a sea-leaping voyaging fish'. But it was the model of Pythagoras himself that Empedocles revered, as:

> a man, knowledgeable beyond measure,
> Who possessed the greatest wealth of organs of thought,
> And most of all was master in wise deeds of all kinds.
> For whenever he stretched forth his mind,
> He saw quite easily everything that might be found
> In ten men's lives, or twenty.

That scale of intelligent understanding, intuitive empathy and a broad appreciation of the powers of the mind was what Empedocles valued. A visionless following of the old inhabitants of Olympus could never deliver the kind of wisdom or contentment that philosophy promised.

> Happy he who possesses the wealth of divine organs of
>   thought;
> Wretched he who cares for an obscure doctrine about
>   the gods.

The physical senses were no better:

> Narrow are the resources spread out along the limbs,
> And numerous the miseries that break in, blunting the mind.
> [Those senses] see in their existence only a small part of
>   life
> And fly off, soon to meet their fate, carried along like
>   smoke,
> Convinced they know whatever each has encountered.

Knowledge from them is all too partial. Anyone who relies on the physical world can have no understanding of the whole. Only those pupils who had 'withdrawn here' to listen to him would learn and come to see that 'human intelligence has never climbed further'.

His range was huge, from the making of the universe through the origins of sex to the genesis of plants, to the working of the body and the nature of the mind. Unbounded energy comes pouring through his verses, which are dedicated to a boy called Pausanias, his lover. Eros, attention and acceptance are applied to soul, city and cosmos in a rigorous and consistent vision. In the troubled world of fifth-century Sicily, Empedocles was the advocate of balance and calm, not one that was still and fixed but with all the entrancing stability of a gyroscope in eternal movement.

His poem addressed the Muse and asks her to give him a kind of straightforward and illuminating voice, not to court popularity, nor to be over-adventurous, but to look carefully at the world, and see the truth in things. He asked to be able to 'think how things are evident' and rely on what he calls in a beautiful expression the *tranōmata glōssēs*, the 'clarities of the tongue'.

His great act of imagination, reconciling many of the contradictory tendencies in the long philosophical inheritance this book has traced, was to conceive of the world as dependent on four combinable elements or 'roots' and two interacting processes. The roots are those which, from their adoption by Aristotle, became foundational for the pre-modern world: earth, water, air and fire. These are the essential things of existence. As Parmenides had shown, nothing can come from nothing and so these roots were 'unborn', eternal, unchangeable and irreducible. In compounds, they are the constituents of everything that exists and so the changes that are apparent in the world are changes not in substance but in the degree to which these elements are combined. Those changes in the combining and separating of elements are brought about by the actions of the two grand motivating forces in the universe, Love and Strife. Love brings together anything that stands apart; Strife drives apart anything that hangs together. 'Birth' is only the name given to a new combination of things, 'death' to their disintegration. The birth of something is always the death of something, nothing is ever actually born and nothing ever actually dies.

Eternity and changeability are fused in this vision. What exists is everlasting but its form is in constant flux. The idea had no sentimentality in it. Love and Strife were each other's intimates. They both contained in some way the seeds of the other. Just as Anaximander and Heraclitus had understood a kind of violence to be essential to the vitality of life, Empedocles embraced something that was voiced with startling force (this in a fragment from a play otherwise lost) by his near contemporary Sophocles, the great Athenian playwright. 'Children,' the Sophoclean fragment begins, talking about the goddess of Love, and summing up the world in which this philosophy had grown,

> Aphrodite is not only Aphrodite,
> But her name is the same as many names.
> She is death, she is eternal life,
> She is crazed and frenzied, she is untrammelled
> Desire, she is weeping. In her is all that is
> Noble, calm, leading to violence.
> For she melts into the lungs of everything
> Alive – what is not hers?
> She is in the shoals of swimming fish,
> She is in the earth's four-footed creatures,
> For birds she is their wings.
> Among animals, the mortals and the gods above,
> Whom does she not catch and overthrow, time and
>   again?
> If it is allowed for me – and it is allowed to say the
>   truth –
> She rules over Zeus himself, no need for spear
> Or sharpened blade. Love cuts short
> Every plan of mortals and of gods.

We live in a universe with roots that are permanent and unchanging but is in a constant eddy of Love-and-Strife, two forces joined at birth, equally powerful, often almost indistinguishable. Love is Strife. Love is in the shoals of swimming fish. Love is everything. Love is death.

This is the vision of a gyrating eternity, the cosmos whirled through time, connecting and disconnecting, whole and not whole, as much as a city gyrates around itself in endless individuated particulars. Just as painters:

> Grasp many-coloured pigments in their hands
> And having mixed them in harmony, some more, others
>   less,
> Out of these they compose forms similar to all things,
> Making trees, and men and women,
> Wild beasts and birds, water-nourished fish,
> And long-lived gods.
> [You must know that the four elementary roots
> When subject to Love and Strife]
> Are the source of all the innumerable mortal things
> Whose existence is evident to us on earth.

At different times in the history of the world, Love has prevailed, at others Strife. In lines that were discovered only in 1994, long preserved and ignored in the library of the University of Strasbourg, written on fragments of papyrus that had been used in Roman Egypt as a support for the gilded copper leaves of a funerary wreath, Empedocles describes the alternation of forces in the cosmic cycle:

> Sometimes by Love we all come together,
> With limbs that the body has received in the flower of
>   blooming life;
> Sometimes in turn, cut apart by evil quarrels . . .
> But as much as [the elements] endlessly exchange their
>   places,
> To that extent they are eternal, immobile,
> Linked in an everlasting cycle of change.

In a phrase from that part of the poem, Empedocles says almost in passing that 'Each of us wanders separately in the surf of life.' For all his grasp of the eternal nature of the universe, his accompanying recognition is that we live in the churn of a breaking sea. Nearly all states of this dynamic, capsizing universe are restlessly creative so that, throughout the history of time, life has 'shot forth in dense eddies', an incessant making, unmaking and remaking of the world. Empedocles' sense of wonder at its multiplicity is undimmed. There are climbing plants and forest trees, vines and hyacinths, microscopic beetles, flocks of birds.

> See this in sea-grazing, heavy-backed seashells,
> and in rocky . . .
> Life living under the strongest possible kind of skin,
> Like a breastplate for the strong-backed,
> Yes, the stone-skinned trumpet shells and the turtles,
> The ashen antler-spears of the horned stags in the
>   mountains . . .
> But I could never finish telling all the species.

From these dense eddies, as much as the plants and animals, all the complexity of being emerged:

> The Earthly was there, and the far-sighted Sun-eyed,
> Bloody Battle and calm-seeing Harmony,
> Beauty and Ugliness, Quickness and Slowness,
> Longed-for Infallibility and black-berried Uncertainty.

These are all quasi-divine presences in Empedocles' vital, animated world, in which every category remains mobile: infallibility hangs away, just out of reach; uncertainty has within it a harvest of shadowed fruits.

When Love is at the centre of this cosmic vortex, the universe assumes the shape of a perfect sphere, tightly gathered into a single round universe surely derived from Parmenides' vision of the everlasting oneness of being. For Empedocles, this state of total love becomes a kind of cosmos-filling god called Sphairos, the Globe-Shaped One:

> He was on all sides equal and entirely without limits,
> Round Sphairos, exulting in his joy-filled and circular
> solitude.

At these moments of stilled perfection nothing but the sphere of Love was in existence. But the tension of Love and Strife inevitably resumed and a mysterious, surreal version developed of a disconnected life. 'Parts of animals, like heads, hands and feet' were born separately and wandered the earth looking to mix together. Races of cow-headed men and man-headed cattle appeared on earth. There were 'many faces without necks', arms with no shoulders and eyes with no brows. Feet whirled through the air accompanied by disconnected hands. Some creatures appeared with two faces and two chests.

But there is a logic by which Love draws like to like, and in time animals appeared in which all parts had an appropriate relation to all others. The two eyes came together in a single face, the functions of respiration and of the blood – Empedocles imagined that thought occurred in the blood around the heart – came into balance.

> Earth, fire, water and the bright-shining radiant air
> Were all anchored in the perfect harbours of Love,
> Some a little more, some a little less,
> And out of these were born blood and flesh.

Thought itself is a function of that harbour ability of Love to unite what is similar. The presence of all the elementary roots in us allows us to encounter and understand, as if by empathy, the realities around us:

> For it is by earth that we see earth, by water water,
> By air divine air and by fire destructive fire,
> Fondness by fondness and strife by hateful strife.

Just as Anaximenes in Miletus had understood our animating breath to be a murmuring of the world-breath, one part of the breathing of the cosmos, Empedocles saw that because we are connected in our physical being to the world as it is, and because we are similarly made, we can love it, know it and, as part of that knowledge, love each other.

It was Love, he says, sounding for a moment like George Herbert, the great seventeenth-century English poet of divine love, that made our 'unyielding, penetrating eyes'. There is no distinction between Love and a close examination of things. With that in mind he ends his poem with an appeal to his listeners that they should think hard and observe hard, and 'with a pure effort of thought gaze on the elements of life with a sense of benevolence towards them'.

Antiquity would laugh at him in the end because they believed the story that he had died by jumping into the burning crater of Mount Etna to prove his immortality – disproved when one of his shoes somehow turned up a little charred – but the final calm and love-filled lines of his poem make a better epitaph:

> If you look carefully and generously
> On all the essential elements of the world
> They will be present to you throughout your life
> And many good things will come to you from them.
> For these roots are what make each thing
> Grow in you, according to your nature.

HOW TO BE

Don't run after all the other things that bring
Countless miseries to men and stupefy the soul.
They will soon abandon you
And go back to the world to which they belong.
For know that all things have a purpose
And do their share of thinking too.

10

THE INVENTION OF
UNDERSTANDING

W hat can we take from these people, so far away in time and mind? Are they simply antiquities, no more to us than some blurred face on the corner of a temple or a piece of pot in an unvisited museum? We have all known how exhausting those things can be, how easily the dream of lunch starts to beckon, that glass of wine in the seaside restaurant. Is there anything to keep us here?

It helps, maybe, to forget the history, both the historical moment to which they belonged and the aeons that spread out between us and them, the vast, troubled plains of European history, and imagine instead that they are here now with us, speaking to us, addressing us as people.

Few would be that easy as dinner companions. Heraclitus would certainly be the worst. He would sit at the table for hours at a time in complete and cantankerous silence. With perhaps an occasional smirk at the idiocy of other human beings. Pythagoras would be so entranced by his own importance he would scarcely notice we were there. Empedocles would, I hope, act the great host, a human harbour, dispensing bonhomie. Parmenides would be dreaming of perfection, Zeno showing off like a lawyer. Odysseus would exert some kind of manipulative charm, leaving us never quite sure of his intentions or motives. Xenophanes slips between self-pity and a little mild pomposity and is considering what to have for pudding. Alcaeus is full of gaiety, I think, and superbly capable of that kind of quick, slight movement from laughter to seriousness that is the mark of friendship and friendliness. Archilochus is grinning at his own smut. Sappho, surely, is the most magnificent, majestic and distant. You would be in no doubt you were being evaluated in her eyes. And would want her to love you.

But what, afterwards, could we say they had to give us?

1. Questioning

First, the habit of *questioning* as the foundation of knowing. Earlier Greeks had been told merely to submit to a world-structure in which Zeus the king of the gods was the undeniable, imperial presence:

> With ease he makes
> The weak man strong, with ease the strong he breaks,
> He brings forth the obscure, he levels the great,
> He withers the tall, and makes the crooked straight.

On the Ionian coast of the Aegean and then in Italy, these thinkers remade that assumption and rejected it. Monarchy, whether in this world or in the cosmos, was not part of their value system. The nature of existence was up for debate and the role of the human mind was not to quake before the world and its powers, nor merely to demonstrate courage in the face of its cruelties, but to interrogate and explain it, in many ways to own it. The new thinkers represent in other words an emergence into self-determination.

2. Liquidity

Second, and implied by that questioning, they set our existence afloat on a certain *liquidity*, that it is better not to cling to what we know but to place what we know and what we are on the seas of what might be. They left behind the tragic permanence of the ancient world-view that prevailed at the deepest levels of, say, Homer in the *Iliad* or in the epic of Gilgamesh. 'Beware the toils of war,' one Lycian hero says to Hector in front of Troy, 'the mesh of the huge dragnet sweeping across the world.' That sense of a careless and brutal destiny, and of human beings skittering like lizards and fledglings in front of its open mouth, or caught helplessly in its webs, is not in these people. They have shaken themselves free of it, and that liberation from the overwhelming fixity of fate is an aspect of what we should think of as the dolphin mind, the mindset of entrepreneurial, adventuring people. It is a form of mercantile courage, of reliance on fluidity.

3. Coherence

Those liquefying qualities are not enough. There is the threat of anarchy in them and anarchy can sustain no city. And so that fluidity must turn towards its opposite, an overarching sense of *coherence*. This was the first instinct of the thinkers in Miletus: what is it that makes the world whole? What is the governing frame of existence? In what ways can soul, city and cosmos be one? It is the fundamental paradox of this early thought that coherence becomes the ally of fluidity, that free thinking to be of any worth can only be systematic, allowing us to work on the assumption that the world we inhabit makes sense in all its dimensions, in a single vision that extends from our own hearts and minds to our companions in life and on to the vastness of everything that is.

4. The valuable self

Fourth comes the *self* as an aspect of value, to be seen not as an object, a fixed thing, nor merely as one node in a network of influences and connections, but as some fusion of those two ways of knowing what we are, so that each of us, like the speaking voice in Sappho's lyrics or in the various heroic-cum-salacious poems written for the symposium, can be seen as a unique organism, but one that is made up of and depends on everything that surrounds us.

The lyric turn taken in the sixth century BC made the self the forum for knowledge. The sense of a person moved centre stage, not as a by-product of social hierarchy, but as someone that both gives and receives, desires others and relies on others, suffers the pain of love and longs for its rewards. If Athena is the goddess of the city, Aphrodite is the goddess of the self.

5. The necessary city

With Xenophanes, some of that emphasis of the lyric poets was pulled back towards the demands of the social. The urges of the ego needed to be held within the embrace of the *city*. Courtesy and seemliness, the preservation of form and even good manners, so easily seen as a truth-denying carapace, were understood by Xenophanes as the armature of wellbeing, the hidden structure that could allow the happiness of a city. No self could be happy unless happy in the city. And if conformity is chosen by the city, and not imposed by an autocracy, then conformity can be one of the names for goodness.

6. Burning

Heraclitus looms over this landscape as the deepest disrupter of order. The tension between the singular and the unified that oscillates through the other thinkers as a form of choice – piratical or civic, self or city, this world or another, transient or eternal – is raised to another level in him so that paradox ripples through every cell of his thought. Coherence consists of a lack of it. Order is the lack of order. Strife is calm. The undeniable presence of things is a universal fire. A conflagration of identity is the core of identity itself.

This is more than the received idea of Heraclitus that

'everything flows'. The astringency of his vision gives less comfort than that. All opposites are one. Life's burning is the source of existence. Doubt is the source of knowing.

7. The dream of completeness

Pythagoras saw, as the seventh core contribution to this invention of understanding, that the experience each human being has of his own individual soul is only the entry point for the knowledge of something more general: the presence of souls throughout all aspects of creation. The philosopher, as he looks into the eyes of a dog, or tastes a bean, or hears the call of a river, sees that all beings have selves. He comes to understand the deep animation of existence. Soul and existence are indistinguishable for him and so death has no final meaning. Souls survive it and return in other forms. The world is full of souls – they are packets or capsules of meaning – in an endless recycling through every form of being. It is the first recognition of the connectedness of all life through time.

For the Pythagoreans, mathematics represented an order that persisted beyond the material existence of which we are usually aware. The harmonies of the lyre seemed to speak of a perfect world. Access could be gained to this conceptual heaven through the music of perfect numbers. Number is where the eternal world manifests itself in this one. And so the essence of Pythagoreanism is double: the recognition of a shared world-soul, allied to the possibility that through mathematics and through the person-reshaping challenges of the Orphic mysteries its nature can be understood. It is the first invitation to the dream of completeness.

8. A multiple vision

In the aftermath of the Pythagorean revolution, one question became fundamental. Which world is real? Is this the world that exists? How are we to know what we know? How can we even start to guess at what reality might exist beyond the unreliable information of our senses? The radical suggestion made by Parmenides, guided by his goddess of the underworld, is that only thought can know what is. And that a final reality exists as one immutable thing in the sphere of being beyond our worldly perceptions. This world is unreal. Only what can be thought can be real.

Little more than a century after the first thinkers in Miletus, this philosophical tradition, driven by its own momentum, had come to the most disruptive of all conclusions: what we assume we know cannot be true; and, for Zeno, Parmenides' follower, what we think we know can be shown to be absurd. There is no actuality to the experience of life as we know it. The delights of a glass of wine or holding someone you love, or swimming in the sea, or rolling up your sleeves, or the grief of losing a friend, or being hurt by life – all are illusory.

Many centuries of stony sleep have followed from the belief that only the ideal is real. It has an unkindness at its heart and its natural conclusion is a form of authoritarian intolerance. It does not love the frail or the broken, nor allow for the beauty of the ordinary or the everyday. And so, of all the ideas in this wonderful cavalcade of thought, it is the one with which it is most difficult to feel in tune. It leaves the world a heap of insignificance, set against the glowing truths of that spectral heaven. The washed spirit of intellectual perfection is elevated above any actual, enriched, mulched and embodied form of life on earth.

But the beauty of Parmenides, having shown the oneness of immaterial being to be the only truth, is that he does not leave it there. Alongside it is the burning, brilliant, beautifying bazaar of life on earth, in all its flesh and desirability. The two worlds coexist. We know both and must live in both, so that in the hands of the great goddess we will be able to surf the waves of being.

9. Love

A warm sun shines over Empedocles' words. Neither an intolerant idealism nor the tragic aspects of existence are allowed to dominate but are held in check and order by the power of clear-eyed *love*, caught in its endless tussle with the forces of strife. Mutability is inescapable but existence is unified, and 'the clarities of the tongue' allow it to be known. Empedocles considers each one of his fellow citizens a harbour. At each one of us, well-laden ships can arrive and unload, only to fill again, depart again and re-encounter all the chance and newness that lies beyond the harbour walls. All of us can take in the wisdom he has to give, which is this: there is strife in a churning world but existence will always carry within it the seeds of its own redemption.

NOTES

I have used Latinized spellings of Greek proper names where they are in common use. In some quotations I have adapted the translations cited in the reference notes.

Introduction: Philosophy has a geography

4 'the attempt to conceive': Bertrand Russell, 'Mysticism and Logic', *Hibbert Journal* (July 1914), reprinted in his *Mysticism and Logic and Other Essays*, George Allen & Unwin, 1917, pp. 1–32 at p. 1

4 'But the greatest': Ibid.

1 Harbour minds

8 All the goods of the world: For the history of the states of Mesopotamia and the Levant in the centuries before and during the period covered by this book, see John Boardman et al. (eds), *The Cambridge Ancient History*, Vol. III, Part 2: *The Assyrian and Babylonian Empires and Other States of the Near East from the Eighth to the Sixth Centuries BC*, 2nd edn, Cambridge University Press, 1991; Cyprian Broodbank, *The Making of the Middle Sea*, Oxford University Press, 2013, pp. 445–592; Jonathan M. Hall, *A History of the Archaic Greek World, ca. 1200–479 BCE*, 2nd edn, Wiley-Blackwell, 2013, pp. 41–59; David W. Tandy, *Warriors into Traders*, University of California Press, 1997, pp. 19–112

8 Where the rest of Europe: See Hall, *A History of the Archaic Greek World*, pp. 41–59

10 Palace and temple ordained: A. Leo Oppenheim, 'The Position of the Intellectual in Mesopotamian Society', *Daedalus*, Vol. 104, No. 2, Wisdom, Revelation, and Doubt: Perspectives on the First Millennium BC (Spring 1975), pp. 37–46 at p. 38

10 The knowledge of writing: Tandy, *Warriors into Traders*, pp. 19–112

10 'the advantage of backwardness': Broodbank, *The Making of the Middle Sea*, p. 466

11 'The unruly Shardana': An inscription by Ramesses II (ruled 1279–1213 BC) on a stele from Tanais. See K. A. Kitchen, *Pharaoh Triumphant: The Life and Times of Ramesses II, King of Egypt*, Aris & Phillips, 1982, pp. 40–1

12 dynamic coastal entrepôts: For the Phoenicians as an invented phenomenon, see Josephine Quinn, *In Search of the Phoenicians*, Princeton University Press, 2018; Sabatino Moscati, *The Phoenicians*, I. B. Tauris, 2001

12 A Phoenician hoard: M. E. Aubet, *The Phoenicians and the West: Politics, Colonies and Trade*, 2nd edn, Cambridge University Press, 2001; Christopher M. Monroe, 'Marginalizing Civilization: The Phoenician Redefinition of Power ca. 1300–800 BCE', in Kristian Kristiansen, Thomas Lindkvist and Janken Myrdal (eds), *Economic Networks and Cultural Ties, from Prehistory to the Early Modern Era*, Cambridge University Press, 2018

12 a 15-acre harbour basin: Ibrahim Noureddine, 'New Light on the Phoenician Harbor at Tyre', *Near Eastern Archaeology*, Vol. 73, Nos. 2–3 (2010), pp. 176–81; N. N. Puckett, 'The Phoenician Trade Network: Tracing a Mediterranean Exchange System', Master's thesis, Texas A&M University, 2012

13 Would the Phoenicians: See Monroe, 'Marginalizing Civilization: The Phoenician Redefinition of Power'; Quinn, *In Search of the Phoenicians*; Moscati, *The Phoenicians*, pp. 60–2 and throughout

13 By about 800 BC: Broodbank, *The Making of the Middle Sea*, pp. 482ff., 506–9. For the house mouse, see p. 495

14 tangled beginnings: For an outline of network theory in the archaic Mediterranean see Diane Harris Cline, 'A Field Map for Untangling the Entangled Sea', *Journal of Eastern Mediterranean Archaeology & Heritage Studies*, Vol. 8, Nos. 3–4 (2020), pp. 226–49

14 'the indicated way': Gregory Vlastos, 'Equality and Justice in Early Greek Cosmologies', *Classical Philology*, July 1947, Vol. 42, No. 3, pp. 156–78 at p. 174. Justice for the early philosophers was one with 'the ineluctable laws of nature herself'

15 When the raft arrived: Pausanias, *Description of Greece* 7.5.5, online at https://www.perseus.tufts.edu/

16 'absolutely Egyptian': Ibid.

17 All animals shrank before him: Aelian, *On Animals* 6.39, online at http://penelope.uchicago.edu/

19 Strength was to be derived: H. A. Shapiro, '"Hêrôs Theos": The Death and Apotheosis of Hercules', *Classical World*, Vol. 77, No. 1 (Sept.–Oct. 1983), pp. 7–18

19 the idea of coinage: E. S. G. Robinson, 'The Date of the Earliest Coins', *Numismatic Chronicle and Journal of the Royal Numismatic Society*, Sixth Series, Vol. 16 (1956), pp. 1–8; Thomas R. Martin,

'Why Did the Greek "Polis" Originally Need Coins?', *Historia: Zeitschrift für Alte Geschichte*, Bd. 45, H. 3 (3rd Qtr, 1996), pp. 257–83

19 'took on board': 'On marvellous things heard', by pseudo-Aristotle, 135, online at penelope.uchicago.edu

20 'Silver King': Herodotus, *Histories* 1.163

20 a merchant explorer: Ibid. 4.152

20 3 million tons: Broodbank, *The Making of the Middle Sea*, p. 515

21 The pollution created: Joseph R. McConnell et al., 'Lead Pollution Recorded in Greenland Ice Indicates European Emissions Tracked Plagues, Wars, and Imperial Expansion during Antiquity', *Proceedings of the National Academy of Sciences of the United States of America*, Vol. 115, No. 22 (29 May 2018), pp. 5726–31; Kevin J. R. Rosman et al., 'Lead from Carthaginian and Roman Spanish Mines Isotopically Identified in Greenland Ice Dated from 600 B.C. to 300 A.D.', *Environ. Sci. Technol.*, Vol. 31, No. 12 (1997), pp. 3413–16; Jack Longman et al., 'Exceptionally High Levels of Lead Pollution in the Balkans from the Early Bronze Age to the Industrial Revolution', *Proceedings of the National Academy of Sciences of the United States of America*, Vol. 115, No. 25 (19 Jun. 2018), pp. E5661–8

22 deep and borrowed roots: Katherine Correa, 'Artemis Ephesia and Sacred Bee Imagery in Ancient Greece', *Symposium*, Vol. 12 (2012), pp. 74–82

22 connects with an earlier object: C. Davaras, 'Μινωικό κηριοφόρο πλοιάριο της Συλλογής Μητσοτάκη', *Archaiologikē Ephēmeris* (1984), pp. 55–93

23 Plato famously compared: Plato, *Phaedo* 109a–b

23 spilling from its jaws: It is still one of the few places where the endangered Mediterranean monk seal survives in any numbers. See https://www.mediterraneanmonkseal.org/

23 a naked satyr: Mando Oeconomides, 'The Human Figure in Archaic Greek Coinage', *Studies in the History of Art*, Vol. 32, Symposium Papers XVI: New Perspectives in Early Greek Art (1991), pp. 272–83

24 Brutal dominance: Sarah P. Morris and John K. Papadopoulos, 'Greek Towers and Slaves: An Archaeology of Exploitation', *American Journal of Archaeology*, Vol. 109, No. 2 (Apr. 2005), pp. 155–225

25 'Without exception': Walter Benjamin, 'On the Concept of History', vii, 1940, written shortly before his suicide when confronted with the prospect of extermination in a Nazi deathcamp. See *Walter Benjamin: 1938–1940*, Vol. 4: *Selected Writings*, ed. H. Eiland and M. W. Jennings, Harvard University Press, 2003, p. 392

27 The number of Athenian slaves: Sara Forsdyke, *Slaves and Slavery in Ancient Greece*, Cambridge University Press, 2021, p. 90

27 Mnason: See Egidia Occhipinti, 'Athenaeus's Sixth Book on Greek and Roman Slavery', *scriptaclassica.org* (2015), p. 121

27 A skilled craftsman: Forsdyke, *Slaves and Slavery in Ancient Greece*, p. 82

27 Slaves came from: David Lewis, 'Near Eastern Slaves in Classical Attica and the Slave Trade with Persian Territories', *Classical Quarterly*, New Series, Vol. 61, No. 1 (May 2011), pp. 91–113

27 The name 'Thratta': Ibid., p. 99

28 'The fragment': Douglas E. Gerber (ed. and trans.), *Greek Iambic Poetry*, Loeb Classical Library, Harvard University Press, 1999, pp. 112–13

29 Timothy Taylor has said: Timothy Taylor, 'Believing the Ancients: Quantitative and Qualitative Dimensions of Slavery and the Slave Trade in Later Prehistoric Eurasia', *World Archaeology*, Vol. 33, No. 1, The Archaeology of Slavery (Jun. 2001), pp. 27–43

29 According to Aristotle: Aristotle, *Nicomachean Ethics* VIII.xi.6–7

29 Where freedom of speech: M. I. Finley, 'Was Greek Civilization Based on Slave Labour?', *Historia: Zeitschrift für Alte Geschichte*, Bd. 8, H. 2 (Apr. 1959), pp. 145–64; Victoria Cuffel, 'The Classical Greek Concept of Slavery', *Journal of the History of Ideas*, Vol. 27, No. 3 (Jul.–Sept. 1966), pp. 323–42; Paul Cartledge, 'Like a Worm i' the Bud? A Heterology of Classical Greek Slavery', *Greece & Rome*, Vol. 40, No. 2 (Oct. 1993), pp. 163–80

29 Philosophy and autocracy: Forsdyke, *Slaves and Slavery in Ancient Greece*, p. 248

29 appear to be half empty: Sarah P. Morris, 'The View from East Greece: Miletus, Samos and Ephesus', in Corinna Riva and Nicolas C. Vella (eds), *Debating Orientalization: Multidisciplinary Approaches to Change in the Ancient Mediterranean*, Equinox, 2006, pp. 66–84

30 more than 26,000: Figures from UNHCR Operational Data Portal: data2.unhcr.org

30 'because the phenomenon': Taylor, 'Believing the Ancients: Quantitative and Qualitative Dimensions of Slavery and the Slave Trade in Later Prehistoric Eurasia', pp. 27–43 at p. 29

32 whose image it bore: Kunsthistorisches Museum Wien, Antikensammlung INV. NO. Antikensammlung, VI 2889

33 'like a star': 'Homeric Hymn to Apollo', in M. L. West, *Homeric Hymns*, Loeb Classical Library, Harvard University Press, 2003, lines 388–442, pp. 100–5

34 Hermes and Hestia: Jean-Pierre Vernant, 'Hestia–Hermès: Sur l'expression religieuse de l'espace et du mouvement chez les Grecs', *L'Homme*, Vol. 3, No. 3 (Sept.–Dec. 1963), pp. 12–50

35 'As a sudden thought': 'Homeric Hymn to Hermes', in West, *Homeric Hymns*, lines 43–6, pp. 116–17

35 'by the sand': Ibid., lines 77–80, pp. 118–19

36 'the divinity of dailiness': Plato, *Cratylus* 401b; Vernant, 'Hestia–Hermès: Sur l'expression religieuse de l'espace et du mouvement chez les Grecs', pp. 12–50; Patricia J. Thompson, 'Dismantling the Master's House: A Hestian/Hermean Deconstruction of Classic Texts', *Hypatia*, Vol. 9, No. 4, Feminist Philosophy of Religion (Autumn 1994), pp. 38–56; Jean Robert, 'Hestia and Hermes: The Greek Imagination of Motion and Space', *International Journal of Illich Studies* (2001), pp. 79–86

36 four independent archaic city states: The cities briefly and apparently not that easily did come together in a federation. See David M. Lewis, 'The Federal Constitution of Keos', *Annual of the British School at Athens*, Vol. 57 (1962), pp. 1–4

37 exploration of the strange: See Jean-Pierre Vernant, *The Origins of Greek Thought*, Cornell University Press, 1982

37 'the crates of lemons': J. Morris, *Trieste*, Faber & Faber, 2001, pp. 15, 30, 32, 56

37 'Here, it is re-assembled': Joseph Roth, *Report from a Parisian Paradise: Essays from France, 1925–1939*, trans. Michael Hofmann, p. 136, quoted in Michael Hofmann, *Messing about in Boats*, Oxford University Press, 2021, p. 106 n. 4

38 'drink *anisette*': Albert Camus, *Lyrical and Critical Essays*, Vintage, 1970, p. 81, 'A short guide to towns without a past'

39 'the tight-lipped little kingdom': A phrase of E. M. Forster's quoted by Philip Mansel, *Levant: Splendour and Catastrophe on the Mediterranean*, John Murray, 2011, p. 142

39 'But don't hurry the journey': Here translated by Edmund Keeley, online at https://www.poetryfoundation.org/; see also C. P. Cavafy, *Complete Poems*, trans. D. Mendelsohn, Harper Press, 2012, pp. 13–14; C. P. Cavafy, *The Collected Poems with Parallel Greek Text*, trans. Evangelos Sachperoglou, ed. Anthony Hirst, Oxford University Press, 2008, p. 367

2 Must I think my own way through the world?

42 'Who are you?': *Odyssey* 1.169–75

42 'polished spear-rack': Ibid. 1.125

43 'down in your heart': Ibid. 1.294

45 Odysseus' fictional homeland: It is frustrating and confusing that Ionia is the name of the Greek province on the eastern side of the Aegean Sea, but the Ionian Sea is the name given to the stretch of water to the west of Greece between Greece and Italy. The etymology is obscure but it may be that the Ionian Sea was

named after those Ionians who left Ionia and sailed westwards to Italy and beyond. Or they may simply be residual names, as 'Ionian' was the name by which all Greeks were known to the people and governors of Egypt and the eastern Mediterranean in the Bronze and Iron Ages. 'Greek' is the Roman name for these people

45 Wherever Homer sang: G. Nagy, 'The Aeolic Component of Homeric Diction', *Proceedings of the 22nd Annual UCLA Indo-European Conference*, ed. S. W. Jamison et al., Los Angeles, CA, 5–6 November 2010, pp. 133–79

46 'a singer at competitive gatherings': Martin West, 'The Homeric Question Today', *Proceedings of the American Philosophical Society*, Vol. 155, No. 4 (Dec. 2011), pp. 383–93 at p. 389

47 '*Odyssey* can't be earlier': Ibid., p. 393

47 these excavated streets: J. M. Cook, 'Old Smyrna, 1948–1951', *Annual of the British School at Athens*, Vol. 53/54 (1958/9), pp. 1–34

49 In a hall house: John Boardman, *Excavations in Chios, 1952–1955: Greek Emporio*, The British School at Athens, Supplementary Volumes, No. 6 (1967), pp. iii–xiv, 1–258

49 the essence of their lives: Cook, 'Old Smyrna, 1948–1951', p. 14

50 a pale and sophisticated city: Ibid., p. 16

52 Most houses had: Ibid., p. 12

52 a description of a city: Ibid.

53 'The curved ships': *Odyssey* 6.3ff., 6.262, 7.39ff.

54 'a man unused': Ibid. 8.158

54 'The gods seldom': Ibid. 8.169–79

55 A Smyrnean called Onomastus: Pausanias, *Description of Greece* 5.7.1, online at https://www.perseus.tufts.edu/

56 found in many Smyrna houses: *Odyssey* 7.98ff.

56 transient things Homer describes: Ibid. 7.345

57 In most of the baths: Cook, 'Old Smyrna, 1948–1951', p. 16

60 easily adapted alphabet: Richard Janko, 'From Gabii and Gordion to Eretria and Methone: The Rise of the Greek Alphabet', *Bulletin of the Institute of Classical Studies*, Vol. 58, No. 1 (Jun. 2015), pp. 1–32 at p. 1

60 A piece of a bronze greave: L. H. Jeffery, 'Old Smyrna: Inscriptions on Sherds and Small Objects', *Annual of the British School at Athens*, Vol. 59 (1964), pp. 39–49 at pp. 40, 42, 45, 47

62 make his presence felt: Ibid., pp. 42, 45

64 Homer sees the young man: *Odyssey* 1.320–4

65 'I have come from heaven': *Iliad* 1.189–210

65 Odysseus thinks of himself: Odysseus as sausage *Odyssey* 20.24–7; his troubled heart 20.5–7; Penelope as nightingale 19.512–34

65 Pondering scenes: Joseph Russo, 'Re-Thinking Homeric Psychology:

Snell, Dodds and their Critics', *Quaderni Urbinati di Cultura Classica*, New Series, Vol. 101, No. 2 (2012), pp. 11–28

66 temple of Athena occupies: In Lindos, Priēnē, Miletus, Notion, Teos, Erythrae, Phocaea, Old Smyrna and others, not to speak of Athens

68 'Just as the mind': *Iliad* 15.75–82

68 'And he sat': *Odyssey* 5.270–5

68 on the shield of Achilles: *Iliad* 18.483–9

70 If he loses concentration: See M. Nielbock, 'Navigation in the Ancient Mediterranean', AstroEDU manuscript no. astroedu1645, online August 2017

71 'in distinguishing shadows': Plato, *Republic* 514

71 practical astronomy: Tomislav Bilić, 'The Myth of Alpheus and Arethusa and Open-Sea Voyages on the Mediterranean – Stellar Navigation in Antiquity', *International Journal of Nautical Archaeology*, Vol. 38, No. 1 (2009), pp. 116–32

72 alive in front of Buchner: G. Buchner and D. Ridgway, *Pithekoussai I: Le necropoli: tombe 1–723 scavate dal 1952–1961*, Monumenti Antichi, Serie Monografica 4, Rome: Bretschneider, 1993

73 She gave me the sherd: See Pietro Monti, 'Homeric Tradition in the Mediterranean Navigation of the Pithekoussans', *Talanta*, Vol. XXX–XXXI (1998–9), pp. 115–33; J. N. Coldstream and G. L. Huxley, 'An Astronomical Graffito from Pithekoussai', *Parole del Passato*, Vol. 288 (1996), pp. 221–4

3 What is existence made of?

74 how those categories meet: Hans Blumenberg, *The Laughter of the Thracian Woman: A Protohistory of Theory*, trans. Spencer Hawkins, New Directions in German Studies, Bloomsbury Academic, 2015

75 His mother was Greek: G. S. Kirk, J. E. Raven and M. Schofield, *The Presocratic Philosophers*, 2nd edn, Cambridge University Press, 1983, p. 77

75 agent and conveyor: André Laks and Glenn W. Most (eds and trans.), *Early Greek Philosophy*, Vol. II: *Beginnings and Early Ionian Thinkers, Pt 1*, Loeb Classical Library, Harvard University Press, 2016, pp. 212–13

76 written a constitution: W. K. C. Guthrie, *A History of Greek Philosophy*, 2 vols, Cambridge University Press, 1962 and 1965, Vol. 1, pp. 45–71; Kirk, Raven and Schofield, *The Presocratic Philosophers*, pp. 74–98; Laks and Most, *Early Greek Philosophy*, Vol. II: *Early Ionian Thinkers, Pt 1*, pp. 212–19, 220–3

76 'What is difficult?': Laks and Most, *Early Greek Philosophy*, Vol. II: *Early Ionian Thinkers, Pt 1*, pp. 226–7

76 'a laughing-stock': Plato, *Theaetetus* 174 b–c; Laks and Most, *Early Greek Philosophy*, Vol. II: *Early Ionian Thinkers, Pt 1*, pp. 218–21

77 'inspecting': Plato, *Symposium* 175 a–b and 220 c–d

77 'The philosopher does not': Plato, *Theaetetus* 173 d–e

78 Cruelty is implicit: Deborah Kamen, 'Sale for the Purpose of Freedom: Slave-Prostitutes and Manumission in Ancient Greece', *Classical Journal*, Vol. 109, No. 3 (Feb.–Mar. 2014), pp. 281–307

79 Cavarero asks: Adriana Cavarero, *In Spite of Plato: A Feminist Rewriting of Ancient Philosophy*, trans. S. Anderlini-D'Onofrio and Aine O'Healy, Cambridge: Polity Press, 1995

80 Northwards lay: Alan M. Greaves, *Miletos: A History*, Routledge, 2002

80 'the ornament of Ionia': Herodotus, *Histories* 5.28; Vanessa B. Gorman, *Miletos, the Ornament of Ionia: History of the City to 400 BCE*, University of Michigan Press, 2001

81 'the entrance of the sea': Ezekiel 26, 27

83 'Javan paid': Ibid. 27.13

83 what is now Ukraine and southern Russia: Nadežda A. Gavriljuk, 'The Graeco-Scythian Slave-Trade in the 6th and 5th Centuries BC', in N. A. Gavriljuk, *Black Sea Studies*, 2003, online at https://antikmuseet.au.dk/fileadmin/www.antikmuseet.au.dk/Pontosfiler/BSS_1/BSS1_08_Gavriljuk.pdf

83 single most valuable commodity: Gorman, *Miletos, the Ornament of Ionia*

84 The idea of making a map: W. Horowitz, 'The Babylonian Map of the World', *Iraq*, Vol. 50 (1988), pp. 147–65; C. Kahn, *Anaximander and the Origins of Greek Cosmology*, New York: Columbia University Press, 1960

84 Homer described the four: Sarah P. Morris, 'The View from East Greece: Miletus, Samos and Ephesus', in Corinna Riva and Nicholas C. Vella (eds), *Debating Orientalization: Multidisciplinary Approaches to Change in the Ancient Mediterranean*, Equinox, 2010; *Odyssey* 17.383–5

87 hill of love: Lana Radloff, '"Placing" a Maritime Territory at Hellenistic Miletus', in Rebecca Döhl and Julian Jansen van Rensburg (eds), *Signs of Place: A Visual Interpretation of Landscape*, Edition Topoi/Exzellenzcluster Topoi der Freien Universität Berlin und der Humboldt-Universität zu Berlin, 2019, pp. 99–120

87 Naukratis: G. Hölbl, 'Funde aus Milet VIII. Die Aegyptiaca vom Aphroditetempel auf dem Zeytintepe', *Archäologischer Anzeiger* (1999), No. 3, pp. 345–71

89 'Aphrodite hear my prayer': Norbert Ehrhardt, Wolfgang Günther and Peter Weiß, 'Funde aus Milet XXVI. Aphrodite-Weihungen mit Ohren-Reliefs aus Oikus', *Archäologischer Anzeiger* (2009), No. 1, pp. 187–203

91 formed a pair with Poseidon: Miroslav Marcovich, 'From Ishtar to Aphrodite', *Journal of Aesthetic Education*, Vol. 30, No. 2, Special Issue: Distinguished Humanities Lectures II (Summer 1996), pp. 43–59

92 The summer salads were made of: Dušanka Kučan, 'Rapport synthétique sur les recherches archéobotaniques dans le sanctuaire d'Héra de l'Île de Samos', *Pallas*, No. 52, Paysage et Alimentation dans le Monde Grec: Les innovations du premier millénaire av. J.C. (2000), pp. 99–108, I–IV

93 'the whole place shadowed with roses': See Sappho, fragment 2, in David A. Campbell (ed. and trans.), *Greek Lyric I: Sappho and Alcaeus*, Loeb Classical Library, Harvard University Press, 1982, pp. 56–7

94 Egyptian mythology: *Odyssey* 11.13

95 with nothing but water: Laks and Most, *Early Greek Philosophy*, Vol. II: *Early Ionian Thinkers, Pt 1*, pp. 230–3, from Aristotle, *Metaphysics*

96 All things, he said: Ibid., pp. 236–7, from Aristotle, *On the Soul*; ibid., pp. 258–61, from Aristotle, *Metaphysics*

99 all needed to come by water: See Greaves, *Miletos: A History*

99 Anaximander was his friend: Laks and Most, *Early Greek Philosophy*, Vol. II: *Early Ionian Thinkers, Pt 1*, pp. 276–7, from Strabo, *Geography*

99 found the colony of Apollonia: Ibid., pp. 276–7, from Aelian, *Historical Miscellany*

99 He was almost certainly a writer: Ibid., pp. 280–1, from Themistius, *Orations*

99 a depiction of the earth: Horowitz, 'The Babylonian Map of the World', pp. 147–65; Laks and Most, *Early Greek Philosophy*, Vol. II: *Early Ionian Thinkers, Pt 1*, pp. 320–1

100 the *apeiron*: Laks and Most, *Early Greek Philosophy*, Vol. II: *Early Ionian Thinkers, Pt 1*, pp. 282–93, from several sources

100 *Peirata*: *Odyssey* 12.162

100 limitless and everlasting reservoir: Laks and Most, *Early Greek Philosophy*, Vol. II: *Early Ionian Thinkers, Pt 1*, pp. 276–7, from Simplicius, *Commentary on Aristotle's On the Heavens*

101 'The source of coming-to-be': Kirk, Raven and Schofield, *The Presocratic Philosophers*, fragment 110, pp. 117–19; Laks and Most, *Early Greek Philosophy*, Vol. II, *Pt 1*, pp. 282–5, from Simplicius, *Commentary on Aristotle's Physics*

101 *kubernaō*: Laks and Most, *Early Greek Philosophy*, Vol. II: *Early Ionian Thinkers, Pt 1*, pp. 288–91, from Aristotle, *Physics*

102 'The Rich': Plutarch, *Moralia*, Vol. IV, fasc. 21, *Quaestiones Graecae* (Αἴτια Ἑλληνικά), 32.298c–d

103 'When the men of influence': Ibid.

103 'At first the Populace': Athenaeus, *Scholars at Dinner* 12.26

104 Thales had thought: Laks and Most, *Early Greek Philosophy*, Vol. II: *Early Ionian Thinkers, Pt 1*, pp. 234–5, from Aristotle, *On the Heavens*

104 'like the drum of a column': Ibid., pp. 284–5, from Hippolytus, *Refutation of All Heresies*; plus ibid., pp. 300–3, from Aëtius and Aristotle, *On the Heavens*

104 'The first living creatures': Aëtius v 19.4; Kirk, Raven and Schofield, *The Presocratic Philosophers*, fragment 133, pp. 140–1; Laks and Most, *Early Greek Philosophy*, Vol. II: *Early Ionian Thinkers, Pt 1*, pp. 308–9

105 'In the beginning': Kirk, Raven and Schofield, *The Presocratic Philosophers*, fragment 134, pp. 140–1; Laks and Most, *Early Greek Philosophy*, Vol. II: *Early Ionian Thinkers, Pt 1*, pp. 308–11, from Pseudo-Plutarch

105 'There arose': Laks and Most, *Early Greek Philosophy*, Vol. II: *Early Ionian Thinkers, Pt 1*, pp. 308–9, from Censorinus, *The Birthday* 4.7; Kirk, Raven and Schofield, *The Presocratic Philosophers*, fragment 135, pp. 140–1

106 An occasional blockage: Laks and Most, *Early Greek Philosophy*, Vol. II: *Early Ionian Thinkers, Pt 1*, pp. 296–9, from Aelian, *Historical Miscellany*

106 those endless worlds: Ibid., pp. 292–3, from Aëtius

107 the self-cycling and recycling world: Ibid., pp. 338–9, from Simplicius, *Commentary on Aristotle's* Physics

107 'Anaximenes of Miletus': Kirk, Raven and Schofield, *The Presocratic Philosophers*, pp. 158–9, from Aëtius 1.3.4

108 Traffic was already rolling: M. L. West, *Early Greek Philosophy and the Orient*, Oxford: Clarendon Press, 1971, pp. 104–5

4 How to be me

109 'is a power': Jean-Pierre Vernant, *Myth and Thought among the Greeks*, trans. J. Lloyd with J. Fort, New York: Zone Books, 2006, p. 366

109 'insubstantial wisp of smoke': Ibid.

110 the woman beside him: Sappho, fragment 31 in David A. Campbell (ed. and trans.), *Greek Lyric I: Sappho and Alcaeus*, Loeb Classical Library, Harvard University Press, 1982, pp. 78–81, from Longinus, *On the Sublime*; see also *Sappho, Poems & Fragments*, 2nd expanded edn, trans. Josephine Balmer, Bloodaxe, 2018

111 'She entered': *Iliad* 14.166–79

111 *ēros angelos imerophōnos*: The word *ēros* here is the genitive of *eär*, meaning 'of spring'. It has nothing to do with *erōs*, the word for 'love' or 'desire'

111 desire-voiced herald of spring: Campbell, *Greek Lyric I: Sappho and Alcaeus*, fragment 136, pp. 152–3

111 'puts the heart': Sappho, fragment 31, lines 8–9, trans. Anne Carson in *If Not, Winter: Fragments of Sappho*, Virago, 2002, pp. 62–3

111 appears in her poems: Campbell, *Greek Lyric I: Sappho and Alcaeus*, fragment 2, pp. 56–7. Found on a potsherd from the third century BC

112 'a grandeur in the beatings of the heart': W. Wordsworth, *The Prelude*, I.414

112 'tongue breaks and thin': Sappho, fragment 31, lines 9–10, trans. Carson in *If Not, Winter*, pp. 62–3

113 Dawn wore golden sandals: Campbell, *Greek Lyric I: Sappho and Alcaeus*, fragment 156, pp. 164–5

113 too high to reach: Ibid., fragment 105a, pp. 130–1

113 'earth is embroidered with its many garlands': Ibid., fragment 168c, pp. 172–3

113 grape hyacinths: Ibid., fragment 105c, pp. 132–3

114 'I want / To remind you': Sappho, fragment 94, trans. Carson in *If Not, Winter*, pp. 185–7; Campbell, *Greek Lyric I: Sappho and Alcaeus*, pp. 116–17

114 'bind your hair with crowns': Sappho, fragment 81, trans. Carson in *If Not, Winter*, p. 157; Campbell, *Greek Lyric I: Sappho and Alcaeus*, pp. 108–9, from Athenaeus, *Scholars at Dinner*

114 'a slender sapling': Campbell, *Greek Lyric I: Sappho and Alcaeus*, fragments 115 and 111, pp. 134–9

115 'May grow rich': This suggestion is borrowed from Pindar 124a, 'A song for the end of a feast', in *The Odes of Pindar*, trans. John Sandys, Loeb Classical Library, Heinemann, 1915, p. 585

116 'Moon has set': Campbell, *Greek Lyric I: Sappho and Alcaeus*, fragment 168B, pp. 170–3; trans. Carson in *If Not, Winter*, p. 343

116 'Now she stands': Campbell, *Greek Lyric I: Sappho and Alcaeus*, fragment 96, pp. 120–1

118 She could be tough-minded: Ibid., fragment 148, pp. 160–1

118 'Black night falls': Ibid., fragment 151, pp. 162–3

118 'bittersweet unmanageable creature': Ibid., fragment 130, pp. 146–7

118 not-singular: Ibid., fragment 1, pp. 52–3; trans. Carson in *If Not, Winter*, pp. 2–3. Others read the text as *poikilothrōn*, to mean 'of the painted throne' or 'dapple-throned', 'throned in all colours'

119 a theatre for the expression: See Oswyn Murray, 'The Culture of the Symposion', in K. A. Raaflaub and Hans van Wees (eds), *A Companion to Archaic Greece*, Wiley-Blackwell, 2009, pp. 508–23

119 'Ye that lie upon': Amos 6.3–7, King James Version

119 'The banquet of them that stretched themselves': J.-M. Dentzer, *Le Motif du banquet couché dans le Proche-Orient et le monde grec du*

VIIIème au IVème siècle avant J-C, Paris/Rome: École Française de Rome, 1982

120 a symposium under way: N. Kaltsas, 'Κλαζομενιακές Σαρκοφάγοι από το Νεκροταφείο της Ακάνθου [Klazomenian sarcophagi from Akanthos]', *Archaiologikon Deltion*, Vol. 51–2 (1996–7), pp. 35–50

120 an eastern scene: Jan Paul Crielaard, 'The Ionians in the Archaic Period: Shifting Identities in a Changing World', in Ton Derks and Nico Roymans (eds), *Ethnic Constructs in Antiquity: The Role of Power and Tradition*, Amsterdam University Press, 2009, pp. 37–84

120 buried in tombs: Inci Delemen, 'An Unplundered Chamber Tomb on Ganos Mountain in Southeastern Thrace', *American Journal of Archaeology*, Vol. 110, No. 2 (Apr. 2006), pp. 251–73

121 celebration of dominance: Leslie Kurke, 'The Politics of ἁβροσύνη in Archaic Greece', *Classical Antiquity*, Vol. 11, No. 1 (Apr. 1992), pp. 91–120

121 Lesbian soldiers: Campbell, *Greek Lyric I: Sappho and Alcaeus*, pp. 206–7, from Strabo, *Geography* 13.2.3

121 'covering the feet with spangled straps': Ibid., pp. 84–5, from Sappho, fragment 39

122 *lydia*: Marian H. Feldman, 'Consuming the East: Near Eastern Luxury Goods in Orientalizing Contexts', in Joan Aruz and Michael Seymour (eds), *Assyria to Iberia: Art and Culture in the Iron Age*, New York: Metropolitan Museum of Art, 2016, pp. 227–33

122 sweetness around them: Athenaeus, *The Deipnosophists* 15.39, online at https://www.perseus.tufts.edu

123 'He stepped out': *Odyssey* 6.130–6

124 'one to health': Athenaeus 2.36, quoted by Murray, 'Culture of the Symposium', p. 516

125 blunt arrowheads were used: François de Callataÿ, 'Did "Dolphins" and Non-Functional Arrowheads Massively Found in and around Olbia, Istros and Apollonia Ever Have a Monetary Function?', online at https://kbr.academia.edu/FrancoisdeCallatay

125 a pre-ordered symposium: Marek Węcowski, 'Wine and the Early History of the Greek Alphabet: Early Greek Vase-Inscriptions and the Symposium' in J. S. Clay, I. Malkin and Y. Z. Tzifopoulos (eds), *Panhellenes at Methone*, Trends in Classics – Supplementary Volumes, Berlin: De Gruyter, 2017, p. 315; L. Dubois, *Inscriptions grecques dialectales d'Olbia du Pont*, Geneva: Droz, 1996, No. 31

125 'He who has written': Dubois, *Inscriptions grecques dialectales d'Olbia du Pont*, p. 74

125 to satisfy their appetites: Plato, *Phaedrus* 241c–d

126 'Bdelycleon': Aristophanes, *The Wasps* lines 1209–15

127 Lovingness: For the so called 'Sarcophagus of the Spouses' see https://www.museoetru.it/en; equivalent Etruscan objects can also be seen in the Louvre, Paris

128 'an island crowned': Douglas E. Gerber (ed. and trans.), *Greek Iambic Poetry*, Loeb Classical Library, Harvard University Press, 1999, pp. 96–7

128 'a thistle with graceful leaves': Meleager in 'The Garland', quoted in Guy Davenport (ed. and trans.), *Carmina Archilochi: The Fragments of Archilochos*, University of California Press, 1964, p. 2

128 'I have no liking for': Gerber, *Greek Iambic Poetry*, pp. 152–3, from Dio Chrysostom, Discourses 33.17

129 'The fox knows many tricks': Ibid., pp. 216–17

129 'O that I might but touch': Ibid., pp. 158–9, here trans. Guy Davenport, in his *7 Greeks*, New York: New Directions, 1995, p. 61

129 'How can I like the way': Willis Barnstone (ed. and trans.), *Sappho and the Greek Lyric Poets*, New York: Schocken Books, 1988, fragment 38, online at http://people.uncw.edu/

129 'His prick swelled up': Gerber, *Greek Iambic Poetry*, pp. 112–13

129 'I do not care for': Archilochus, fragment 22, online at https://sententiaeantiquae.com/, 'Reflections on Tyranny'

130 'I caressed the beauty': Guy Davenport, 'Archilochos: "Epode: Fireworks on the Grass"', *Hudson Review*, Vol. 28, No. 3 (Autumn 1975), pp. 352–6; for a different take on the same poem see Gerber, *Greek Iambic Poetry*, pp. 210–15

130 'Charilaus, son of Erasmon': Gerber, *Greek Iambic Poetry*, pp. 180–1

131 'You have turned your back': Ibid., pp. 186–7

131 'How many times': Davenport, *7 Greeks*, fragment 279, p. 67

131 'Why should the sea be fat': Ibid., fragment 129, p. 47; also Gerber, *Greek Iambic Poetry*, pp. 84–9, where the text is separated into several fragments

132 'In the hospitality of war': Davenport, *7 Greeks*, fragment 184, p. 55

132 'to await Resurrection Day in linen and gold': Davenport, 'Archilochos: "Epode: Fireworks on the Grass"', pp. 352–6

132 sent into exile: Campbell, *Greek Lyric I: Sappho and Alcaeus*, pp. 206–19, for ancient references to the political turmoil in Lesbos

133 'Let's drink!': Ibid., pp. 379–81

133 'a window into men's souls': Ibid., p. 373

133 'his conciseness': Ibid., p. 227, from Dionysius of Halicarnassus, *On Imitation*

133 'a steward of yourself': Ibid., p. 365

133 'rule of the rich': Kurt A. Raaflaub, 'The Newest Sappho and Archaic Greek–Near Eastern Interactions', in Anton Bierl and André Lardinois (eds), *The Newest Sappho: P. Sapph. Obbink and P. GC inv. 105, Frs. 1-4: Studies in Archaic and Classical Greek Song*, Vol. 2, Leiden: Brill, 2016, pp. 127–47

133 For the *tyrannoi* themselves: Greg Anderson, 'Before *Turannoi* Were Tyrants: Rethinking a Chapter of Early Greek History', *Classical Antiquity*, Vol. 24, No. 2 (Oct. 2005), pp. 173–222 at p. 203; Alexander Dale, 'Alcaeus on the Career of Myrsilos: Greeks, Lydians and Luwians at the East Aegean–West Anatolian Interface', *Journal of Hellenic Studies*, Vol. 131 (2011), pp. 15–24 at p. 21

134 'climbing up on': Campbell, *Greek Lyric I: Sappho and Alcaeus*, fragment 6, pp. 238–41

134 '. . . from fathers': Ibid., fragment 6, pp. 240–1

135 One of his poems describes: Ibid., fragment 43, pp. 258–9

135 'As we leave the Peloponnese': Ibid., fragment 34, pp. 246–7, from papyrus at Oxyrhynchus

135 'I cannot understand': Ibid., fragment 208, pp. 321–3

136 '. . . the whole cargo': Ibid., fragment 73, pp. 276–9

136 '. . . the North wind': Ibid., fragment 38B, pp. 252–3

136 'impossible for anybody': Herodotus, *Histories* 4.152

137 'I belong to Aeginetan Apollo': Raaflaub, 'The Newest Sappho and Archaic Greek-Near Eastern Interactions', p. 136

137 A woven web of goods: J. M. Cook, *The Greeks in Ionia and the East*, New York: Praeger, 1963, p. 95; Hermippus, fragment 63 K-A

138 'I would rather see her lovely step': Campbell, *Greek Lyric I: Sappho and Alcaeus*, fragment 16, pp. 66–7

138 'what you passionately desire': Ibid. The word she uses in this poem, *eramai*, does not mean merely to love in an abstract or disembodied way but to desire and lust after, passionately and sexually

139 5 tons of the precious liquids: Elizabeth S. Greene et al., 'Inconspicuous Consumption: The Sixth-Century BCE Shipwreck at Pabuç Burnu, Turkey', *American Journal of Archaeology*, Vol. 112, No. 4 (Oct. 2008), pp. 685–711

139 One large wreck: Rosalba Panvini, *The Archaic Greek Ship at Gela*, trans. Brian E. McConnell, Palermo: Salvatore Sciascia, 2001

140 none reveals more: Ulrike Krotscheck, 'Pointe Lequin 1A: Wine Cups and Economic Networks in the Western Mediterranean', *Ancient West & East*, Vol. 14 (2015), pp. 169–89 at p. 170

140 *pentekonters*: Herodotus, *Histories* 1.163

140 the product of a standardized workshop: Krotscheck, 'Pointe Lequin 1A: Wine Cups and Economic Networks in the Western Mediterranean', p. 172

140 A chemical comparison: Ibid., p. 178

141 It is impossible to know what proportion of marine traffic: Up until 2016, when the survey was discontinued, the US NOAA charted 10,000 submerged wrecks in American coastal waters,

perhaps 0.1 per cent or one in a thousand of the wrecks that are there: https://nauticalcharts.noaa.gov/data/wrecks-and-obstructions. html

142 One lead letter: Esther Eidinow and Claire Taylor, 'Lead-letter Days: Writing, Communication and Crisis in the Ancient Greek World', *Classical Quarterly*, New Series, Vol. 60, No. 1 (May 2010), pp. 30–62 at pp. 55, 57–8

142 written by a merchant from Phocaea: Enric Sanmarti-Grego and Rosa. A. Santiago, 'La lettre grecque d'Emporion et son contexte archéologique', *Revue Archéologique de Narbonnaise*, Vol. 21 (1988), pp. 3–17

143 '[You must take care]': Ibid. for this suggested translation (in French) and their rationale

144 The number of people: There are eight named guests at Plato's symposium

144 One wreck discovered at Kyrenia: H. W. Swiny and M. L. Katzev, 'The Kyrenia Shipwreck: A Fourth-Century BC Greek Merchant Ship', in D. J. Blackman (ed.), *Marine Archaeology*, Colston Papers No. 23, Archon Books, 1973, p. 345

144 The sails did most of the work: G. A. Cariolou, 'Kyrenia II: The Return from Cyprus to Greece of the Replica of a Hellenic Merchant Ship', in S. Swiny et al. (eds), *Res Maritimae: Cyprus and the Eastern Mediterranean from Prehistory to Late Antiquity*, American Schools of Oriental Research, Atlanta: Scholars Press, 1997, pp. 83–97; Justin Leidwanger, 'Modeling Distance with Time in Ancient Mediterranean Seafaring: A GIS Application for the Interpretation of Maritime Connectivity', *Journal of Archaeological Science*, Vol. 40, Issue 8 (August 2013), pp. 3302–8

145 As the cups go quickly round: R. C. Jebb (ed.), *Bacchylides: The Poems and Fragments,* Cambridge University Press, 1905, p. 418

145 'He that is penniless': Pindar 124 to Thrasybulus of Acragas, 'A song for the end of a feast', *The Odes of Pindar*, trans. John Sandys, Loeb Classical Library, Heinemann, 1915, p. 585 (adapted), online at https://ryanfb.github.io/loebolus-data/L056. pdf; a fragment S. T. Coleridge copied into his notebooks at a particularly low moment, Kathleen Coburn, *The Notebooks of Samuel Taylor Coleridge*, Vol. III: 1808–1819, Routledge & Kegan Paul, 1973, p. 3732

147 an archaic Greek vision of heaven on earth: Albert Henrichs, 'Myth Visualized: Dionysos and his Circle in Sixth-Century Attic Vase-Painting', in *Papers on the Amasis Painter and his World*, Malibu: J. Paul Getty Museum, 1987, pp. 92–194

NOTES

5 Is politeness a virtue?

148 He was the first sage: Douglas E. Gerber (ed. and trans.), *Greek Elegiac Poetry from the Seventh to the Fifth Centuries BC*, Loeb Classical Library, Harvard University Press, 1999, pp. 408–25

149 Ionian ideas first began to spread: Ibid., pp. 422–3, from Diogenes Laërtius, *Lives of the Philosophers*

150 a fog of sensuality: See ibid., pp. 418–19, from Athenaeus, *Scholars at Dinner*

150 the story of how a man called Gyges: Herodotus, *Histories* 1.8–12

150 'I will put you behind': Ibid. 1.9

151 'Take your choice': Ibid. 1.11

151 Only the queen: Richard Wenghofer, 'Sexual Promiscuity of Non-Greeks in Herodotus' "Histories"', *Classical World*, Vol. 107, No. 4 (Summer 2014), pp. 515–34

152 'All the daughters': Herodotus, *Histories* 1.93.4

152 'To put the Colophon on it': Strabo, *Geography* 1.14.28

153 'For now the floor is swept clean': Gerber, *Greek Elegiac Poetry*, pp. 412–13 (adapted), from Athenaeus, *Scholars at Dinner*

154 'It is the right thing': See ibid., pp. 412–13, from Athenaeus, *Scholars at Dinner*

154 'those who came before us': Ibid., pp. 412–15, from Athenaeus, *Scholars at Dinner*

154 'There is no good, wholesome use': See ibid.

154 the wellbeing of your peers: Miroslav Marcovich, 'Xenophanes on Drinking-Parties and Olympic Games', *Illinois Classical Studies*, Vol. 3 (1978), pp. 1–26

156 archaeological campaign has been conducted by Donald Haggis: David B. Small, 'The Archaic Polis of Azoria: A Window into Cretan "Polital" Social Structure', *Journal of Mediterranean Archaeology*, Vol. 23, No. 2 (2010), pp. 197–217

157 Azoria is a model of its kind: Ruth Westgate, 'Space and Social Complexity in Greece from the Early Iron Age to the Classical Period', *Hesperia: The Journal of the American School of Classical Studies at Athens*, Vol. 84, No. 1 (Jan.–Mar. 2015), pp. 47–95

157 Social, political and psychological impulses: Rodney D. Fitzsimons, 'Urbanization and the Emergence of the Greek *Polis*: The Case of Azoria, Crete', in Andrew T. Creekmore III and Kevin D. Fisher (eds), *Making Ancient Cities: Space and Place in Early Urban Societies*, New York: Cambridge University Press, 2014, pp. 220–56

160 Azoria is the equivalent in stone: Manolis I. Stefanakis et al., 'Excavations at Azoria, 2003–2004, Part 1: The Archaic Civic Complex', *Hesperia: The Journal of the American School of Classical Studies at Athens*, Vol. 76, No. 2 (Apr.–Jun. 2007), pp. 243–321; Donald C. Haggis et al., 'Excavations in the Archaic Civic

Buildings at Azoria in 2005–2006', *Hesperia: The Journal of the American School of Classical Studies at Athens*, Vol. 80, No. 1 (Jan.–Mar. 2011), pp. 1–70

160 'Most things': André Laks and Glenn Most (eds and trans.), *Early Greek Philosophy*, Vol. III: *Early Ionian Thinkers, Pt 2*, Loeb Classical Library, Harvard University Press, 2016, pp. 20–1, from Diogenes Laërtius

161 'or in the pentathlon': See Gerber, *Greek Elegiac Poetry*, pp. 414–17, from Athenaeus, *Scholars at Dinner*

161 'For those things': See ibid.

161 Xenophanes pointed out: Laks and Most, *Early Greek Philosophy*, Vol. III: *Early Ionian Thinkers, Pt 2*, pp. 28–31; G. S. Kirk, J. E. Raven and M. Schofield, *The Presocratic Philosophers*, 2nd edn, Cambridge University Press, 1983, pp. 168–9. The word for red hair is *purrous*

162 'if cattle or horses': Laks and Most, *Early Greek Philosophy*, Vol. III: *Early Ionian Thinkers, Pt 2*, pp. 30–1; Kirk, Raven and Schofield, *The Presocratic Philosophers*, pp. 168–9

162 'rests always in the same state': Laks and Most, *Early Greek Philosophy*, Vol. III: *Early Ionian Thinkers, Pt 2*, pp. 34–5; Kirk, Raven and Schofield, *The Presocratic Philosophers*, pp. 169–70

162 'All of him sees': Laks and Most, *Early Greek Philosophy*, Vol. III: *Early Ionian Thinkers, Pt 2*, pp. 32–3; Kirk, Raven and Schofield, *The Presocratic Philosophers*, pp. 169–70

162 'Without toil he shapes': Laks and Most, *Early Greek Philosophy*, Vol. III: *Early Ionian Thinkers, Pt 2*, pp. 34–5; Kirk, Raven and Schofield, *The Presocratic Philosophers*, pp. 169–70

162 'No man knows': Laks and Most, *Early Greek Philosophy*, Vol. III: *Early Ionian Thinkers, Pt 2*, pp. 54–5; Kirk, Raven and Schofield, *The Presocratic Philosophers*, p. 179. 'Seeming' can be translated as the equally unreliable 'opinion'

163 'If God had not made yellow honey': Laks and Most, *Early Greek Philosophy*, Vol. III: *Early Ionian Thinkers, Pt 2*, pp. 56–7; Kirk, Raven and Schofield, *The Presocratic Philosophers*, p. 179

163 'purple, red and yellow to the eye': Laks and Most, *Early Greek Philosophy*, Vol. III: *Early Ionian Thinkers, Pt 2*, pp. 48–9; Kirk, Raven and Schofield, *The Presocratic Philosophers*, p. 173

163 What more evidence: Laks and Most, *Early Greek Philosophy*, Vol. III: *Early Ionian Thinkers, Pt 2*, pp. 18–19, from Aristotle, *Rhetoric*

163 They were only ever meant: See John Boardman, *Greek Sculpture: The Archaic Period, a Handbook*, Thames & Hudson, 1978; Josephine Crawley Quinn, 'Herms, Kouroi and the Political Anatomy of Athens', *Greece & Rome*, Second Series, Vol. 54, No. 1 (Apr. 2007), pp. 82–105

164 An unexaggerated fullness of muscle: Larissa Bonfante, 'Nudity as a

Costume in Classical Art', *American Journal of Archaeology*, Vol. 93, No. 4 (Oct. 1989), pp. 543–70

166 They represent human beauty: Evelyn B. Harrison, 'The Dress of the Archaic Greek Korai', *Studies in the History of Art*, Vol. 32, Symposium Papers XVI: New Perspectives in Early Greek Art (1991), pp. 216–39

167 'like poured chocolate sauce': Boardman, *Greek Sculpture: The Archaic Period*, p. 70; Elizabeth P. Baughan, 'Sculpted Symposiasts of Ionia', *American Journal of Archaeology*, Vol. 115, No. 1 (Jan. 2011), pp. 19–53

167 a member of the male elite: Elizabeth P. Baughan, 'Sculpted Symposiasts of Ionia', *American Journal of Archaeology*, Vol. 115, No. 1 (Jan. 2011), pp. 19–53

167 'the fat': Herodotus, *Histories* 5.30, 5.77, 6.91, 7.156

167 'luxury in belly, sides and feet': Plutarch, *Solon* 21.1–4, online at https://www.perseus.tufts.edu

169 'wetting': Strabo, *Geography* 14

169 'These Ionians': Herodotus, *Histories* 1.142

170 Is it not just as likely: C. Doumas, *Wall Paintings of Thera*, trans. A. Doumas, Athens: The Thera Foundation, 1992

171 'For sixty-seven years now': Gerber, *Greek Elegiac Poetry*, p. 422–3, from Diogenes Laërtius; ibid., pp. 58–9 from Athenaeus

171 'While they were still free from': Ibid., pp. 418–19, from Athenaeus, *Scholars at Dinner*

172 found by metal detectors on the acropolis at Notion: Henry S. Kim and John H. Kroll, 'A Hoard of Archaic Coins of Colophon and Unminted Silver (*CH* I.3)', *American Journal of Numismatics*, Vol. 20 (2008), pp. 53–103

173 Characters in ancient Greek comedy: Euelpides in Aristophanes, *The Birds*. He swallows an obol when he trips

174 tucked inside his cheek: Nicholas Cahill and John H. Kroll, 'New Archaic Coin Finds at Sardis', *American Journal of Archaeology*, Vol. 109, No. 4 (Oct. 2005), pp. 589–617

6 Is life a fire?

177 'Come in, the gods are here too': André Laks and Glenn Most (eds and trans.), *Early Greek Philosophy*, Vol. III: *Early Ionian Thinkers, Pt 2*, Loeb Classical Library, Harvard University Press, 2016, pp. 130–1, from Aristotle, *Parts of Animals*, A.5, 645a.17ff.

177 A much later bronze head: Ibid., pp. 126–9, from Diogenes Laërtius

177 'The waste of semen': Jonathan Barnes, *The Presocratic Philosophers*, Routledge, 1982, p. 160

177 'Heraclitus the obscure': See e.g. Laks and Most, *Early Greek*

Philosophy, Vol. III: *Early Ionian Thinkers, Pt 2*, pp. 210–11, from Clement of Alexandria; G. S. Kirk, J. E. Raven and M. Schofield, *The Presocratic Philosophers*, 2nd edn, Cambridge University Press, 1983, p. 183; Cicero, e.g. *De finibus bonorum et malorum* 2.15

177 'The soul wants to be wet': Laks and Most, *Early Greek Philosophy*, Vol. III: *Early Ionian Thinkers, Pt 2*, pp. 190–1, from Clement of Alexandria

177 'A dry soul': Ibid., pp. 190–1, from Stobaeus, *Anthology*

178 He loathed the ancient gods: Ibid., pp. 144–5, from Clement of Alexandria, *Protreptic*; ibid., pp. 148–9, from Hippolytus, *Refutation of All Heresies*

178 He preferred playing knucklebones: Ibid., pp. 124–7, from Diogenes Laërtius

178 renounced it in favour of his brother: Ibid., pp. 124–5, from Diogenes Laërtius

178 Democracy was far from his mind: Ibid., pp. 124–7, from Diogenes Laërtius

178 'It would be a good idea': Ibid., pp. 142–3, from Strabo, *Geography*, and referring to someone called Hermodorus of whom nothing more is known than his name

179 'kindling by measures': Ibid., pp. 178–9; Kirk, Raven and Schofield, *The Presocratic Philosophers*, p. 197

179 'One thing': Laks and Most, *Early Greek Philosophy*, Vol. III: *Early Ionian Thinkers, Pt 2*, pp. 158–9

179 'the tension of incompatibles': Barnes, *The Presocratic Philosophers*, p. 60

179 'being pulled apart it is brought together with itself': Laks and Most, *Early Greek Philosophy*, Vol. III: *Early Ionian Thinkers, Pt 2*, pp. 160–1, from Hippolytus, *Refutation*; Kirk, Raven and Schofield, *The Presocratic Philosophers*, p. 192

180 'Strife is justice': Laks and Most, *Early Greek Philosophy*, Vol. III: *Early Ionian Thinkers, Pt 2*, pp. 166–7, from Origen; Kirk, Raven and Schofield, *The Presocratic Philosophers*, p. 193

180 'falls apart if it is not stirred': Laks and Most, *Early Greek Philosophy*, Vol. III: *Early Ionian Thinkers, Pt 2*, pp. 164–5, from Theophrastus, *On Dizziness*

183 all in a world lit: Friedrich Brein, 'Ear Studs for Greek Ladies', *Anatolian Studies*, Vol. 32 (1982), pp. 89–92

183 It was a city without walls: There is no archaeological evidence for a wall before the fourth century BC even though Herodotus mentions one (I.26) as part of his unlikely story that the Ephesians tied their city walls to the Artemision. M. Kerschner et al., 'Ephesus in archaischer und klassischer Zeit. Die Ausgrabungen in der Siedlung Smyrna', in F. Krinzinger (ed.), *Die Ägäis und das Westliche Mittelmeer. Beziehungen und Wechselwirkungen 8. Bis 5.*

Jh. v. Chr., Vienna: Verlag der österreichischen Akademie der Wissenschaften, 2000, pp. 45–54

184 The Hebrews called it a *saq*: Jerker Blomqvist, review of Rafał Rosół, *Frühe semitische Lehnwörter im Griechischen*, Frankfurt am Main: Peter Lang, 2013, *Bryn Mawr Classical Review 2013.11.54*

184 Grouse, hare, sesame pancakes: Douglas E. Gerber (ed. and trans.), *Greek Iambic Poetry*, Loeb Classical Library, Harvard University Press, 1999, pp. 372–3, in a fragment from Hipponax via Athenaeus, *Scholars at Dinner*

184 *eborboruze*: Ibid., pp. 374–5, from Photios, *Lexicon*

184 'And one of them': Ibid., pp. 112–13, 370–3

185 the grim labour: Alexander Dale, 'A Feast Fit for a Eunuch: Hipponax Frs. 26, 26a, and Martial 3.77', *Phoenix*, Vol. 71, No. 3/4 (Fall–Winter/automne–hiver 2017), pp. 215–29

185 'They set the victim': Gerber, *Greek Iambic Poetry*, pp. 58–9, 448–9

186 Croesus paid for them: M. Kerschner, 'The Lydians and their Ionian and Aiolian Neighbours', in N. D. Cahill (ed.), *Lidyalılar ve Dünyaları/The Lydians and their World*, Istanbul: Yapı Kredi Yayınları, 2010, pp. 247–66

187 a listener to people: F. Sokolowski, 'A New Testimony on the Cult of Artemis of Ephesus', *Harvard Theological Review*, Vol. 58, No. 4 (Oct. 1965), pp. 427–31

188 dressed in women's clothes: Tuna Şare, 'An Archaic Ivory from a Tumulus near Elmali: Cultural Hybridization and a New Anatolian Style', *Journal of the American School of Classical Studies at Athens*, Vol. 79, No. 1 (Jan.–Mar. 2010), pp. 53–78

188 sacrificed to her power: L. R. LiDonnici, 'The Images of Artemis Ephesia and Greco-Roman Worship: A Reconsideration', *Harvard Theological Review*, Vol. 85, No. 4 (Oct. 1992), pp. 389–415

188 preserved in the Artemision: Laks and Most, *Early Greek Philosophy*, Vol. III: *Early Ionian Thinkers, Pt 2*, pp. 130–1, from Diogenes Laërtius

188 'The name of the bow': Ibid., pp. 162–3

188 '*hola kai ouch hola*': Ibid., pp. 160–1, from Pseudo-Aristotle, *On the World*

189 '*Potamoisi toisin autoisin embainousin*': Ibid., pp. 168–9

190 '*Puros te antamoibē ta panta*': Ibid., pp. 178–9, from Plutarch; Kirk, Raven and Schofield, *The Presocratic Philosophers*, p. 197; Cels Veira, 'Heraclitus' Bow Composition', *Classical Quarterly*, New Series, Vol. 63, No. 2 (Dec. 2013), pp. 473–90

190 '*Physis kruptesthai philei*': Laks and Most, *Early Greek Philosophy*, Vol. III: *Early Ionian Thinkers, Pt 2*, pp. 124–7, from Themistius, *Oration*

191 'If one does not expect': Ibid., pp. 156–7, from Clement of Alexandria, *Stromata*

191 point at it with his finger: Aristotle, *Metaphysics*, 1010a1–15
191 'Although *logos*': Laks and Most, *Early Greek Philosophy*, Vol. III:
    Early Ionian Thinkers, Pt 2, pp. 124–5, 138–9, from Sextus
    Empiricus, *Against the Logicians*
192 'God: day dusk': Ibid., pp. 160–1, from Hippolytus, *Refutation*;
    Jonathan Barnes, *Early Greek Philosophy*, Penguin, 1987, p. 52
192 he urged on his compatriots: Laks and Most, *Early Greek
    Philosophy*, Vol. III: *Early Ionian Thinkers, Pt 2*, pp. 146–7;
    Diogenes Laërtius, *Lives of Eminent Philosophers*, ed. R. D. Hicks,
    Loeb Classical Library, Harvard University Press, Book IX, Chapter
    1, Part 12, quoting Diodotus
193 penetrate its depths: M. L. West, *Early Greek Philosophy and the
    Orient*, Oxford: Clarendon Press, 1971, p. 112
193 'Everything goes': F. Nietzsche, *Thus Spoke Zarathustra*, trans. R. J.
    Hollingdale, Penguin, 1961, p. 234 (adapted)
194 'At long last': Michael Allen Gillespie & Tracy B. Strong (eds),
    Nietzsche's New Seas, University of Chicago Press, 1988, p. 6
194 But others: Herodotus, *Histories* 1.169
195 large numbers of Greeks: Gisela M. A. Richter, 'Greeks in
    Persia', *American Journal of Archaeology*, Vol. 50, No. 1 (Jan.–Mar.
    1946), pp. 15–30 at p. 28
196 The Greek physician Democedes was so admired: John Boardman
    et al. (eds), *The Cambridge Ancient History*, Vol. IV: *Persia, Greece
    and the Western Mediterranean, c. 525 to 479 BC*, 2nd edn,
    Cambridge University Press, 1988, pp. 205–8
196 The Indian laughed and asked: E. H. Gifford, *Eusebius of Caesarea:
    Preparation for the Gospel*, Oxford: Clarendon Press, 1903, Book 11
196 castrated for the job: Jan N. Bremmer, 'Priestly Personnel of the
    Ephesian Artemision: Anatolian, Persian, Greek and Roman
    Aspects', online at http://www.rug.nl/research/portal
196 Heraclitus refused: Laks and Most, *Early Greek Philosophy*, Vol. III:
    Early Ionian Thinkers, Pt 2, pp. 126–7; Diogenes Laërtius, *Lives of
    Eminent Philosophers*, ed. Hicks, Book IX, Chapter 1, Parts 13–14
197 recognized under the name of Zeus the Lawgiver: Even though
    Herodotus was clear that the Persians were not interested in anthro-
    pomorphic gods like the Greeks'. See Herodotus, *Histories* 1.131
197 the choice between good and bad: West, *Early Greek Philosophy
    and the Orient*; M. L. West, *The Hymns of Zoroaster*, Bloomsbury
    Academic, 2010
198 yet another symptom of luxury: See Jacques Duchesne-Guillemin,
    'Heraclitus and Iran', *History of Religions*, Vol. 3, No. 1 (Summer
    1963), pp. 34–49; for a Jewish connection see James Barr, 'The
    Question of Religious Influence: The Case of Zoroastrianism,
    Judaism, and Christianity', *Journal of the American Academy of
    Religion*, Vol. 53, No. 2 (Jun. 1985), pp. 201–35

198 righteousness emerged from the flames: West, *The Hymns of Zoroaster*, pp. 165–202

198 it was in fire itself: Ibid.

198 'The parts of the world': West, *Early Greek Philosophy and the Orient*, pp. 30–2

199 'Fraigneau: There must be': Jean Cocteau and André Fraigneau, *Entretiens: Jean Cocteau et André Fraigneau*, ed. Jean-Paul Bertrand, Monaco: Editions du Rocher, 1988, pp. 80–1. The interviews were broadcast from 26 January to 28 March 1951. See also Nick Laird, 'Property', *New Yorker*, 20 May 2022

7 Is the world full of souls?

202 difficult to extract: See the introduction to Pythagoras' teachings in G. S. Kirk, J. E. Raven and M. Schofield, *The Presocratic Philosophers*, 2nd edn, Cambridge University Press, 1983, pp. 222–8; André Laks and Glenn W. Most (eds and trans), *Early Greek Philosophy*, Vol. IV: *Western Greek Thinkers, Pt 1*, Loeb Classical Library, Harvard University Press, 2016, pp. 40–1, from Iamblichus; and Walter Burkert, *Lore and Science in Ancient Pythagoreanism*, trans. Edwin L. Minar, Harvard University Press, 1972

203 you would have thought him a wizard: https://www.perseus.tufts. edu/: reference to the verb used by Antiphon the fifth-century Athenian sophist, Speeches 226.8

203 'The Man': Laks and Most, *Early Greek Philosophy*, Vol. IV: *Western Greek Thinkers, Pt 1*, pp. 66–7, from Iamblichus, *Life of Pythagoras*

203 'persuading them': Plato, *Republic* II.364

204 heir to all the interminglings: Laks and Most, *Early Greek Philosophy*, Vol. IV: *Western Greek Thinkers, Pt 1*, pp. 14–15, 22–3, from Diogenes Laërtius and Porphyry; Burkert, *Lore and Science in Ancient Pythagoreanism*, p. 111 n. 12

204 learned on his travels: Laks and Most, *Early Greek Philosophy*, Vol. IV: *Western Greek Thinkers, Pt 1*, pp. 24–9; Burkert, *Lore and Science in Ancient Pythagoreanism*, p. 112

205 flowers brought in from Egypt: David A. Campbell (ed. and trans.), *Greek Lyric II: Anacreon, Anacreonta*, Loeb Classical Library, Harvard University Press, 1988, pp. 136–7

205 'filled with the excited gaze': Ibid., pp. 130–1

205 'thighs twined around thighs': Ibid., pp. 108–9

205 'with hips swaying': Ibid., pp. 118–19

205 on into the night: Ibid., pp. 142–3

205 'O boy with the girlish glance': Ibid., pp. 58–9

205 'Because they are my gods': Ibid., pp. 28–9

205 'So you too, Polycrates': See G. Nagy, 'Polycrates and his Patronage

NOTES

of Two Lyric Masters, Anacreon and Ibycus', presented at Princeton symposium on 'The Lyric Age in Greece', September 2017, online at https://classical-inquiries.chs.harvard.edu/

206 consider exercising tyranny himself?: Laks and Most, *Early Greek Philosophy*, Vol. IV: *Western Greek Thinkers, Pt 1*, pp. 28–9; see Burkert, *Lore and Science in Ancient Pythagoreanism*, pp. 110, 119

206 'slaves to their belly and lovers of luxury': Diodorus Siculus, *Library of History* 8.18.1

208 dance tunes on their trumpets: For ancient accounts of the Sybarites, see: Strabo, *Geography* 6.1.13; Diodorus Siculus, *Library of History* 12.9.2; Herodotus, *Histories* 5.44; Claudius Aelianus, *His Various History* 9.24; and Athenaeus, *Scholars at Dinner* 12.58

208 'like the skeleton': Plato, *Critias* 111b

209 timber of the forests in the hills above: Greta Balzanelli and Maria Rosaria Luberto, 'Kroton in the Archaic Period', in *SAIA: Annuario della Scuola Archeologica di Atene e delle Missioni Italiane in Oriente, Supplemento 3, 2019*, pp. 301–21

209 'tossed . . . restlessly up': Kirk, Raven and Schofield, *The Presocratic Philosophers*, p. 163

209 for generation after generation: Balzanelli and Luberto, 'Kroton in the Archaic Period', pp. 301–21

210 Kroton to the Greek world: Pausanias, *Description of Greece* 6.14.5, online at https://www.theoi.com/Text/Pausanias6A.html

211 bound by rules they were not allowed to divulge: Laks and Most, *Early Greek Philosophy*, Vol. IV: *Western Greek Thinkers, Pt 1*, pp. 66–8, from Porphyry and Isocrates

211 'wrote to their relatives': Ibid., pp. 32–3

211 'One ought to sacrifice': Diogenes Laërtius, *Life of Pythagoras* VI

212 Persephone, queen of the underworld: Laks and Most, *Early Greek Philosophy*, Vol. IV: *Western Greek Thinkers, Pt 1*, pp. 54–5, from Diogenes Laërtius

212 'He built a little underground room': Ibid., pp. 46–7, from Diogenes Laërtius quoting Hermippus

212 Walter Burkert saw echoes: Burkert, *Lore and Science in Ancient Pythagoreanism*, p. 159

213 'Hesiod's soul': Laks and Most, *Early Greek Philosophy*, Vol. IV: *Western Greek Thinkers, Pt 1*, pp. 44–5, from Diogenes Laërtius

214 All property was held in common: Ibid., pp. 58–9, from Diogenes Laërtius

214 there was no rationale behind them: Ibid., pp. 122–3, from Diogenes Laërtius

214 he killed a poisonous snake: Ibid., pp. 48–51, from Aristotle in Apollonius, *Wonders*; Kirk, Raven and Schofield, *The Presocratic Philosophers*, pp. 228–9

215 lord of all the lifeless dead: *Odyssey* 11.488

215 cult of Orpheus: Laks and Most, *Early Greek Philosophy*, Vol. IV: *Western Greek Thinkers, Pt 1*, pp. 24–5, for Pythagoras' original instruction in the ways of Orpheus

216 In the Dionysiac mysteries: M. P. Nilsson, *The Dionysiac Mysteries of the Hellenistic and Roman Age*, Lund: Gleerup, 1957, pp. 21–37; Walter Burkert, *Ancient Mystery Cults*, Harvard University Press, 1987, pp. 9–10

216 'she knows her share of the beautiful': In *Supplementum Epigraphicum Graecum*, 17.503 (an annual collection of newly published or discussed Greek inscriptions, online at https://scholarlyeditions.brill.com/)

217 'At first there was wandering': Plutarch in Stobaeus, *Anthology* 4.52.49, quoted in Yulia Ustinova, 'To Live in Joy and Die with Hope: Experiential Aspects of Ancient Greek Mystery Rites', *Bulletin of the Institute of Classical Studies*, Vol. 56, No. 2, Ancient History Issue (2013), pp. 105–23

217 'During altered states of consciousness': Ustinova, 'To Live in Joy and Die with Hope: Experiential Aspects of Ancient Greek Mystery Rites', pp. 105–23

219 'is a spring on the right side': Fritz Graf and Sarah Iles Johnston, *Ritual Texts for the Afterlife: Orpheus and the Bacchic Gold Tablets*, 2nd edn, Routledge, 2013, p. 5

220 the claims he made: Laks and Most, *Early Greek Philosophy*, Vol. IV: *Western Greek Thinkers, Pt 1*, pp. 40–5, from Diogenes Laërtius and Porphyry

220 'They say that once': Kirk, Raven and Schofield, *The Presocratic Philosophers*, p. 219; Douglas E. Gerber (ed. and trans.), *Greek Elegiac Poetry from the Seventh to the Fifth Centuries BC*, Loeb Classical Library, Harvard University Press, 1999, pp. 422–3, from Diogenes Laërtius

221 could one escape the endless return?: Laks and Most, *Early Greek Philosophy*, Vol. IV: *Western Greek Thinkers, Pt 1*, pp. 102–3, from Porphyry

221 'a power that was much better for developing strength': Ibid., pp. 62–3, from Porphyry, *Life of Pythagoras*

221 part of their system of belief: Ibid.

221 'daily praise of virtue': Burkert, *Lore and Science in Ancient Pythagoreanism*, p. 116

221 'hear the harmony': Laks and Most, *Early Greek Philosophy*, Vol. IV: *Western Greek Thinkers, Pt 1*, pp. 38–9, from Porphyry, claiming to quote Empedocles

222 'The *tetraktys*': Ibid., pp. 118–19, from Iamblichus

222 'Past and present': Burkert, *Lore and Science in Ancient Pythagoreanism*, p. 136

223 five years of silent discipline: Ibid., p. 115; Laks and Most, *Early*

Greek Philosophy, Vol. IV: *Western Greek Thinkers, Pt 1*, pp. 68–9, from Diogenes Laërtius

223 must have looked reassuring: Burkert, *Lore and Science in Ancient Pythagoreanism*, p. 482

224 parading in a pair of pure white shoes to celebrate his victory: His Nikē trainers. Diodorus Siculus, *Library of History* 12.9.6

224 'Once, when he was travelling': Strabo, *Geography* 6.12

224 populist movement against the self-serving, self-satisfied elite: Laks and Most, *Early Greek Philosophy*, Vol. IV: *Western Greek Thinkers, Pt 1*, pp. 54–5, from Iamblichus. Pythagoreans avoided friendship with non-Pythagoreans

224 expelled to Metapontum: Ibid., pp. 50–3, from Diogenes Laërtius; ibid., pp. 82–3, from Iamblichus. Different accounts survive of his death: starving himself when exiled or killed by his enemies who caught him after he would not enter a field of beans

224 soothed by the music he made: Aldo Brancacci, 'The Origins of the Reflection on Music in Greek Archaic Poetry', *Revue de Philosophie Ancienne*, Vol. 34, No. 1 (2016), pp. 3–36

225 power of the Pythagorean elite was broken: Balzanelli and Luberto, 'Kroton in the Archaic Period', pp. 301–21

226 made of a tortoiseshell: From a fragmentary poem by the Hellenistic poet Phanocles, *Erotēs h Kaloi*, quoted in Sarah Burges Watson, 'Orpheus' Erotic Mysteries: Plato, Pederasty and the Zagreus Myth in Phanocles', *Bulletin of the Institute of Classical Studies*, Vol. 57, No. 2 (Dec. 2014), pp. 47–71

227 unknown white cypress: Tonio Hölscher, *Der Taucher von Paestum: Jugend, Eros und das Meer im antiken Griechenland*, Stuttgart: Klett-Cotta Verlag, 2021, comes to the firm view that the image of the diver is not symbolic but a depiction of everyday life in Poseidonia

228 Is the Orphic dream somehow there, *within* the fire?: It is the question that has entranced our culture, whenever it has raised its eyes beyond the material. See the great poem by Gerard Manley Hopkins, 'That Nature is a Heraclitean Fire and of the Comfort of the Resurrection': on the one hand, 'Million-fuelèd, nature's bonfire burns on / . . . Is any of [Man] at all so stark / But vastness blurs and time beats level . . . / [and] World's wildfire leave but ash': the hope of the Resurrection, which for the priest-poet Hopkins is the Christian descendant of the Orphic mystery, brings 'A beacon, an eternal beam' in the light of which mutability fades and humanity – 'This Jack, joke, poor potsherd, patch, matchwood' – becomes 'immortal diamond, / Is immortal diamond'

8 Can I live in multiple realities?

231 'not in round freight-ships but in fifty-oared vessels': Herodotus, *Histories* 1.163

232 'in preparation for collective exile': Ibid. 1.164

232 What was a harbour compared to a people?: See the remark of Thucydides' Nikias (7.77.7), 'Men *are* the polis', in P. A. Cartledge, 'The Peculiar Position of Sparta in the Development of the Greek City-State', *Proceedings of the Royal Irish Academy: Archaeology, Culture, History, Literature*, Vol. 80C (1980), pp. 91–108 at p. 92

232 slaughtered every one of them: Herodotus, *Histories* 1.165

232 a beam of about 14 or 15 feet: The Gela wreck is 15m × 4.5m: Rosalba Panvini, *The Archaic Greek Ship at Gela*, trans. Brian E. McConnell, Palermo: Salvatore Sciascia, 2001

234 Half that could be expected for daylight sailing alone: Lionel Casson, 'Speed under Sail of Ancient Ships', *Transactions and Proceedings of the American Philological Association*, Vol. 82 (1951), pp. 136–48

234 his years of trouble: *Odyssey* 9.82

235 'When you round Cape Malea': Strabo, *Geography* 8.6.20

235 harbour cities of the western Mediterranean: Herodotus, *Histories* 1.166

236 to become Elea: Ibid. 1.167

237 Misenum on the bay of Naples: Tombstone in *L'Année Épigraphique*, Paris: Presses Universitaires de France, 1978, p. 257, and 1998, 399; see Lloyd Hopkins, 'Fleets and Manpower on Land and Sea: The Italian *Classes* and the Roman Empire 31 BC–AD 193', PhD thesis, University of Oxford, 2014

237 'a retired, healthy, and pretty spot': Horace, Epistle 1.15, online at https://www.poetryintranslation.com/; Cicero, *Letters to his Friends*, VII.20, to Gaius Trebatius, online at https://topostext.org/work/136

238 as far as Taras and Kroton: Herodotus, *Histories* 3.125

239 Athens a foreign country: E. Miranda, 'Nuove iscrizioni sacre di Velia', *Mélanges de l'École Française de Rome*, Vol. 94, No. 1 (1982), pp. 163–74

239 *Greek* Athena, *Greek* Zeus: Giovanna Greco, 'Elea/Velia: Lo spazio del sacro e le evidenze di culti e rituali', *Empúries*, Vol. 56 (2009–2011), pp. 101–22

240 spoke Greek rather than Latin to arriving travellers: V. Nutton, 'Velia and the School of Salerno', *Medical History*, Vol. 15, No. 1 (Jan. 1971), pp. 1–11, online at cambridge.org

241 'an official narrative': D. M. Spitzer, 'Broken Light on the Ground of Home: Non-Being and Diasporic Trauma in the Parmenidean Poem', *Diacritics*, Vol. 48, No. 1 (2020), pp. 108–26

241 'he beautified': André Laks and Glenn W. Most (eds and trans.),

Early Greek Philosophy, Vol. V: *Western Greek Thinkers, Pt 2*, Loeb Classical Library, Harvard University Press, 2016, pp. 28–9, from Plutarch, *Against Colotes*

241 Body and soul could both be cured there: Nutton, 'Velia and the School of Salerno', pp. 1–11

242 his beloved boy: Laks and Most, *Early Greek Philosophy*, Vol. V: *Western Greek Thinkers, Pt 2*, pp. 22–5, from Plato, *Parmenides* 127b and others

242 perhaps in June 450: In Plato, *Parmenides* 127a–c; Laks and Most, *Early Greek Philosophy*, Vol. V: *Western Greek Thinkers, Pt 2*, pp. 16–17

242 clustering for wisdom: Plato, *Phaedo* 109b

242 *On Being* or *On Nature*: Laks and Most, *Early Greek Philosophy*, Vol. V: *Western Greek Thinkers, Pt 2*, pp. 30–101

243 abstract and immovable: Ibid., pp. 18–19, from Aristotle, *Metaphysics*; for Xenophanes' God see André Laks and Glenn Most, *Early Greek Philosophy*, Vol. III: *Early Ionian Thinkers, Pt 2*, Loeb Classical Library, Harvard University Press, 2016, pp. 34–5; G. S. Kirk, J. E. Raven and M. Schofield, *The Presocratic Philosophers*, 2nd edn, Cambridge University Press, 1983, pp. 169–70

243 in the light of the everyday: For the tradition that Parmenides followed the Pythagoreans see Laks and Most, *Early Greek Philosophy*, Vol. V: *Western Greek Thinkers, Pt 2*, pp. 20–3, from Diogenes Laërtius and Strabo

244 This is no calm and rational introduction: Ibid., pp. 32–3

244 the goddess of truth and understanding: Ibid., pp. 34–5

245 'Come now, I shall tell you': Ibid., pp. 38–9

246 What-is-thought *is* what-is: Ibid., pp. 42–3

247 'By thinking': Kirk, Raven and Schofield, *The Presocratic Philosophers*, p. 262, from Simplicius

247 '. . . what-is is unborn': Laks and Most, *Early Greek Philosophy*, Vol. V: *Western Greek Thinkers, Pt 2*, pp. 42–3

248 knowledge of an unchanging, eternal idea: Plato, *Republic* 597a

248 'Birth has been extinguished': For this impenetrably difficult text see Laks and Most, *Early Greek Philosophy*, Vol. V: *Western Greek Thinkers, Pt 2*, pp. 46–7; also Robin Waterfield, *The First Philosophers*, Oxford University Press, 2000, p. 60; and Jonathan Barnes, *Early Greek Philosophy*, Penguin, 1987, p. 83 (I have adapted the text to make use of all three of these translations)

249 'Everything is one to me': Laks and Most, *Early Greek Philosophy*, Vol. V: *Western Greek Thinkers, Pt 2*, pp. 36–7

249 'borne along deaf and blind': Ibid., pp. 40–1; also Waterfield, *The First Philosophers*, p. 58; Barnes, *Early Greek Philosophy*, p. 81 (again I have used all three translations)

250 path to truth and understanding: Ibid., pp. 42–3

250 'horseness': From Diogenes Laërtius, quoted in Kojin Karatani, *Isonomia*, Durham, NC: Duke University Press, 2017, pp. 36–7. Other Cynic philosophers, when faced with Zeno's paradox about the impossibility of movement, stood up and walked away

250 'is one and immobile': Laks and Most, *Early Greek Philosophy*, Vol. V: *Western Greek Thinkers, Pt 2*, pp. 126–7, from Aristotle, *On Generation and Corruption*

250 'He was not unaware': Simplicius, *On Aristotle, On the Heavens* 559–60

251 'Parmenides abolishes everything': Laks and Most, *Early Greek Philosophy*, Vol. V: *Western Greek Thinkers, Pt 2*, pp. 136–7, from Plutarch, *Against Colotes*

251 'Here I end': Ibid., pp. 50–1; Barnes, *Early Greek Philosophy*, p. 85

251 'The unshaken heart of well-rounded truth': Laks and Most, *Early Greek Philosophy*, Vol. V: *Western Greek Thinkers, Pt 2*, pp. 336–7; Kirk, Raven and Schofield, *The Presocratic Philosophers*, p. 243

251 'the wandering works of the round-eyed moon': Laks and Most, *Early Greek Philosophy*, Vol. V: *Western Greek Thinkers, Pt 2*, pp. 66–7

251 preserved in such fragmentary form that little more can be said of his system: For fragments from the second half of the poem see ibid., pp. 50–87; Kirk, Raven and Schofield, *The Presocratic Philosophers*, pp. 254–62

252 The two forms of reality: John Palmer, 'Parmenides', in Edward N. Zalta (ed.), *The Stanford Encyclopedia of Philosophy* (Winter 2020), online at https://plato.stanford.edu/

252 The conceptual world and the sensuous world: Palmer revived an answer that was already at least suggested in antiquity. Laks and Most, *Early Greek Philosophy*, Vol. V: *Western Greek Thinkers, Pt 2*, pp. 216–17, from Aristotle, *Sophistic Refutations*

254 'was a gallant man': Ibid., pp. 164–5; Diogenes Laërtius, IX.28

254 whether to make his arguments public: Plato, *Parmenides* 128d7–e1

255 'We are told that': Laks and Most, *Early Greek Philosophy*, Vol. V: *Western Greek Thinkers, Pt 2*, pp. 170–1; Diogenes Laërtius IX.28

255 'Many men had mocked Parmenides': Jonathan Barnes, *The Presocratic Philosophers*, Routledge, 1982, p. 236

256 enough to feed sixty families for a year: Laks and Most, *Early Greek Philosophy*, Vol. V: *Western Greek Thinkers, Pt 2*, pp. 164–5; Plato, *Alcibiades* 119a.3–6; *Parmenides* 126b–c; Michael Vickers, 'Golden Greece: Relative Values, Minae, and Temple Inventories', *American Journal of Archaeology*, Vol. 94, No. 4 (Oct. 1990), pp. 613–25

257 never be overtaken by the fastest: Laks and Most, *Early Greek*

Philosophy, Vol. V: *Western Greek Thinkers, Pt 2*, pp. 184–7, from Aristotle's *Physics*

257 an arrow in flight never moves: Ibid., pp. 186–9, from Aristotle's *Physics*. The paradox depends on the idea that time exists in moments. At any one moment the arrow can only be where it is. It cannot half be somewhere. But if time is continuous, indivisible and single, and hours, minutes and seconds are merely accounting conveniences, the arrow can of course fly. This was Aristotle's refutation, *Physics* 6.9 239b, Laks and Most, *Early Greek Philosophy*, Vol. V: *Western Greek Thinkers, Pt 2*, pp. 210–11

257 the things of which the world is made must be infinitely small: Laks and Most, *Early Greek Philosophy*, Vol. V: *Western Greek Thinkers, Pt 2*, pp. 176–7, from Simplicius, *Commentary on Aristotle's* Physics

257 the infinitely small can have no existence: Ibid., pp. 176–9, from Simplicius, *Commentary on Aristotle's* Physics

258 existence can only be a single vast immobile thing: Ibid.

258 'What you've said': Ibid., pp. 192–3, from Plato, *Parmenides* 128a6–b6

258 'against those who say': Ibid., pp. 190–5, from Plato, *Parmenides* 128c6–d6

258 'a god of refutation': Plato, *Sophist* 216a–b

258 'a controversialist and paradox-monger': See John Palmer, 'Zeno', in Edward N. Zalta (ed.), *The Stanford Encyclopedia of Philosophy* (Winter 2020), online at https://plato.stanford.edu/

259 'discoursing on nature': Laks and Most, *Early Greek Philosophy*, Vol. V: *Western Greek Thinkers, Pt 2*, pp. 196–7, from Plutarch, *Pericles* 4.5

259 a recognition that the answers are not to be had: 'To be a philosopher you need only three things. First, infinite intellectual eros: endless curiosity about everything. Second, the ability to pay attention: to be rapt by what is in front of you without seizing it yourself, the care of concentration . . . Third, acceptance of pathlessness (*aporia*): that there may be no solutions to questions, only the clarification of their statement.' Gillian Rose, *Paradiso*, 2nd edn, Swindon: Shearsman Books, 2015, p. 45 (with thanks to Tim Dee for alerting me to this wonderful paragraph)

9 Does love rule the universe?

261 The colonists made the harbour: J. W. Hanson and S. G. Ortman, 'A Systematic Method for Estimating the Populations of Greek and Roman Settlements, online at https://www.colorado.edu/

262 its assertive Greekness: Gianfranco Adornato, 'Phalaris: Literary Myth or Historical Reality? Reassessing Archaic Acragas', *American Journal of Archaeology*, Vol. 116, No. 3 (Jul. 2012), pp. 483–506

262 'But how will you react': Lucian, *Phalaris* I, online at http://www.perseus.tufts.edu/

263 thrown off the cliffs: Diodorus Siculus, *Library of History* 9.19.1, online at https://penelope.uchicago.edu/

264 'he was conducted': Ibid., 13.82.7, online at https://penelope.uchicago.edu/

264 'who had several apartments': Ibid., 13.83, online at https://penelope.uchicago.edu/

264 'Tellias was quite plain': Ibid.

265 'more than eight hundred': Ibid., 13.84, online at https://penelope.uchicago.edu/

265 'they became so wild': Sean Corner, 'Transcendent Drinking: The Symposium at Sea Reconsidered', *Classical Quarterly*, Vol. 60, No. 2 (2010), pp. 352–80

266 too comfortable: Diodorus Siculus, *Library of History* 13.84.5, online at https://penelope.uchicago.edu/

267 a sense of grandeur: Ibid., 13.81.1, online at https://penelope.uchicago.edu/

267 'with a multitude of fish': Alfred Burns, 'Ancient Greek Water Supply and City Planning: A Study of Syracuse and Acragas', *Technology and Culture*, Vol. 15, No. 3 (Jul. 1974), pp. 389–412; Diodorus Siculus, *Library of History* 11.25.3-5, online at https://penelope.uchicago.edu/

267 pollution from the streets: Aristotle, *Politics* 7.1330

268 slaves enough to carry it: Burns, 'Ancient Greek Water Supply and City Planning: A Study of Syracuse and Acragas', pp. 389–412

269 entirely Egyptian: Diodorus Siculus, *Library of History* 13.82, online at https://penelope.uchicago.edu/

270 slaves could be used: Maria Pavlou, 'Pindar Olympian 3: Mapping Acragas on the Periphery of the Earth', *Classical Quarterly*, New Series, Vol. 60, No. 2 (Dec. 2010), pp. 313–26

271 'reached across the sea': Pindar, *Olympian 3* composed for Theron of Acragas after his victory in the Chariot Race, 476 BC, online at http://www.perseus.tufts.edu/; Pavlou, 'Pindar Olympian 3: Mapping Acragas on the Periphery of the Earth', pp. 313–26

274 *peripteron*: Tapio Prokkola, *The Optical Corrections of the Doric Temple*, privately published, 2011; Vincent Scully, *The Earth, the Temple, and the Gods: Greek Sacred Architecture*, Yale University Press, 1962, rev. edn 1979

274 Not that there is anything light: Tapio Prokkola, *The Optical Corrections of the Doric Temple*, privately published, 2011; Vincent Scully, *The Earth, the Temple, and the Gods: Greek Sacred Architecture*, Yale University Press, 1962, rev. edn 1979

275 'Stand near': Douglas E. Gerber (ed. and trans.), *Greek Elegiac Poetry from the Seventh to the Fifth Centuries BC*, Loeb Classical

Library, Harvard University Press, 1999, p. 56; quoted Prokkola, *The Optical Corrections of the Doric Temple*, p. 52. Tyrtaios is following closely on a passage from the *Iliad*: 'locking spear by spear, shield against shield at the base, so buckler / leaned on buckler, helmet on helmet, man against man, and the horse-hair crests along the horns of their shining helmets / touched as they bent their heads, so dense were they formed on each other …' – *Iliad* 13.130–3, trans. Richmond Lattimore

275 an image of justice: Prokkola, *The Optical Corrections of the Doric Temple*, p. 186

275 'the ultimate manifestation': Ibid., p. 27

276 finely graded grey bands: Ibid., pp. 194–5

276 'Living on the high acropolis': André Laks and Glenn W. Most (eds and trans.), *Early Greek Philosophy, Vol. V: Western Greek Thinkers, Pt 2*, Loeb Classical Library, Harvard University Press, 2016, pp. 362–3

277 The people of Acragas treated him: Ibid., pp. 347–8

277 'For you I am an immortal': Ibid., pp. 362–3

277 bogus theatricality: Ibid., pp. 348–9

278 'belonged not only to the Rich': Ibid., pp. 346–7

278 'as though I were': Ibid., pp. 364–5

278 prohibition on bay leaves: Ibid., pp. 380–1

278 'both a youth and girl': Ibid., pp. 370–1

278 'a man, knowledgeable beyond': Ibid., pp. 384–5

279 'Happy he who possesses': Ibid., pp. 366–7

279 'Narrow are the resources': Ibid., pp. 386–9

279 'human intelligence': Ibid., pp. 388–9

280 'clarities of the tongue': Ibid., pp. 390–3

280 earth, water, air and fire: Suggestions of the same kind had been made by the philosophers in Miletus

280 'unborn': Laks and Most, *Early Greek Philosophy*, Vol. V: *Western Greek Thinkers*, Pt 2, pp. 400–1

280 nothing ever actually dies: Ibid., pp. 396–7

281 'Aphrodite is not only Aphrodite': André Laks and Glenn W. Most (eds and trans.), *Early Greek Philosophy*, Vol. II: *Beginnings and Early Ionian Thinkers, Pt 1*, Loeb Classical Library, Harvard University Press, 2016, p. 93

282 'Grasp many-coloured pigments': Laks and Most, *Early Greek Philosophy*, Vol. V: *Western Greek Thinkers, Pt 2*, p. 403

282 the cosmic cycle: N. van der Ben, 'The Strasbourg Papyrus of Empedocles: Some Preliminary Remarks', *Mnemosyne*, Fourth Series, Vol. 52, Fasc. 5 (Oct. 1999), pp. 525–44

282 'Sometimes by Love': Laks and Most, *Early Greek Philosophy*, Vol. V: *Western Greek Thinkers, Pt 2*, pp. 420–3

282 'But as much as': Ibid., pp. 412–13

283 'shot forth in dense eddies': Ibid., pp. 416–17
283 'See this in sea-grazing': Ibid., pp. 422–3
283 'The Earthly was there': Ibid., pp. 372–5
284 'He was on all sides equal': Ibid., p. 449
284 Some creatures: Ibid., pp. 496–501
284 Empedocles imagined that thought: Ibid., pp. 566–7
284 'Earth, fire, water': Ibid., pp. 524–5
285 'For it is by earth': Ibid., pp. 540–1
285 'unyielding, penetrating eyes': Ibid., pp. 544–5
285 'with a pure effort': Ibid., pp. 578–9
285 'If you look carefully': Ibid., pp. 578–81

10 The invention of understanding

288 'With ease he makes': Hesiod, *Works and Days*, trans. A. E.
    Stallings, Penguin, 2018, lines 5–8
289 'Beware the toils of war': *Iliad* 5.487–8; in the translation by
    Robert Fagles at 5.559–60, Penguin, 1990, p. 180
292 The washed spirit: See Karl Popper, *The Open Society and its
    Enemies*, Routledge, 1945, for a sustained argument along that line

BIBLIOGRAPHY

Primary texts

Josephine Balmer (ed. and trans.), *Sappho: Poems & Fragments*, 2nd expanded edn, Bloodaxe, 2018

Jonathan Barnes, *Early Greek Philosophy*, Penguin, 1987

David A. Campbell (ed. and trans.), *Greek Lyric I: Sappho and Alcaeus*, Loeb Classical Library, Harvard University Press, 1982

David A. Campbell (ed. and trans.), *Greek Lyric II: Anacreon, Anacreonta*, Loeb Classical Library, Harvard University Press, 1988

Anne Carson (ed. and trans.), *If Not, Winter: Fragments of Sappho*, Virago, 2002

Guy Davenport (ed. and trans.), *Carmina Archilochi: The Fragments of Archilochos*, University of California Press, 1964

Guy Davenport, 'Archilochos: "Epode: Fireworks on the Grass"', *Hudson Review*, Vol. 28, No. 3 (Autumn 1975), pp. 352–6

Guy Davenport, *7 Greeks*, New York: New Directions, 1995

Robert Fagles (trans.), *The Iliad*, Penguin, 1990

Robert Fagles (trans.), *The Odyssey*, Penguin, 1997

Douglas E. Gerber (ed. and trans.), *Greek Elegiac Poetry from the Seventh to the Fifth Centuries BC*, Loeb Classical Library, Harvard University Press, 1999

Douglas E. Gerber (ed. and trans.), *Greek Iambic Poetry*, Loeb Classical Library, Harvard University Press, 1999

R. C. Jebb (ed. and trans.), *Bacchylides: The Poems and Fragments*, Cambridge University Press, 1905

G. S. Kirk, J. E. Raven and M. Schofield, *The Presocratic Philosophers*, 2nd edn, Cambridge University Press, 1983

André Laks and Glenn W. Most (eds and trans.), *Early Greek Philosophy*:
   Vol. I: *Introductory and Reference Materials*, Loeb Classical Library, Harvard University Press, 2016
   Vol. II: *Beginnings and Early Ionian Thinkers, Pt 1*, Loeb Classical Library, Harvard University Press, 2016

Vol. III: *Early Ionian Thinkers, Pt 2*, Loeb Classical Library, Harvard University Press, 2016

Vol. IV: *Western Greek Thinkers, Pt 1*, Loeb Classical Library, Harvard University Press, 2016

Vol. V: *Western Greek Thinkers, Pt 2*, Loeb Classical Library, Harvard University Press, 2016

A. T. Murray (ed. and trans.), *The Iliad*, 2 vols, rev. William F. Wyatt, Loeb Classical Library, Harvard University Press, 1999

A. T. Murray (ed. and trans.), *The Odyssey*, 2 vols, rev. George E. Dimock, Loeb Classical Library, Harvard University Press, 1995

John Sandys (trans.), *Pindar: The Odes*, Loeb Classical Library, Heinemann, 1915

Aubrey de Sélincourt (trans.), *Herodotus: Histories*, rev. John M. Marincola, Penguin, 2003

A. E. Stallings (trans.), *Hesiod: Works and Days*, Penguin, 2018

Robin Waterfield, *The First Philosophers: The Presocratics and Sophists*, Oxford University Press, 2000

M. L. West, *Homeric Hymns*, Loeb Classical Library, Harvard University Press, 2003

M. L. West, *The Hymns of Zoroaster*, Bloomsbury Academic, 2010

A wide range of ancient texts, in Greek or Latin and English, are accessible online at www.perseus.tufts.edu/hopper or at www.penelope.uchicago.edu/

Guide book

George E. Bean, *Aegean Turkey: An Archaeological Guide*, Ernest Benn, 1966

Philosophical background

Jonathan Barnes, *The Presocratic Philosophers*, Routledge, 1982

Walter Benjamin: 1938–1940, Vol. 4: *Selected Writings*, ed. H. Eiland and M. W. Jennings, Harvard University Press, 2003

Hans Blumenberg, *The Laughter of the Thracian Woman: A Protohistory of Theory*, trans. Spencer Hawkins, New Directions in German Studies, Bloomsbury Academic, 2015

Adriana Cavarero, *In Spite of Plato: A Feminist Rewriting of Ancient Philosophy*, trans. S. Anderlini-D'Onofrio and Aine O'Healy, Cambridge: Polity Press, 1995

Patricia Curd and Daniel W. Graham, *The Oxford Handbook of Presocratic Philosophy*, Oxford University Press, 2008

E. R. Dodds, *The Greeks and the Irrational*, University of California Press, 1951

W. K. C. Guthrie, *A History of Greek Philosophy*, 2 vols, Cambridge University Press, 1962 and 1965

Martin Heidegger, *The Beginning of Western Philosophy (Anaximander and Parmenides)*, trans. Richard Rojcewicz, Indiana University Press, 2015

Edward Hussey, *The Presocratics*, Duckworth, 1972

David C. Jacobs, *The Presocratics after Heidegger*, Albany, NY: State University of New York Press, 1999

Julian Jaynes, *The Origin of Consciousness in the Breakdown of the Bicameral Mind*, Houghton Mifflin, 1976

A. A. Long (ed.), *The Cambridge Companion to Early Greek Philosophy*, Cambridge University Press, 1999

Manussos Marangudakis, 'The Social Sources and Environmental Consequences of Axial Thinking: Mesopotamia, China, and Greece in Comparative Perspective', *European Journal of Sociology/Archives Européennes de Sociologie/Europäisches Archiv für Soziologie*, Vol. 47, No. 1 (2006), pp. 59–91

Karl Popper, *The Open Society and its Enemies*, Routledge, 1945

Gillian Rose, *Paradiso*, 2nd edn, Swindon: Shearsman Books, 2015

Bertrand Russell, 'Mysticism and Logic', *Hibbert Journal* (July 1914), reprinted in his *Mysticism and Logic and Other Essays*, George Allen & Unwin, 1917

Richard Seaford, *Money and the Early Greek Mind: Homer, Philosophy, Tragedy*, Cambridge University Press, 2004

Bruno Snell, *The Discovery of the Mind in Greek Philosophy and Literature*, trans. T. G. Rosenmeyer, New York: Harper, 1960

Jean-Pierre Vernant, *The Origins of Greek Thought*, Cornell University Press, 1982

Jean-Pierre Vernant, *Myth and Thought among the Greeks*, trans. J. Lloyd with J. Fort, New York: Zone Books, 2006

M. L. West, *Early Greek Philosophy and the Orient*, Oxford: Clarendon Press, 1971

Historical background

David Abulafia, *The Great Sea: A Human History of the Mediterranean*, Allen Lane, 2011

M. E. Aubet, *The Phoenicians and the West: Politics, Colonies and Trade*, 2nd edn, Cambridge University Press, 2001

Marie-Claire Beaulieu, *The Sea in the Greek Imagination*, University of Pennsylvania Press, 2016

Robert N. Bellah and Hans Joas, *The Axial Age and its Consequences*, Belknap/Harvard University Press, 2012

John Boardman (ed.), *The Cambridge Ancient History: Plates to Volume III:*

The Middle East, the Greek World and the Balkans to the Sixth Century BC, 2nd edn, Cambridge University Press, 1984

John Boardman, *The Greeks Overseas*, 4th edn, Thames & Hudson, 1999

John Boardman and N. G. L. Hammond (eds), *The Cambridge Ancient History*, Vol. III, Pt 3: *The Expansion of the Greek World Eighth to the Sixth Centuries BC*, 2nd edn, Cambridge University Press, 1982

John Boardman et al. (eds), *The Cambridge Ancient History*, Vol. III, Pt 2: *The Assyrian and Babylonian Empires and Other States of the Near East from the Eighth to the Sixth Centuries BC*, 2nd edn, Cambridge University Press, 1991

John Boardman et al. (eds), *The Cambridge Ancient History*, Vol. IV: *Persia, Greece and the Western Mediterranean, c. 525 to 479 BC*, 2nd edn, Cambridge University Press, 1988

Fernand Braudel, *The Mediterranean in the Ancient World*, trans. Siân Reynolds, Penguin, 2001

Cyprian Broodbank, *The Making of the Middle Sea*, Oxford University Press, 2013

Walter Burkert, *The Orientalizing Revolution: Near Eastern Influence on Greek Culture in the Early Archaic Age*, Harvard University Press, 1992

Walter Burkert, *Babylon, Memphis, Persepolis: Eastern Contexts of Greek Culture*, Harvard University Press, 2004

Jan-Mathieu Carbon, 'Dolphin-Pillars', *Epigraphica Anatolica*, Vol. 46 (2013), pp. 27–34

Paul Cartledge, 'Like a Worm i' the Bud? A Heterology of Classical Greek Slavery', *Greece & Rome*, Vol. 40, No. 2 (Oct. 1993), pp. 163–80

Lionel Casson, *Ships and Seamanship in the Ancient World*, Johns Hopkins University Press, 1971

Lionel Casson, *The Ancient Mariners*, 2nd edn, Princeton University Press, 1991

Diane Harris Cline, 'A Field Map for Untangling the Entangled Sea', *Journal of Eastern Mediterranean Archaeology & Heritage Studies*, Vol. 8, Nos. 3–4 (2020), pp. 226–49

J. M. Cook, *The Greeks in Ionia and the East*, New York: Frederick A. Praeger, 1973

Katherine Correa, 'Artemis Ephesia and Sacred Bee Imagery in Ancient Greece', *Symposium*, Vol. 12 (2012), pp. 74–82

David Cosandey, *Le Secret de l'Occident: Vers un théorie générale du progrès scientifique*, 2nd edn, Paris: Flammarion, 2007

Jan Paul Crielaard, 'The Ionians in the Archaic Period: Shifting Identities in a Changing World', in Ton Derks and Nico Roymans (eds), *Ethnic Constructs in Antiquity: The Role of Power and Tradition*, Amsterdam University Press, 2009, pp. 37–84

Victoria Cuffel, 'The Classical Greek Concept of Slavery', *Journal of the History of Ideas*, Vol. 27, No. 3 (Jul.–Sept. 1966), pp. 323–42

C. Davaras, 'Μινωικό κηριοφόρο πλοιάριο της Συλλογής Μητσοτάκη', *Archaiologikē Ephēmeris* (1984), pp. 55–93

Ton Derks and Nico Roymans (eds), *Ethnic Constructs in Antiquity: The Role of Power and Tradition*, Amsterdam University Press, 2009

M. I. Finley, 'Was Greek Civilization Based on Slave Labour?', *Historia: Zeitschrift für Alte Geschichte*, Bd. 8, H. 2 (Apr. 1959), pp. 145–64

Sara Forsdyke, *Slaves and Slavery in Ancient Greece*, Cambridge University Press, 2021

Alan M. Greaves, *The Land of Ionia: Society and Economy in the Archaic Period*, Wiley-Blackwell, 2015

Jonathan M. Hall, *A History of the Archaic Greek World, ca. 1200–479 BCE*, 2nd edn, Wiley-Blackwell, 2013

J. W. Hanson and S. G. Ortman, 'A Systematic Method for Estimating the Populations of Greek and Roman Settlements', online at https://www.colorado.edu/

Peregrine Horden and Nicholas Purcell, *The Corrupting Sea: A Study of Mediterranean History*, Blackwell, 2000

Daniel Hoyer and Jenny Reddish, *Seshat History of the Axial Age*, Chaplin, Conn.: Beresta Books, 2019

K. A. Kitchen, *Pharaoh Triumphant: The Life and Times of Ramesses II, King of Egypt*, Oxford: Aris & Phillips, 1982

Kristian Kristiansen, Thomas Lindkvist and Janken Myrdal (eds), *Economic Networks and Cultural Ties, from Prehistory to the Early Modern Era*, Cambridge University Press, 2018

Dušanka Kučan, 'Rapport synthétique sur les recherches archéobotaniques dans le sanctuaire d'Héra de l'Île de Samos', *Pallas*, No. 52, Paysage et Alimentation dans le Monde Grec: Les innovations du premier millénaire av. J.C. (2000), pp. 99–108, I–IV

Brian M. Lavelle, *Archaic Greece: The Age of New Reckonings*, Wiley-Blackwell, 2020

Justin Leidwanger and Carl Knappett (eds), *Maritime Networks in the Ancient Mediterranean World*, Cambridge University Press, 2018

David Lewis, 'Near Eastern Slaves in Classical Attica and the Slave Trade with Persian Territories', *Classical Quarterly*, New Series, Vol. 61, No. 1 (May 2011), pp. 91–113

David M. Lewis, 'The Federal Constitution of Keos', *Annual of the British School at Athens*, Vol. 57 (1962), pp. 1–4

Jack Longman et al., 'Exceptionally High Levels of Lead Pollution in the Balkans from the Early Bronze Age to the Industrial Revolution', *Proceedings of the National Academy of Sciences of the United States of America*, Vol. 115, No. 25 (19 Jun. 2018), pp. E5661–8

Joseph R. McConnell et al., 'Lead Pollution Recorded in Greenland Ice Indicates European Emissions Tracked Plagues, Wars, and Imperial Expansion during Antiquity', *Proceedings of the National Academy of*

Sciences of the United States of America, Vol. 115, No. 22 (29 May 2018), pp. 5726–31

J. G. Macqueen, *The Hittites and their Contemporaries in Asia Minor*, 2nd edn, Thames & Hudson, 1986

Irad Malkin, *A Small Greek World: Networks in the Ancient Mediterranean*, Oxford University Press, 2011

Thomas R. Martin, 'Why Did the Greek "Polis" Originally Need Coins?', *Historia: Zeitschrift für Alte Geschichte*, Bd. 45, H. 3 (3rd Qtr, 1996), pp. 257–83

Lynette G. Mitchell and P. J. Rhodes (eds), *The Development of the Polis in Archaic Greece*, Routledge, 1997

Christopher M. Monroe, 'Marginalizing Civilization: The Phoenician Redefinition of Power ca. 1300–800 BCE', in Kristian Kristiansen, Thomas Lindkvist and Janken Myrdal (eds), *Economic Networks and Cultural Ties, from Prehistory to the Early Modern Era*, Cambridge University Press, 2018, pp. 195–241

Sarah P. Morris and John K. Papadopoulos, 'Greek Towers and Slaves: An Archaeology of Exploitation', *American Journal of Archaeology*, Vol. 109, No. 2 (Apr. 2005), pp. 155–225

Sabatino Moscati, *The Phoenicians*, I. B. Tauris, 2001

Oswyn Murray and Simon Price, *The Greek City from Homer to Alexander*, Oxford: Clarendon Press, 1990

Ibrahim Noureddine, 'New Light on the Phoenician Harbor at Tyre', *Near Eastern Archaeology*, Vol. 73, Nos. 2–3 (2010), pp. 176–81

Egidia Occhipinti, 'Athenaeus's Sixth Book on Greek and Roman Slavery', scriptaclassica.org (2015)

Mando Oeconomides, 'The Human Figure in Archaic Greek Coinage', *Studies in the History of Art*, Vol. 32, Symposium Papers XVI: New Perspectives in Early Greek Art (1991), pp. 272–83

Leo Oppenheim, 'The Position of the Intellectual in Mesopotamian Society', *Daedalus*, Vol. 104, No. 2, Wisdom, Revelation, and Doubt: Perspectives on the First Millennium BC (Spring 1975), pp. 37–46

Barry B. Powell, *Homer and the Origin of the Greek Alphabet*, Cambridge University Press, 1991

N. N. Puckett, 'The Phoenician Trade Network: Tracing a Mediterranean Exchange System', Master's thesis, Texas A&M University, 2012

Josephine Quinn, *In Search of the Phoenicians*, Princeton University Press, 2018

K. A. Raaflaub and Hans van Wees (eds), *A Companion to Archaic Greece*, Wiley-Blackwell, 2009

P. J. Rhodes, *The Greek City States: A Source Book*, 2nd edn, Cambridge University Press, 2007

Jean Robert, 'Hestia and Hermes: The Greek Imagination of Motion and Space', *International Journal of Illich Studies* (2001), pp. 79–86

E. S. G. Robinson, 'The Date of the Earliest Coins', *Numismatic Chronicle* and *Journal of the Royal Numismatic Society*, Sixth Series, Vol. 16 (1956), pp. 1–8

Carl Roebuck, *Ionian Trade and Colonization*, Chicago: Ares Publishers, 1984

Kevin J. R. Rosman et al., 'Lead from Carthaginian and Roman Spanish Mines Isotopically Identified in Greenland Ice Dated from 600 BC to 300 AD', *Environ. Sci. Technol.*, Vol. 31, No. 12 (1997), pp. 3413–16

Georges Roux, *Ancient Iraq*, 3rd edn, Penguin, 1992

H. A. Shapiro, '"Hērôs Theos": The Death and Apotheosis of Hercules', *Classical World*, Vol. 77, No. 1 (Sept.–Oct. 1983), pp. 7–18

Anthony Snodgrass, *Archaic Greece: The Age of Experiment*, University of California Press, 1980

David W. Tandy, *Warriors into Traders*, University of California Press, 1997

Timothy Taylor, 'Believing the Ancients: Quantitative and Qualitative Dimensions of Slavery and the Slave Trade in Later Prehistoric Eurasia', *World Archaeology*, Vol. 33, No. 1, The Archaeology of Slavery (Jun. 2001), pp. 27–43

Taco Terpstra, *Trade in the Ancient Mediterranean: Private Order and Public Institutions*, Princeton University Press, 2019

Patricia J. Thompson, 'Dismantling the Master's House: A Hestian/ Hermean Deconstruction of Classic Texts', *Hypatia*, Vol. 9, No. 4, Feminist Philosophy of Religion (Autumn 1994), pp. 38–56

Marc Van De Mieroop, *Philosophy before the Greeks: The Pursuit of Truth in Ancient Babylonia*, Princeton University Press, 2016

Jean-Pierre Vernant, 'Hestia–Hermès: Sur l'expression religieuse de l'espace et du mouvement chez les Grecs', *L'Homme*, Vol. 3, No. 3 (Sept.–Dec. 1963), pp. 12–50

Cultural background

C. P. Cavafy, *The Collected Poems with Text*, trans. Evangelos Sachperoglou, ed. Anthony Hirst, Oxford University Press, 2008

C. P. Cavafy, *Complete Poems*, trans. D. Mendelsohn, Harper Press, 2012

Michael Hofmann, *Messing about in Boats*, Oxford University Press, 2021

Philip Mansel, *Levant: Splendour and Catastrophe on the Mediterranean*, John Murray, 2011

J. Morris, *Trieste*, Faber & Faber, 2001

Jonathan Wordsworth (ed.), *W. Wordsworth, The Prelude: The Four Texts*, Penguin, 1995

Homer

Tomislav Bilić, 'The Myth of Alpheus and Arethusa and Open-Sea Voyages on the Mediterranean – Stellar Navigation in Antiquity', *International Journal of Nautical Archaeology*, Vol. 38, No. 1 (2009), pp. 116–32

G. Buchner and D. Ridgway, *Pithekoussai I: Le necropoli: tombe 1–723 scavate dal 1952–1961*, Monumenti Antichi, Serie Monografica 4, Rome: Bretschneider, 1993

J. N. Coldstream and G. L. Huxley, 'An Astronomical Graffito from Pithekoussai', *Parole del Passato*, Vol. 288 (1996), pp. 221–4

Richard Janko, 'From Gabii and Gordion to Etetria and Methonea: The Rise of the Greek Alphabet', *Bulletin of the Institute of Classical Studies*, Vol. 58, No. 1 (Jun. 2015), pp. 1–32

Pietro Monti, 'Homeric Tradition in the Mediterranean Navigation of the Pithekoussans', *Talanta*, Vol. XXX–XXXI (1998–9), pp. 115–33

G. Nagy, 'The Aeolic Component of Homeric Diction', *Proceedings of the 22nd Annual UCLA Indo-European Conference*, ed. S. W. Jamison et al., Los Angeles, 5–6 November 2010, pp. 133–79

M. Nielbock, 'Navigation in the Ancient Mediterranean', AstroEDU manuscript no. astroedu1645, online August 2017

Joseph Russo, 'Re-Thinking Homeric Psychology: Snell, Dodds and their Critics', *Quaderni Urbinati di Cultura Classica*, New Series, Vol. 101, No. 2 (2012), pp. 11–28

Martin West, 'The Homeric Question Today', *Proceedings of the American Philosophical Society*, Vol. 155, No. 4 (Dec. 2011), pp. 383–93

Homer's Smyrna

John Boardman, *Excavations in Chios, 1952–1955: Greek Emporio*, The British School at Athens, Supplementary Volumes, No. 6 (1967), pp. iii–xiv, 1–258

J. M. Cook, 'Old Smyrna, 1948–1951', *Annual of the British School at Athens*, Vol. 53/54 (1958/9), pp. 1–34

Miletus

Rebecca Döhl and Julian Jansen van Rensburg (eds), *Signs of Place: A Visual Interpretation of Landscape*, Edition Topoi/Exzellenzcluster Topoi der Freien Universität Berlin und der Humboldt-Universität zu Berlin, 2019

Norbert Ehrhardt, Wolfgang Günther and Peter Weiß, 'Funde aus Milet XXVI. Aphrodite-Weihungen mit Ohren-Reliefs aus Oikus', *Archäologischer Anzeiger* (2009), No. 1, pp. 187–203

N. A. Gavriljuk, *Black Sea Studies*, 2003, online at https://antikmuseet.au.dk/fileadmin/www.antikmuseet.au.dk/Pontosfiler/BSS_1/BSS1_08_Gavriljuk.pdf

Vanessa B. Gorman, *Miletos, the Ornament of Ionia: A History of the City to 400 BCE*, University of Michigan Press, 2001

Alan M. Greaves, *Miletos: A History*, Routledge, 2002

G. Hölbl, 'Funde aus Milet VIII. Die Aegyptiaca vom Aphroditetempel auf dem Zeytintepe', *Archäologischer Anzeiger* (1999), No. 3, pp. 345–71

W. Horowitz, 'The Babylonian Map of the World', *Iraq*, Vol. 50 (1988), pp. 147–65

C. Kahn, *Anaximander and the Origins of Greek Cosmology*, New York: Columbia University Press, 1960

Deborah Kamen, 'Sale for the Purpose of Freedom: Slave-Prostitutes and Manumission in Ancient Greece', *Classical Journal*, Vol. 109, No. 3 (Feb.–Mar. 2014), pp. 281–307

Miroslav Marcovich, 'From Ishtar to Aphrodite', *Journal of Aesthetic Education*, Vol. 30, No. 2, Special Issue: Distinguished Humanities Lectures II (Summer 1996), pp. 43–59

Sarah P. Morris, 'The View from East Greece: Miletus, Samos and Ephesus', in Corinna Riva and Nicholas C. Vella (eds), *Debating Orientalization: Multidisciplinary Approaches to Change in the Ancient Mediterranean*, Equinox, 2010, pp. 66–84

F. Nietzsche, *Thus Spoke Zarathustra*, trans. R. J. Hollingdale, Penguin, 1961

Philipp Niewöhner, *Miletus/Balat*, Istanbul: Ege Yaylinari, 2016

Lana Radloff, '"Placing" a Maritime Territory at Hellenistic Miletus', in Rebecca Döhl and Julian Jansen van Rensburg (eds), *Signs of Place: A Visual Interpretation of Landscape*, Edition Topoi/Exzellenzcluster Topoi der Freien Universität Berlin und der Humboldt-Universität zu Berlin, 2019, pp. 99–120

Corinna Riva and Nicholas C. Vella (eds), *Debating Orientalization: Multidisciplinary Approaches to Change in the Ancient Mediterranean*, Equinox, 2010

The lyric poets

Joan Aruz and Michael Seymour (eds), *Assyria to Iberia: Art and Culture in the Iron Age*, New York: Metropolitan Museum of Art, 2016

Willis Barnstone (ed. and trans.), *Sappho and the Greek Lyric Poets*, New York: Schocken Books, 1988, fragment 38, online at http://people .uncw.edu/

Anton Bierl and André Lardinois (eds), *The Newest Sappho: P. Sapph. Obbink and P. GC inv. 105, Frs. 1-4: Studies in Archaic and Classical Greek Song*, Vol. 2, Leiden: Brill, 2016

Felix Budelmann (ed.), *The Cambridge Companion to Greek Lyric*, Cambridge University Press, 2009

A. R. Burn, *The Lyric Age of Greece*, Edward Arnold, 1960

François de Callataÿ, 'Did "Dolphins" and Non-Functional Arrowheads Massively Found in and around Olbia, Istros and Apollonia Ever Have a Monetary Function?', online at https://kbr.academia.edu /FrancoisdeCallatay

G. A. Cariolou, 'Kyrenia II: The Return from Cyprus to Greece of the Replica of a Hellenic Merchant Ship', in S. Swiny et al. (eds), *Res*

Maritimae: Cyprus and the Eastern Mediterranean from Prehistory to Late Antiquity, American Schools of Oriental Research, Atlanta: Scholars Press, 1997, pp. 83–97

J. S. Clay, I. Malkin and Y. Z. Tzifopoulos (eds), *Panhellenes at Methone*, Trends in Classics – Supplementary Volumes, Berlin: De Gruyter, 2017

Inci Delemen, 'An Unplundered Chamber Tomb on Ganos Mountain in Southeastern Thrace', *American Journal of Archaeology*, Vol. 110, No. 2 (Apr. 2006), pp. 251–73

J.-M. Dentzer, *Le Motif du banquet couché dans le Proche-Orient et le monde grec du VIIIème au IVème siècle avant J-C*, Paris/Rome: École Française de Rome, 1982

L. Dubois, *Inscriptions grecques dialectales d'Olbia du Pont*, Geneva: Droz, 1996, No. 31

Esther Eidinow and Claire Taylor, 'Lead-letter Days: Writing, Communication and Crisis in the Ancient Greek World', *Classical Quarterly*, New Series, Vol. 60, No. 1 (May 2010), pp. 30–62

Marian H. Feldman, 'Consuming the East: Near Eastern Luxury Goods in Orientalizing Contexts', in Joan Aruz and Michael Seymour (eds), *Assyria to Iberia: Art and Culture in the Iron Age*, New York: Metropolitan Museum of Art, 2016, pp. 227–33

P. J. Finglass and Adrian Kelly, *The Cambridge Companion to Sappho*, Cambridge University Press, 2021

Elizabeth S. Greene et al., 'Inconspicuous Consumption: The Sixth-Century BCE Shipwreck at Pabuç Burnu, Turkey', *American Journal of Archaeology*, Vol. 112, No. 4 (Oct. 2008), pp. 685–711

Albert Henrichs, 'Myth Visualized: Dionysos and his Circle in Sixth-Century Attic Vase-Painting', in *Papers on the Amasis Painter and his World*, Malibu: J. Paul Getty Museum, 1987, pp. 92–194

N. Kaltsas, 'Κλαζομενιακές Σαρκοφάγοι από το Νεκροταφείο της Ακάνθου [Klazomenian sarcophagi from Akanthos]', *Archaiologikon Deltion*, Vol. 51–2 (1996–7), pp. 35–50

Ulrike Krotscheck, 'Pointe Lequin 1A: Wine Cups and Economic Networks in the Western Mediterranean', *Ancient West & East*, Vol. 14 (2015), pp. 169–89

Leslie Kurke, 'The Politics of ἀβροσύνη in Archaic Greece', *Classical Antiquity*, Vol. 11, No. 1 (Apr. 1992), pp. 91–120

Justin Leidwanger, 'Modeling Distance with Time in Ancient Mediterranean Seafaring: A GIS Application for the Interpretation of Maritime Connectivity', *Journal of Archaeological Science*, Vol. 40, Issue 8 (Aug. 2013), pp. 3302–8

Oswyn Murray, 'The Culture of the Symposion', in K. A. Raaflaub and Hans van Wees (eds), *A Companion to Archaic Greece*, Wiley-Blackwell, 2009, pp. 508–23

Rosalba Panvini, *The Archaic Greek Ship at Gela*, trans. Brian E. McConnell, Palermo: Salvatore Sciascia, 2001

Kurt A. Raaflaub, 'The Newest Sappho and Archaic Greek–Near Eastern Interactions', in Anton Bierl and André Lardinois (eds), *The Newest Sappho: P. Sapph. Obbink and P. GC inv. 105, Frs. 1-4: Studies in Archaic and Classical Greek Song*, Vol. 2, Leiden: Brill, 2016, pp. 127–47

Enric Sanmarti-Grego and Rosa. A. Santiago, 'La lettre grecque d'Emporion et son contexte archéologique', *Revue archéologique de Narbonnaise*, Vol. 21 (1988), pp. 3–17

H. W. Swiny and M. L. Katzev, 'The Kyrenia Shipwreck: A Fourth-Century BC Greek Merchant Ship', in D. J. Blackman (ed.), *Marine Archaeology*, Colston Papers No. 23, Archon Books, 1973, pp. 339–60

Marek Węcowski, 'Wine and the Early History of the Greek Alphabet: Early Greek Vase-Inscriptions and the Symposium', in J. S. Clay, I. Malkin and Y. Z. Tzifopoulos (eds), *Panhellenes at Methone*, Trends in Classics – Supplementary Volumes, Berlin: De Gruyter, 2017, pp. 309–20

Xenophanes

Elizabeth P. Baughan, 'Sculpted Symposiasts of Ionia', *American Journal of Archaeology*, Vol. 115, No. 1 (Jan. 2011), pp. 19–53

John Boardman, *Greek Sculpture: The Archaic Period, a Handbook*, Thames & Hudson, 1978

Larissa Bonfante, 'Nudity as a Costume in Classical Art', *American Journal of Archaeology*, Vol. 93, No. 4 (Oct. 1989), pp. 543–70

Nicholas Cahill and John H. Kroll, 'New Archaic Coin Finds at Sardis', *American Journal of Archaeology*, Vol. 109, No. 4 (Oct. 2005), pp. 589–617

Andrew T. Creekmore III and Kevin D. Fisher (eds), *Making Ancient Cities: Space and Place in Early Urban Societies*, New York: Cambridge University Press, 2014

C. Doumas, *Wall Paintings of Thera*, trans. A. Doumas, Athens: The Thera Foundation, 1992

Alain Duplouy, 'Les Mille du Colophon: "Totalité symbolique" d'une cité d'Ionie (VI e–II e s. av. J.-C.)', *Historia: Zeitschrift für Alte Geschichte*, Bd. 62, H. 2 (2013), pp. 146–66

Elspeth R. M. Dusinberre, *Aspects of Empire in Achaemenid Sardis*, Cambridge University Press, 2003

Rodney D. Fitzsimons, 'Urbanization and the Emergence of the Greek *Polis*: The Case of Azoria, Crete', in Andrew T. Creekmore III and Kevin D. Fisher (eds), *Making Ancient Cities: Space and Place in Early Urban Societies*, New York: Cambridge University Press, 2014, pp. 220–56

Donald C. Haggis et al., 'Excavations in the Archaic Civic Buildings at Azoria in 2005–2006', *Hesperia: The Journal of the American School of Classical Studies at Athens*, Vol. 80, No. 1 (Jan.–Mar. 2011), pp. 1–70

Evelyn B. Harrison, 'The Dress of the Archaic Greek Korai', *Studies in the History of Art*, Vol. 32, Symposium Papers XVI: New Perspectives in Early Greek Art (1991), pp. 216–39

Henry S. Kim and John H. Kroll, 'A Hoard of Archaic Coins of Colophon and Unminted Silver (*CH* I.3)', *American Journal of Numismatics*, Vol. 20 (2008), pp. 53–103

James H. Lesher, 'Xenophanes' Scepticism', *Phronesis*, Vol. 23, No. 1 (1978), pp. 1–21

Miroslav Marcovich, 'Xenophanes on Drinking-Parties and Olympic Games', *Illinois Classical Studies*, Vol. 3 (1978), pp. 1–26

Josephine Crawley Quinn, 'Herms, Kouroi and the Political Anatomy of Athens', *Greece & Rome*, Second Series, Vol. 54, No. 1 (Apr. 2007), pp. 82–105

David B. Small, 'The Archaic Polis of Azoria: A Window into Cretan "Polital" Social Structure', *Journal of Mediterranean Archaeology*, Vol. 23, No. 2 (2010), pp. 197–217

Manolis I. Stefanakis et al., 'Excavations at Azoria, 2003–2004, Part 1: The Archaic Civic Complex', *Hesperia: The Journal of the American School of Classical Studies at Athens*, Vol. 76, No. 2 (Apr.–Jun. 2007), pp. 243–321

Richard Wenghofer, 'Sexual Promiscuity of Non-Greeks in Herodotus' "Histories"', *Classical World*, Vol. 107, No. 4 (Summer 2014), pp. 515–34

Ruth Westgate, 'Space and Social Complexity in Greece from the Early Iron Age to the Classical Period', *Hesperia: The Journal of the American School of Classical Studies at Athens*, Vol. 84, No. 1 (Jan.–Mar. 2015), pp. 47–95

Heraclitus

James Barr, 'The Question of Religious Influence: The Case of Zoroastrianism, Judaism, and Christianity', *Journal of the American Academy of Religion*, Vol. 53, No. 2 (Jun. 1985), pp. 201–35

Jerker Blomqvist, review of Rafał Rosół, *Frühe semitische Lehnwörter im Griechischen*, Frankfurt am Main: Peter Lang, 2013, *Bryn Mawr Classical Review 2013.11.54*

Friedrich Brein, 'Ear Studs for Greek Ladies', *Anatolian Studies*, Vol. 32 (1982), pp. 89–92

Jan N. Bremmer, 'Priestly Personnel of the Ephesian Artemision: Anatolian, Persian, Greek and Roman Aspects', online at http://www.rug.nl/research/portal

Maria Brosius, *A History of Ancient Persia: The Achaemenid Empire*, Wiley-Blackwell, 2021

N. D. Cahill (ed.), *Lidyalılar ve Dünyaları/The Lydians and their World*, Istanbul: Yapı Kredi Yayınları, 2010

Jean Cocteau and André Fraigneau, *Entretiens: Jean Cocteau et André Fraigneau*, ed. Jean-Paul Bertrand, Monaco: Editions du Rocher, 1988

Alexander Dale, 'A Feast Fit for a Eunuch: Hipponax Frs. 26, 26a, and Martial 3.77', *Phoenix*, Vol. 71, No. 3/4 (Fall–Winter/automne–hiver 2017), pp. 215–29

Jacques Duchesne-Guillemin, 'Heraclitus and Iran', *History of Religions*, Vol. 3, No. 1 (Summer 1963), pp. 34–49

E. H. Gifford, *Eusebius of Caesarea: Preparation for the Gospel*, Oxford: Clarendon Press, 1903

Michael Allen Gillespie and Tracy B. Strong (eds), *Nietzsche's New Seas*, University of Chicago Press, 1988

Martin Heidegger, *Heraclitus*, trans. Julia Goesser Assaiante and S. Montgomery Ewegen, Bloomsbury Academic, 2018

Charles H. Kahn, *The Art and Thought of Heraclitus*, Cambridge University Press, 1979

M. Kerschner et al., 'Ephesus in archaischer und klassischer Zeit. Die Ausgrabungen in der Siedlung Smyrna', in F. Krinzinger (ed.), *Die Ägäis und das Westliche Mittelmeer. Beziehungen und Wechselwirkungen 8. Bis 5. Jh. v. Chr.*, Vienna: Verlag der österreichischen Akademie der Wissenschaften, 2000, pp. 45–54

M. Kerschner, 'The Lydians and their Ionian and Aiolian Neighbours', in N. D. Cahill (ed.), *Lidyalılar ve Dünyaları/The Lydians and their World*, Istanbul: Yapı Kredi Yayınları, 2010, pp. 247–66

L. R. LiDonnici, 'The Images of Artemis Ephesia and Greco-Roman Worship: A Reconsideration', *Harvard Theological Review*, Vol. 85, No. 4 (Oct. 1992), pp. 389–415

Tuna Şare, 'An Archaic Ivory Figurine from a Tumulus near Elmali: Cultural Hybridization and a New Anatolian Style', *Journal of the American School of Classical Studies at Athens*, Vol. 79, No. 1 (Jan.–Mar. 2010), pp. 53–78

F. Sokolowski, 'A New Testimony on the Cult of Artemis of Ephesus', *Harvard Theological Review*, Vol. 58, No. 4 (Oct. 1965), pp. 427–31

Cels Veira, 'Heraclitus' Bow Composition', *Classical Quarterly*, New Series, Vol. 63, No. 2 (Dec. 2013), pp. 473–90

Pythagoras

Greta Balzanelli and Maria Rosaria Luberto, 'Kroton in the Archaic Period', in *SAIA: Annuario della Scuola Archeologica di Atene e delle Missioni Italiane in Oriente*, Supplemento 3, 2019, pp. 301–21

Aldo Brancacci, 'The Origins of the Reflection on Music in Greek Archaic Poetry', *Revue de Philosophie Ancienne*, Vol. 34, No. 1 (2016), pp. 3–36

Walter Burkert, *Lore and Science in Ancient Pythagoreanism*, trans. Edwin L. Minar, Harvard University Press, 1972

Walter Burkert, *Ancient Mystery Cults*, Harvard University Press, 1987

Fritz Graf and Sarah Iles Johnston, *Ritual Texts for the Afterlife: Orpheus and the Bacchic Gold Tablets*, 2nd edn, Routledge, 2013

R. Ross Holloway, 'The Tomb of the Diver', *American Journal of Archaeology*, Vol. 110, No. 3 (Jul. 2006), pp. 365–88

Tonio Hölscher, *Der Taucher von Paestum: Jugend, Eros und das Meer im antiken Griechenland*, Stuttgart: Klett-Cotta Verlag 2021

Boris Kayachev, 'The So-Called Orphic Gold Tablets in Ancient Poetry and Poetics', *Zeitschrift für Papyrologie und Epigraphik*, Bd. 180 (2012), pp. 17–37

G. Nagy, 'Polycrates and his Patronage of Two Lyric Masters, Anacreon and Ibycus', presented at Princeton symposium on 'The Lyric Age in Greece', September 2017, online at https://classical-inquiries.chs.harvard.edu/

M. P. Nilsson, *The Dionysiac Mysteries of the Hellenistic and Roman Age*, Lund: Gleerup, 1957

Walter Duvall Penrose, 'Before Queerness? Visions of a homoerotic heaven in ancient Greco-Italic tomb paintings', in Mark Masterson, Nancy Sorkin Rabinowitz and James Robson (eds), *Sex in Antiquity*, Routledge, 2014, pp. 137–56

Yulia Ustinova, 'To Live in Joy and Die with Hope: Experiential Aspects of Ancient Greek Mystery Rites', *Bulletin of the Institute of Classical Studies*, Vol. 56, No. 2, Ancient History Issue (2013), pp. 105–23

Sarah Burges Watson, 'Orpheus Erotic Mysteries: Plato, Pederasty and the Zagreus Myth in Phanocles', *Bulletin of the Institute of Classical Studies*, Vol. 57, No. 2 (Dec. 2014), pp. 47–71

Margaret Wertheim, 'Pythagoras' Trousers', Math Horizons, Vol. 3, No. 3 (February 1996), pp. 5–7

Leonid Zhmud, 'Pythagoras' Northern Connections', *Classical Quarterly*, New Series, Vol. 66, No. 2 (Dec. 2016), pp. 446–62

Parmenides and Zeno

P. A. Cartledge, 'The Peculiar Position of Sparta in the Development of the Greek City-State', *Proceedings of the Royal Irish Academy: Archaeology, Culture, History, Literature, Vol. 80C (1980)*, pp. 91–108

Lionel Casson, 'Speed under Sail of Ancient Ships', *Transactions and Proceedings of the American Philological Association*, Vol. 82 (1951), pp. 136–48

Giovanna Greco, 'Elea/Velia: Lo spazio del sacro e le evidenze di culti e rituali', *Empúries*, Vol. 56 (2009–11), pp. 101–22

Lloyd Hopkins, 'Fleets and Manpower on Land and Sea: The Italian *Classes* and the Roman Empire 31 BC–AD 193', PhD thesis, University of Oxford, 2014

Kojin Karatani, *Isonomia*, Durham, NC: Duke University Press, 2017

E. Miranda, 'Nuove iscrizioni sacre di Velia', *Mélanges de l'École Française de Rome*, Vol. 94, No. 1 (1982), pp. 163–74

V. Nutton, 'Velia and the School of Salerno', *Medical History*, Vol. 15, No. 1 (Jan. 1971), pp. 1–11, online at cambridge.org

John Palmer, 'Parmenides', in Edward N. Zalta (ed.), *The Stanford Encyclopedia of Philosophy* (Winter 2020), online at https://plato .stanford.edu/

John Palmer, 'Zeno', in Edward N. Zalta (ed.), *The Stanford Encyclopedia of Philosophy* (Winter 2020), online at https://plato.stanford.edu/

Rosalba Panvini, *The Archaic Greek Ship at Gela*, trans. Brian E. McConnell, Palermo: Salvatore Sciascia, 2001

D. M. Spitzer, 'Broken Light on the Ground of Home: Non-Being and Diasporic Trauma in the Parmenidean Poem', *Diacritics*, Vol. 48, No. 1 (2020), pp. 108–26

Michael Vickers, 'Golden Greece: Relative Values, Minae, and Temple Inventories', *American Journal of Archaeology*, Vol. 94, No. 4 (Oct. 1990), pp. 613–25

Edward N. Zalta (ed.), *The Stanford Encyclopedia of Philosophy* (Winter 2020), online at https://plato.stanford.edu/

Empedocles

Gianfranco Adornato, 'Phalaris: Literary Myth or Historical Reality? Reassessing Archaic Acragas', *American Journal of Archaeology*, Vol. 116, No. 3 (Jul. 2012), pp. 483–506

N. van der Ben, 'The Strasbourg Papyrus of Empedocles: Some Preliminary Remarks', *Mnemosyne*, Fourth Series, Vol. 52, Fasc. 5 (Oct. 1999), pp. 525–44

Alfred Burns, 'Ancient Greek Water Supply and City Planning: A Study of Syracuse and Acragas', *Technology and Culture*, Vol. 15, No. 3 (Jul. 1974), pp. 389–412

Sean Corner, 'Transcendent Drinking: The Symposium at Sea Reconsidered', *Classical Quarterly*, Vol. 60, No. 2 (2010), pp. 352–80

Maria Pavlou, 'Pindar Olympian 3: Mapping Acragas on the Periphery of the Earth', *Classical Quarterly*, New Series, Vol. 60, No. 2 (Dec. 2010), pp. 313–26

Tapio Prokkola, *The Optical Corrections of the Doric Temple*, privately published, 2011

Vincent Scully, *The Earth, the Temple, and the Gods: Greek Sacred Architecture*, Yale University Press, 1962, rev. edn 1979

ACKNOWLEDGEMENTS

My thanks go, above all, to the team at William Collins, the most broad-minded, skilled, painstaking and generous set of people you could hope for, who care about books in a way few people outside publishing might recognise. The atmosphere they generate (and this is the fifteenth book I have written for them) is of course entirely professional but goes way beyond anything that word might suggest. The team that Arabella Pike leads is somehow animated by a feeling of joint enterprise, both with each other and with the author, at times as close as a ship's crew or a gathering of friends who have come together for a celebratory symposium.

I have sometimes thought, when writing this book and responding to the careful mending and smoothing to which my chapters have been subjected, that the process could be seen as a reflection of the virtues the ancient philosophers cherished: a belief in the sane as a governing ideal; not indifferent to higher or more esoteric ideas but needing to see them in the context of the lives we all live; inculcating a set of relationships that are collegiate, warm and social; a frame of mind that is intellectually open but dissatisfied with any lack of clarity or exactness; needing a good story to be told but consistently holding in mind ideals and values that go beyond the mere exercise or imposition of self-interest or private obsession. Essentially the whole process is governed by a belief in the book as an act of civilisation.

That team has been: Arabella Pike, publishing director at HarperCollins, who like her predecessor Susan Watt has never hesitated to say 'Do it again' and who in my experience has always presided over a subtle, iterative, conversational sifting of the good from the bad, the necessary from the unnecessary, the understood from the frankly unintelligible; the supremely helpful Sam Harding; Iain Hunt, senior editor, urging us all gently and firmly onwards to the conclusion you now hold in your hands; the brilliantly acute Peter James, who edited the text in the style of a Dior sempstress, a masterclass in elegant precision, no stitch to go astray, no flourish to be excessive; Emma Pidsley, who designed the jacket with the diving man, which I think of as an invitation to plunge in beneath the surface of these lives; Mark Wells, who made the index; and Martin Brown, who made the many graceful maps and charts from my rough sketches. For years Helen Ellis was the inimitable and now much-missed publicity director at William Collins, her shoes filled by the wonderful Laura Meyer.

To all of them nothing but thanks for the privilege of being published by and with them.

I have also been lucky enough to find the sympathetic ear of Paul Cartledge, now Emeritus A. G. Leventis Professor of Greek Culture at the University of Cambridge, who has not only tolerated the repeated suggesting and questioning of my drafts but sat on stages with me at literary festivals and showed a rare generosity from a professor to a non-academic writer, all of which has been a unique combination of balm and stimulus to me.

At Farrar, Straus and Giroux, Jonathan Galassi and Katie Liptak have given me just the encouragement and welcome an author needs, ever urging me on towards the sense of lived reality beyond any crust antiquity has grown.

As ever Georgina Capel and Zoe Pagnamenta have been my stalwart friends and guides.

And my wife Sarah has with absolute love and care allowed me over the years to pursue these figures down their strange and distant paths. No human being could ask for more.

INDEX

Page references in *italics* refer to illustrations.

INDEX

INDEX

INDEX

Demeter (earth mother goddess), 212, 213, 218, 219, 273, *274*; Dionysus/Bacchus, 32, 124, 145–7, *146*, 154, 211, 216, 219, 226; *epichthonioi* (*on-earths*), 36; Eros (god of longing), 32, 34, 118, 279; great gods of Greece, 34–5; Hades, 17, 35, 54, 212–13, 215, 219; healing gods, 241; Helios, daughters of, 244; Hephaestus, 34, 68; Hera, 19, 34, 67–8, 92, 110–11, *166*, 166–7; Hercules, 14–18, *15*, *18*, 34, 58, 224; Hermes, 34–6, 38, 40, 51, 85, 86–7, 220; Hestia, 34–6, 38, 40, 51; nymphs, 30, 32, 91; Persephone (queen of the underworld), 212, 218, 219, 244–50, *245*, 251, 252, 254, 292; Poseidon, 31, 34, 52–3, 63, 86, 91, 239; Rape of Europa, 24–5; Zeus, 34, 162, 197, 239, 268–70, 271, 276, 288 *see also* Apollo; Athena

Mytilene, city of, 110, 115, 132–8

Myus, city of, 95, *96*, 167–8

Naukratis (colony of Miletus), 87, 99

Nebuchadnezzar II, Babylonian king, 88

Nemea, the Peloponnese, 17, 210

neo-Babylonian empire, 14

Neoplatonism, 250

Nervilius Iustus, Caius, 237

Nicholls, Richard, *53*

Nietzsche, Friedrich, *Thus Spoke Zarathustra*, 193–4

Notion (Colophon's harbour), 3, 149, 169–70, *170*, 172, 173, 174

the *Odyssey* (Homer): Bronze Age roots of, 45–6; dating of production of, 45, 46–7, 48–9, 50; encounter with Achilles in Hades, 215; forms of thought in, 41–5, 61–7; framed as sequel to *Iliad*, 47; and *Homeric Hymn to Apollo*, 32; human decision-making in, 43–4, 63–7; Ithaca in, 42, 45; Mentes (Athena), 42–4, 63; Nausicaa, 122–4, *123*; navigation in, 41, 68–70, *69*, 71, 73; Odysseus, 41–5, 52–5, 61–3, 65–73, 100, 112, 122–4, 215, 234, 287; Old Smyrna as Scheria in, 53–7; origins on coast of Ionia, 45–6, 47; Penelope, 64, 65, 66; the Sirens, 100; story/plot, 43, 52–6, 68; Telemachus, 42, 43, 63, 64

Olbia, Greek city of, 30, 33, 124–5, 142, 218

Olympia, 34; Olympic games, 55, 161, 209–10, 214, 224, 263–4, 271, 277

Onomastus (Smyrnean boxer), 55

Oppenheim, Leo, 8–10

Orpheus, cult of, 215–20, 226–8, 229, 243–4, 253, 291

Ortygia, island of, 30

Palmer, John, 252, 253

Panionius (slave merchant), 27

Parmenides, 287; criticism/ridicule of, 250–1, 255, 258; Elea as home of, 230, 237, 238, 240–1, 254; followers of, 254; great work/poem of, 241, 242–50, 251–4, 292; and the idea/idealism, 245–54, 255–9, 291–2; influence on Empedocles, 278, 284; as inspiration for Plato, 230, 247, 248, 254; Italian emphasis of, 243; as maybe a healer, 241; oneness of truth/unity of existence, 243, 245–54, 255–9, 278, 280, 284, 292; and Pythagorean /Orphic mysteries, 243–4, 253; *stēlē and portrait bust of, 240*, 241; two forms of reality for, 251, 252–4, 292; Zeno as pupil/follower, 241–2, 254–9, 292

Paros, island of, 149

Pausanias (traveller), 14–18

the Peloponnese, 17, 30, 200, 210, 232, 234

Pericles, 259

Persepolis, Persian capital, 195, 196

Persian empire: conquest of Greek world (mid-sixth-century), 148–9, 151, 169, 170–1, 172, 174, 194–8, 230–2; conquest of Lydian empire (mid-sixth-century), 151, 169, 172, 194, 197; destruction of Miletus, 195; influence on Greek world, 84, 172–4, 194–8; Ionian revolt against (499 BC), 195; Phocaeans abandon city to, 230–2; and Phoenicians, 197, 238; road and postal system, 195; and slavery, 27, 29, 195–6; statues/sculpture, *195*, 195, 196; vast expansion under Cyrus and Darius, 194–8; wars with Greeks in fifth century, 150, 271; Zarathuṣtra (Zoroaster), 196–7, 198–9

Phalaris (tyrant of Acragas), 262–3

Phidias (sculptor), 34

philosophy: Anaximander's *apeiron*, 100–2, 103–4, 105, 106, 180; Anaximenes' theory of air, 106–8; and architectural form, 275–6; birth of western philosophy, 3–6, 7–14; co-emergence with slave society, 24–5, 29, 76–7, 78–9; connectedness, 5–6, 193; early ecological visions, 101–2; earth's

ILLUSTRATION CREDITS

In the Text

Title page: Currents of the Mediterranean, *NASA/Goddard Space Flight Center Scientific Visualization Studio*

17: Erythrae coin of Hercules Ionia/erythrae/BMC_41. *With permission of wildwinds.com, ex Freeman & Sear MBS, 15, June 2008*

18: Stone head from Old Smyrna, *Museum of History And Art T.C. Kültür ve*

22: A Minoan honey boat, *public domain*

24: Coins from Larissa, *Coinweek*; from Delos, *Wildwinds*; from Metapontum, *Münzkabinett, Staatliche Museen zu Berlin, 18225405. Photograph by Dirk Sonnenwald*; from Aegina, *Münzkabinett, Staatliche Museen zu Berlin, 18246445. Photograph by Lutz-Jürgen Lübke (Lübke und Wiedemann)*; from Apollonia, *Münzkabinett, Staatliche Museen zu Berlin, 18200133. Photograph by Lutz-Jürgen Lübke (Lübke und Wiedemann)*; from Thasos, *Münzkabinett, Staatliche Museen zu Berlin, 18203251. Photograph by Dirk Sonnenwald*

28: A fifth-century BC plate, *Museuo Taranto*

31: Coins from Thera, Syracuse, *Numisbids*; from Dankle, *Münzkabinett, Staatliche Museen zu Berlin, 18216051. Photograph by Dirk Sonnenwald*; from Taranto, *Münzkabinett, Staatliche Museen zu Berlin, 18202672. Photograph by Lutz-Jürgen Lübke (Lübke und Wiedemann)*; from Cyzicus, *Coinweek*

32: Discus from Gela, *KHM-Museumsverband*

34: Altar of Apollo at Miletus, *Author's image*

46: A silver-gilt bowl, *Musei Vaticani*

49: Emborio on Chios, *British School at Athens*

50: Photos of Old Smyrna and model, *Author's image*

51: Photos of Old Smyrna, *Author's image*

53: A sketch of Old Smyrna, *British School at Athens*

55: A gold necklace from Rhodes, *British Museum*

56: Part of a silver banqueting service, *Musei Vaticani*
57: Friezes of wild goats, *İzmir Arkeoloji ve Etnografya Müzesi*
58: A bath from Old Smyrna, *British School at Athens*; capitals from the archaic temple, *İzmir Tarih ve Sanat Müzesi*
59: Capitals from seventh-century, *Israel Museum*; lion from Old Smyrna, *İzmir Tarih ve Sanat Müzesi*
60: Ownership marks, *British School at Athens*
61: Graffiti, *British School at Athens*
62: Reconstructed temple at Old Smyrna, *Author's image*
75: Wells in Miletus, *Author's image*
87: Bronze head of Horus, *Archäologischer Anzeiger*; stary-eyed Egyptian, *Milet Müzesi*
88: Partridges, *Milet Müzesi*; oil jars from Zeytintepe, *Milet Müzesi*
89: The listening stones, *Archäologischer Anzeiger*
90: Canaanite figurines, *Israel Museum*; figurines found at Miletus, *Milet Müzesi*
92: The stony rubbish of Miletus, *Author's image*
94: Lion in Miletus, *Milet Müzesi*; lion in the Louvre, *Author's image*
96: The harbour works and city wall, *Author's image*
98: Ship graffiti, *Author's image*
120: Scenes from a symposium, *Archaiologikon Deltion*
121: Perfume bottles: man and helmeted head, *Universal History Archive/Getty*; horse, *World History Archive/Alamy*; swallow, *GRANGER – Historical Picture Archive/Alamy*
123: A wine jug, *J. Paul Getty Museum*; fifth-century *kantharos*, *British Museum*
127: Etruscan Sarcophagus, *National Etruscan Museum of Villa Giulia*
138: Port Sigri, *H.M. Denham, The Aegean*
139: Pointe Lequin wreck, *Philippe Foliot/Fonds Drassm/CNRS Ministère de la Culture*
141: Drawing of wine cup, *public domain*
142: The lead letter, *Javier Velaza*
146: Dionysus, *Staatliche Antikensammlungen Munich*
155: Aerial view of Azoria, *Courtesy of the Azoria Project, University of North Carolina at Chapel Hill*
157: *Pithoi* under reconstruction, *Courtesy of the Azoria Project, University of North Carolina at Chapel Hill*
159: The equipment of a kitchen, *Courtesy of the Azoria Project, University of North Carolina at Chapel Hill*
165: *Kouroi* in Izmir, *İzmir Tarih ve Sanat Müzesi*; *kouroi* in London, *British Museum*; a kore in mid song, *İzmir Tarih ve Sanat Müzesi*; a kore in the Louvre, *Author's image*
166: Reconstruction of the Geneleos group, *Bjanka Kadic/Alamy*

167: Reclining Geneleos figure, *American Journal of Archaeology*

168: Symposiasts from Myus, *Staatliche Museen zu Berlin, Antikensammlung /CC BY-NC-SA 4.0*; Fat man with beer, *Staatliche Museen zu Berlin, Antikensammlung /CC BY-NC-SA 4.0*

170: Boats dressed for a pleasure, *public domain*; modern boats, *Author's image*

172: A Colophon coin, *American Journal of Numismatics*

178: The head of a philosopher, *Selcuk Ephesus Archaeology Museum*

181, 182: Ephesus, *Author's image*

183: Jewellery from Ephesus, *British Museum*

186: Capital from one of the Artemision's columns, *British Museum*

187: Almost-smiling archaic face, *British Museum*; copies of the cult figure of Artemis, *Selcuk Ephesus Archaeology Museum*

195: Fragment of the foot of a statue of Darius, *American Journal of Archaeology*

207: A Sybarite *aryballos*, *National Archaeological Museum of Sibaritide*

210: Plain of Sybaris, *Author's image*

218: The golden letter in Vibo, *Author's image*

222: The *tetraktys*, *public domain*

225: Chains and shackles from Kroton, *National Archaeological Museum of Crotone*

227: Paestum, *Author's image*

229: The Tyrrhenian shore, *Author's image*

231: Foça, *Author's image*

234: A modern replica of Phocaean ship, *Author's image*

235: Aléria in Corsica, *public domain*

236: The valley of Elea, *Author's image*

238: Shrine to Kybele, *Museo Archeologico Nazionale di Paestum*

239: IPH bowl, *Museo Archeologico Nazionale di Paestum*

240: Parmenides, *Museo Archeologico Nazionale di Paestum*

245: Persephone, *Agrigento Pietro Griffo Regional Archaeology Museum*

256: A mid-fifth-century drinking cup, *National Etruscan Museum of Villa Giulia*

261: Skyline temples, *Author's image*

262: Olive and almond orchards, *Author's image*

265: Acragas' coinage, *Wildwinds*

268: A Doric capital, *Author's image*

269: A reconstructed stone giant, *Author's image*

270: A recumbent giant, *Author's image*

271: A cork model, *Agrigento Pietro Griffo Regional Archaeology Museum*

273: Temple of Concordia, *Author's image*

274: Archaic clay figurines, *Agrigento Pietro Griffo Regional Archaeology Museum*

Insert

1: Odysseus sherd, *Chiara Goia*
2: Temple of Athena, *Author's image*
3: Teos quay, *Author's image*
4: Priēnē, *Author's image*
5: Panionion, *Author's image*
6: Ephesus coin, *Author's image*
7: Miletus lion, *Author's image*
8: Zeytintepe, *Author's image*
9: Young man at Didyma, *Author's image*
10: Symposium, Paestum, *Author's image*
11: Symposium, Thera/Istanbul, *Author's image*
12: Egyptian, *Sotheby's*
13: Kouros, *Jebulon*
14: Letter, *J. Paul Getty Museum*
15: Diving boy, Paestum, *Author's image*
16: Persephone, Acragas, *Author's image*
17: Cornice, Metapontum, *Author's image*